ONTOPOWER

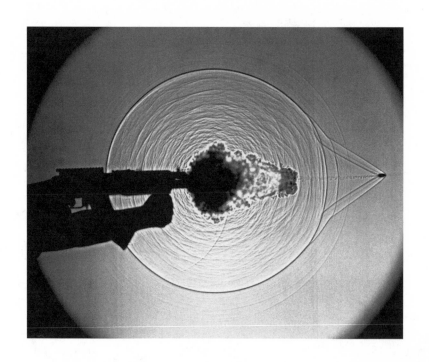

BRIAN MASSUMI

# Ontopower: War, Powers, and the State of Perception

DUKE UNIVERSITY PRESS   DURHAM AND LONDON   2015

Designed by Natalie F. Smith

Typeset in Quadraat Pro by Westchester Book Group

Library of Congress Cataloging-in-Publication Data
Massumi, Brian, author.
Ontopower : war, powers, and the state of perception / Brian Massumi.
pages cm
Includes bibliographical references and index.
ISBN 978-0-8223-5952-4 (hardcover : alk. paper)
ISBN 978-0-8223-5995-1 (pbk. : alk. paper)
ISBN 978-0-8223-7519-7 (e-book)
1. Power (Social sciences)—United States—History—21st century. 2. War on Terrorism,
2001–2009. 3. National security—United States—History—21st century. I. Title.
HN90.P6M37 2015
320.01'1—dc23   2015001928

Frontispiece art: AK-47 firing, shadowgraph, Dr. Gary S. Settles/Science Photo Library.
Cover art: Erin Manning, 9/11 (2001), acrylic and mixed media, detail. Courtesy of the artist.
Photo by Leslie Plumb.

The author acknowledges the generous support of the Social Science and Humanities Research
Council of Canada (SSHRC).

# CONTENTS

PREFACE

This book began on September 11, 2001: "The day the world changed."

Hyperbole, of course. There is no event that changes everything. Still, something changed, and the change was significant. In the aftermath of 9/11, many aspects of contemporary life reconfigured themselves around a new dominant: preemption. It is the thesis of this book that the doctrine of preemption that was the hallmark of George W. Bush's "war on terror" became the driving force for a reconfiguration of powers that has survived his administration and whose full impact we have yet to come to terms with. More than a doctrine, preemption has taken on a life of its own. It launches into operation wherever threat is felt. In today's multidimensional "threat environment," that is everywhere.

This book will argue that preemption, as it operates today, lies at the heart of a newly consolidated mode of power. A new mode of power deserves a new name. In the chapters that follow, it is dubbed "ontopower." Ontopower does not replace prior powers. Rather, it reorganizes and reintegrates them around the new fulcrum of preemption, changing their object and mode of operation in the process. Ontopower designates a changing "ecology of powers." The way in which this ecology of powers pivots on preemption brings new urgency to what can only be called metaphysical problems. Preemption is a time concept. It denotes acting on the time before: the time of threat, before it has emerged as a clear and present danger. What is this time of the before? How can it be acted upon? How can that acting upon already constitute a decision, given the ungraspability of that which has yet to eventuate and may yet take another form?

Preemption does not idly pose these problems concerning the nature of time, perception, action, and decision: it *operationalizes* them. It weaponizes them. Paradoxically, it weaponizes them in a way that is productive. Ontopower is not a negative power, a power-over. It is a power-to: a power to incite and orient emergence that insinuates itself into the pores of the world where life is just stirring, on the verge of being what it will become, as yet barely there. It is a positive power for bringing into being (hence the prefix "onto"). The goal of *Ontopower* is to explore how this operationalization works. In particular, the book seeks to plumb the paradox that a power so productive centers on preemption. Ontopowers are many and diverse. Preemption is their keystone and cutting edge.

This is not a book of history. It is in equal parts pragmatic (how does it work?) and speculative (what does how it works tell us philosophically about the way in which the present-day ecology of powers obliges us to rethink fundamental categories?). Each chapter sparks from very particular events in the history of post-9/11 culture and politics. The object of the analyses, however, is less these historical moments per se than the driving force of their formation as it passes through them. Preemption is treated as a formative tendency moving *through* historical moments. It is transhistorical.

The project of diagnosing a transhistorical tendency that concerns nothing so much as what has yet to emerge is fraught with difficulties. It not only raises fundamental philosophical questions; it also raises questions about how a philosophical consideration of the formative movement of history relates to historiography. This is the problem of the relation between speculatively pragmatic thought and empirical study. This problem is treated in chapter 5, in a self-reflective pause midstream. It is returned to in the afterword, which is a belated meditation on what comes before: an afterthought on how the project of thinking the transhistorical force of the not-yet-fully-emerged must conceive itself, paradoxically, as a "history of the present."

The afterword deals with the conceptual issues raised by the speculative-pragmatic nature of the project at great length, at the same time as it fulfils many of the functions of an introduction (including a chapter-by-chapter synopsis). Its main job is to delve into the status of what throughout the book is called an "operative logic." This is a term designating that transhistorical tendencies are *in and of themselves* speculatively pragmatic formative forces: they effectively carry a conceptual force of change (in their way of formatively posing and operationalizing metaphysical problems). It is also a term for concepts themselves, in that when they succeed in their mission to speculate pragmatically on the history of the present, they have the power to carry over as transhistorical tendencies. In and of themselves, concepts may be operative logics: forces for change. At this point, the difference between a concept and a formative force of history becomes a question of perspective—which is why, try as it might, historiography can never disentangle itself from philosophy, especially when it is a question of such fundamentally quizzical issues as preemption and ontopower. Alone, historiography cannot approach them—much less the crucial question for the future of what a counter-ontopower might be.

Readers of a particularly philosophical bent may enjoy reading the afterword first, as an introduction. Others may wish to enter the preemptive thick of things directly with chapter 1. Readers curious for more detail on how preemption has carried over from the Bush administration into and through the Obama administration, an issue sporadically addressed at various points in the book, may be directed to the lengthy aside inserted halfway through the afterword in indented text titled "Bush on Steroids?."

# PART ONE

# Powers

# 1   The Primacy of Preemption

## The Operative Logic of Threat

If we wait for threats to fully materialize, we will have waited too long. We must take
the battle to the enemy, disrupt his plans and confront the worst threats before they
emerge. In the world we have entered, the only path to safety is the path to action.
And this nation will act.
—George W. Bush

It was with these words, uttered in June 2002 in a speech before the grad-
uating class of the United States Military Academy at West Point, that
George W. Bush first gave explicit expression to the approach that would
become the hallmark of his administration's foreign policy (2002).[1] The
doctrine of preemption would lead the United States from the invasion
of Afghanistan to the War in Iraq, and carry Bush himself to reelection
in 2004. It would also lead, after another two short but eventful years
punctuated by the turbulence of a hurricane and the near-death of a great
American city, to the dramatic defeat of the president's party in the 2006
midterm congressional elections. The most immediate casualty of that
defeat would not be President Bush himself. Secretary of Defense Donald Rumsfeld, the individual most identified in the public's mind with the
doctrine of preemption and its translation into action in Iraq, would take
the fall. He would be out of office within twenty-four hours of the vote
count. The reason universally cited for the election defeat was the growing
dissatisfaction of the American public with the fact that there had been no
palpable change in the situation in Iraq.

One thing that had changed in the lead-up to the election lay half a
world away from Iraq, in North Korea. Although the North Korean government's October 2006 announcement that it had tested a nuclear weapon
barely created a ripple on the surface of the American electorate's general awareness and was not cited in press analyses as having had an

appreciable influence on the election outcome, it seemed to be one more sign that the Bush administration's defining doctrine of preemption was fast becoming history. For here was a "fully materialized" threat, and the Bush administration was not rushing to take a unilateral "path to action." Instead, it was emphasizing just the kind of multilateral, nonmilitary response it had brushed aside in its rush to invade Iraq. In his first press conference following the North Korean announcement, Bush reassured the world that "the United States affirmed that we have no nuclear weapons on the Korean Peninsula. We affirmed that we have no intention of attacking North Korea. . . . The United States remains committed to diplomacy" (Bush 2006). In the same appearance, Bush changed his tune on Iraq for the first time. In response to polls already registering the devastating impact of the War in Iraq on Republican Party popularity, he reinterpreted the mantra on Iraq he had intoned for months. "Stay the course," he said, really means "don't leave before the job is done," and getting the job done, he continued, sometimes means "change tactics."[2]

Coming from a president so intransigent that he had never before been able to bring himself to so much as entertain the possibility that his administration's decisions had been anything less than perfect, this semantic metacommentary seemed momentous. The statement was picked up by the press, repeated, commented upon, blogged, analyzed, and variously cited as a sudden attack of wisdom and ridiculed as a bumbling too-little-too-late. Either way, it had popular play. The statement on North Korea, although duly reported, did not. It is likely that only an infinitesimal percentage of the American electorate would be able to correctly identify its own government's policy on North Korea, but only the most severely news- and entertainment-deprived would fail to have registered that the president was no longer exactly "staying the course" on Iraq. The president's own admission of the need for a change and the Democrats' subsequent regaining of control of both houses of Congress led many to the conclusion that the direction of the country was about to take a major turn.

It is important to note, however, that Bush referred to a change in "tactics" not a change in "strategy." Preemption remained the official military strategy of the United States to the end of the Bush administration. More than that, in essential respects the concept has effectively continued to underpin U.S. national security strategy throughout President Obama's two terms in office, as discussed in the afterword.[3]

Preemption is far more than a specific military doctrine of a particular administration. It can be plausibly argued that preemption is an *operative logic of power* defining a political epoch in as infinitely space-filling and insidiously infiltrating a way as the logic of "deterrence" defined the Cold War era. By an "operative" logic I mean one that combines an *ontology* with an *epistemology* in such a way as to trace itself out as a self-propelling *tendency* that is not in the sway of any particular existing formation but sweeps across them all and where possible sweeps them up in its own dynamic.

### Preemption, Prevention, Deterrence

Preemption is not *prevention*. Although the goal of both is to neutralize threat, they fundamentally differ epistemologically and ontologically. Epistemologically, prevention assumes an ability to assess threats empirically and identify their causes. Once the causes are identified, appropriate curative methods are sought to avoid their realization. Prevention operates in an objectively knowable world in which uncertainty is a function of a lack of information, and in which events run a predictable, linear course from cause to effect. As we will see, this is very different from the epistemological premise of preemption, which entails a divergence from prevention on the ontological level as well. Prevention, in fact, has no ontology of its own because it assumes that what it must deal with has an objectively given existence prior to its own intervention. In practice, this means that its object is given to it predefined by other formations, in whose terms and on whose terrain it must then operate. A preventive approach to social conflict might analyze it, for example, as an effect of poverty, objectively quantifiable in terms of economic and health indexes. Each index is defined by a specialist formation (economics, medicine) in relation to a norm specific to that domain and against which goals may be set and success measured (annual income, mortality rates, life expectancy, etc.). The preventive measures will then operate as a political extension of the concerned specialist domains (economic analysis extended into politics as aid and development, medicine extended into vaccination programs, etc.). They will be regulated by the specialist logics proper to those fields.

Prevention has no proper object, no operational sphere of its own, and no proprietary logic. It is derivative. It is a *means* toward a given end. Because of this, preventive measures are not self-sustaining. They must be *applied*, by an outside source. They are not an organizing force in their own right. They run on borrowed power.

*Deterrence* takes over at the end of this same process, when the means of prevention have failed. Deterrence makes use of the same epistemology prevention does, in that it assumes knowability and objective measurability. However, because it starts where prevention ends, it has no margin of error. It must know with *certainty* because the threat at hand is fully formed and ready to detonate: the enemy has the bomb and the means to deliver it. The imminence of the threat means that deterrence cannot afford to subordinate itself to objects, norms, and criteria passed on to it from other domains. If it did, its ability to respond with an immediacy proportional to the imminence of the threat would be compromised. Since it would not hold the key to its own knowledge, in the urgency of the situation it would be haunted internally by the specter of a possible incompleteness of the knowledge coming from the outside. Since its operations would be mediated by that outside domain, neither would it hold a direct key to its own actions. Since it would be responding to causes outside its specific purview, it would not be master of its own effects.

The only way to have the kind of epistemological immediacy necessary for deterrence is for its process to *have its own cause* and to hold it fast within itself. The quickest and most direct way for a process to acquire its own cause is for it to *produce* one. The easiest way to do this is to take the *imminence* of the very threat prevention has failed to neutralize and make it the foundation of a new process. In other words, the process must take the effect it seeks to avoid (nuclear annihilation) and organize itself around it, as the cause of its very own dynamic (deterrence). It must convert an effect that has yet to eventuate into a cause: a *future cause*. Past causes are in any case already spoken for. They have been claimed as objects of knowledge and operational spheres by a crowded world of other already-functioning formations.

For a future cause to have any palpable effect it must somehow be able to act on the present. This is much easier to do and much less mysterious than it might sound. You start by translating the imminent *threat* into a clear and present *danger*. You do this by acquiring a capability to realize the threat rather than prevent it. If your neighbor has a nuke, you build the nuclear weaponry that would enable you to annihilate the adversary, even at the price of annihilating yourself by precipitating a "nuclear winter." In fact, the more capable you are of destroying yourself along with your enemy, the better. You can be certain the enemy will follow your lead in acquiring the capability to annihilate you, and themselves as well. The imminent threat is then so imminent on both sides, so immediately present in its menacing futurity, that only a madman or suicidal regime would ever tip the balance and press the button. This gives rise to a unique logic of mutuality: "mutually assured destruction" (MAD).

Mutually assured destruction is equilibrium-seeking. It tends toward the creation of a "balance of terror." MAD is certainty squared: to the certainty that there is objectively a threat is added the certainty that it is balanced out. The second certainty is dynamic, and requires maintenance. The assurance must be maintained by continuing to produce the conditions that bring the cause so vividly into the present. You have to keep moving into the dangerous future. You have to race forward ever faster. You have to build more weapons, faster and better, to be sure that your systems match the lethality of your opponent's, give or take a few half-lives. The process soon becomes self-driving. The logic of mutually assured destruction becomes its own motor. It becomes self-propelling. Now that you've started, you can't very well stop.

What began as an epistemological condition (a certainty about what you and your opponent are capable of doing) dynamizes into an ontology or mode of being (a race for dear life). Deterrence thus qualifies as an operative logic, in that it combines its own proprietary epistemology with a unique ontology. For the process to run smoothly, of course, it still needs to mobilize other logics borrowed from other domains. It needs, for example, quantitative measures of destructive load and delivery capacity, a continual intelligence feed, and good geographical data, to mention just a few. The necessary measures are provided by other formations operating in annex domains having their own logics. But this does not compromise deterrence's status as an operative logic because it is not the measures themselves or their specialist logics that count so much as the criterion imposed upon them by the logic of deterrence itself: the quantitative balance necessary to achieve lethal life-defining mutuality.

The equilibrium deterrence achieves is not a stable one. It is a meta-stability, or dynamic equilibrium, built on constant movement. *Deterrence is when a threat is held in futurity by being fully realized as the concretest of possibilities in the present in such a way as to define a self-propelling movement all its own.* Because the threat's futurity is firmly held in the present, it short-circuits its own effect. It self-deters. This does not mean it ceases to operate as a cause. It means that its causality is displaced. It is no longer in a position to realize its original effect, annihilation. Instead, it becomes the determinant of something else: a race. It remains a cause, to different effect. Deterrence captures a future effect (mutual annihilation) in order to make it the cause of its own movement (which ends up going elsewhere). It captures this potential difference in end-effect as a means toward its becoming self-causing. It takes the potential of the end as the means whereby it makes itself. Its logic succeeds when it closes in on itself to form a self-causal loop of its own self-making. Because it operates in this closed self-causal loop, its epistemology is univocal (centered on a single certainty) and its ontology is monolithic (both sides are taken up in a single global dynamic that coagulates in a bipolar structure). It may seem odd to say so, but deterrence can be seen as the apotheosis of humanism in the technoscientific age, in the sense that in the face of the imminent annihilation of the species it still reposes on an implicit psychological premise: that an at-least-residual concern for humanity and a minimum of shared sanity can be mobilized to place a limit on conflict.

Deterrence does not work across different orders of magnitude. Only powers perceiving themselves to be of potentially equal military stature can mutually assure destruction. Neither does it work if one of the adversaries considers the other inhuman or potentially suicidal (just plain mad, uncapitalized). Where the conditions of deterrence are not met, the irruption of a nuclear threat feeds a different operative logic. This is the case with North Korea. Kim Jong-un's nuclear capabilities will never counterbalance those of the established nuclear powers. In the Western press and policy literature, he, like his father before him, is regularly portrayed as unbalanced, mad enough to have the inhumanity to come to the point of willing the destruction of his own country to assure the (unlikely) destruction of his enemy. Prevention has failed, and neither the quantitative conditions nor the psychological premise necessary for deterrence is in place. In view of this, a different operative logic must be used to understand the current nuclear situation, in North Korea and elsewhere. That logic, of course, is preemption. The superficial condition of the presence of a nuclear threat should not be mistaken for a return to a Cold War logic.

## To Move and Make Move

Preemption shares certain characteristics with deterrence. Like deterrence, it operates in the present on a future threat. It also does this in such a way as to make that present futurity the motor of its process. The process, however, is qualitatively different. President Bush began the 2002 speech at which he first announced that preemption would be the guiding principle of his national defense strategy by asserting a difference in nature between the deterrence paradigm of the Cold War and the "war on terror." His military policy of preemption, he says, is predicated on the "*inability to deter* a potential attacker," which defines the contemporary state of things.[4]

The epistemology of preemption is distinguished from that of deterrence in that it is unabashedly one of *uncertainty*—and not due to a simple lack of knowledge. There is uncertainty because the threat has not only not yet fully formed but, according to Bush's opening definition of preemption, it has *not yet even emerged*. In other words, the threat is still indeterminately in potential. This is an ontological premise: the nature of threat cannot be specified. It might in some circumstances involve weapons of mass destruction, but in others it will not. It might come in the form of strange white powder, or then again it might be an improvised explosive device. The enemy is also unspecifiable. It might come from without, or rise up unexpectedly from within. You might, stereotypically, expect the enemy to be a member of a certain ethnic or religious group, an Arab or a Muslim, but you can never be sure. It might turn out be a white Briton wearing sneakers, or a Puerto Rican from the heartland of America (to mention just two well-known cases, those of John Reid and Jose Padilla). It might be an anonymous member of a cell, or the supreme leader of a "rogue" state. The lack of knowledge about the nature of the threat can never be overcome. It is part of what defines the objective conditions of the situation: threat has become proteiform and it tends to proliferate unpredictably.

The situation is objectively one in which the only certainty is that threat will emerge where it is least expected. This is because what is ever-present is not a particular threat or set of threats, but the *potential* for still more threats to emerge without warning (it is impossible "to deter a potential attacker"). The global situation is not so much threatening as threat *generating*: threat-o-genic. It is the world's capacity to produce *new* threats at any and every moment that defines this situation. We are in a world that has passed from what Rumsfeld called the "known unknown" (uncertainty that can be analyzed and circumscribed) to the "unknown unknown" (objective uncertainty) (Rumsfeld 2002a). Objective uncertainty is as directly an ontological category as an epistemological one. The threat is known to have the ontological status of indeterminate potentiality.

The unknown unknown is inexpungible because its potentiality belongs to the objective conditions of life today. Consequently, no amount of effort to understand will ever bring a definitive answer. Thinking about it will only reopen the same uncomprehending question, why do they hate us so? This question, asked over and over again by the U.S. media in the years following 9/11, expresses the impossibility of basing a contemporary logic of conflict on a psychological premise. The nature and motives of the adversary strike us as purely incomprehensible. The only hypothesis left is that they are just plain "evil," capable of the worst "crimes against humanity." They are simply "inhuman." The only way to identify the enemy collectively is, in Bush's formulation, as an "axis of evil." That characterization does not add new knowledge. It is the moral equivalent of ignorance. Its function is to concentrate "humanity" entirely on one side in order to legitimate acts on "our" side that would be considered crimes against humanity were the enemy given the benefit of being considered human (torture, targeting civilian populations, contraventions of human rights and the laws of war). The ostensibly moral judgment of "evil" functions very pragmatically as a device for giving oneself unlimited tactical options freed from moral constraint. This is the only sense in which something like deterrence continues to function: moral judgment is used in such a way as to deter any properly moral or ethical logic from becoming operative. The operative logic will function on an entirely different plane.

The situation within which the logic of preemption arises is far-from-equilibrium by nature. There is no hope for balance, so it is not even sought. The disequilibrium occurs on many levels. There is the post-humanist moral imbalance just mentioned between the human and the "inhuman." Militarily, the imbalance goes by the name of "asymmetrical warfare." This refers to the difference in order of magnitude between the adversaries' capacities for attack. The quantitative superiority of the state players in terms of the size of their armed forces, technological resources, weaponry, and funding does not necessarily give them an advantage on the ground. This is because there is another asymmetry in play that takes the form of an ontological difference. The mode of being of the "terrorist" is wed to the potential of the unspecified threat. That of the terrorist's state enemy is all-too concrete, fully actualized in a top-heavy defense structure. This gives the "terrorist" the very significant advantage of surprise. It also gives him or her an epistemological edge over the lumbering state formation, which is at an order of magnitude that makes it easily visible, whereas the proteiform "terrorist" is by nature imperceptible from the opposing vantage point of the state. This situation is what is commonly referred to as "imbalance of terror."

In the face of the "imbalance of terror," the state adversary must transform a part of its own structure *in the image of what it fights*. You cannot engage the enemy if the situation is so asymmetrical that there is no ground in common to serve as a battlefield. You have to become, at least in part, what hates you and what you hate back. You have to undertake a becoming-terrorist of your own.[5]

Rumsfeld's project of "transforming the military," known more broadly as the "revolution in military affairs," involved tipping the defense structure into this movement of becoming-terrorist by realigning it on smaller-scale rapid-deployment and rapid-response capabilities mirroring the ways of the enemy.[6] Eyal Weizman has documented a similarly, remarkably lucid project of mimicking the enemy within the Israeli Defense Forces, considered (at least up until the Lebanese War of 2006) the most advanced and effective state fighting force.[7] The realignment on less-specified, more potentialized capabilities must be backed up by technologically assisted means of perception: monitoring systems to detect the slightest signs of enemy action. But any detection system is still prone to error or evasion. In fact, since the enemy is indeterminate, it is certain that he will remain undetectable until he makes a move. You look to detect the movements, at as emergent a level as possible. But given the speed with which a terrorist attack can unfold, once the movement has detectably begun it might already be over. A defensive posture, even backed up with the best monitoring technology, is not enough. The military machinery must go on the offensive.[8] It is not safe to wait for the enemy to make the first move. You have to move first, to make them move.[9] You have to "flush them out." You test and prod, you move as randomly and unpredictably and ubiquitously as they do, in the hopes that you will brush close enough to provoke a response. You avoid making yourself a sitting target. You move like the enemy, in order to make the enemy move. He will be flushed out into taking some active form, and in taking active form will become detectable and thus attackable. In other words, you go on the offensive to make the enemy emerge from its state of potential and take actual shape. The exercise of your power is *incitatory*. It is contributes to the actual emergence of the threat. In other words, since the threat is proliferative in any case, your best option is to help *make it proliferate more*—that is (hopefully) more on your own terms. The most effective way to fight an unspecified threat is to actively contribute to *producing* it.

## Potential Politics

This co-productive logic is well illustrated in the policies and statements of the Bush administration, and explains why Bush never admitted that the War in Iraq was a failure, even as he was coming to accept that it wasn't exactly a victory yet and that midstream "tactical changes" were necessary. Consider this statement from June 2005: "Some may agree with my decision to remove Saddam Hussein from power, but all of us can agree that the world's terrorists have now made Iraq a central front in the war on terror" (Bush 2005a). This was Bush's way of admitting that there were no weapons of mass destruction in Iraq. Objectively, his reasons for invading were false. But threat in today's world is not objective. It is potential. Potential threat calls for a potential politics. As Bush and many members of his administration have repeatedly argued, Saddam Hussein *could have* had weapons of mass destruction and that *if* he had had them, he *would have* used them. Could have, would have, if: the potential nature of the threat requires a *conditional* logic. A conditional statement cannot be wrong. First because it only asserts a potential, and second because, especially in the case of something so slippery as a potential, you can't prove the negative. Even if it wasn't *actually* there, it will always still have been there potentially: Saddam *could have* restarted his weapons projects at any moment. When you act on "could haves" and "would haves" you are right *by definition* as long as your reasons for acting are *not objective*.[10] It is simply a category error to give empirical reasons for your actions with respect to potential politics. This is what the Bush administration insiders meant when they ridiculed "the reality-based community" as being hopelessly behind the times (Suskind 2004). Nowadays, your action is right by definition as long as you go politically conditional and have a good reason for doing so.

*Fear* is always a good reason to go politically conditional. Fear is the palpable action in the present of a threatening future cause. It acts just as palpably whether the threat is determinate or not. It weakens your resolve, creates stress, lowers consumer confidence, and may ultimately lead to individual and/or economic paralysis. To avoid the paralysis, which would make yourself even more of a target and carry the fear to an even higher level, you must simply act. In Bush administration parlance, you "go kinetic" (Woodward 2002, 150).[11] You leap into action on a level with the potential that frightens you. You do that, once again, by inciting the potential to take an actual shape you can respond to. You trigger a *production of what you fear. You turn the objectively indeterminate cause into an actual effect* so you can actually deal with it in some way. Any time you feel the need to act, then all you have to do is actuate a fear.[12] The production of the effect follows as smoothly as a reflex. This *affective* dynamic is still very much in place. It will remain in place as long as fear remains politically actuatable.

The logic of preemption operates on this affective plane, in this proliferative or *ontogenetic* way: in a way that contributes to the reflex production of the specific being of the threat. You're afraid Iraq is a breeding ground for terrorists? It could have been. If it could have been, it would have been. So go ahead, make it one. "Bring 'em on," the president said, following his Hollywood-trained reflex (Loughlin 2003). He knew it in his "guts."[13] He couldn't have gone wrong. His reflex was right. Because "now we can all agree" that Iraq is in actual fact a breeding ground for "terrorists." That just goes to *prove* that the potential was always there. Before, there was doubt in some quarters that Saddam had to be removed from power. Some agreed he had to go; some didn't. Now we can all agree. It was right to remove him because doing so made Iraq *become what it always could have been*. And that's the truth.

Truth, in this new world order, is by nature retroactive. Fact grows conditionally in the affective soil of an indeterminately present futurity. It *becomes objective* as that present reflexively plays out, as an *effect* of the preemptive action taken. The reality-based community wastes time studying empirical reality, the Bushites said: "We *create* it." And because of that, "we" the preemptors will always be right. We always will have been right to preempt, because we have objectively produced a recursive truth-effect for your judicious study. And while you are looking back studying the truth of it, we will have acted with reflex speed again, effecting a new reality.[14] We will always have had no choice but to prosecute the "war on terror," ever more vigilantly and ever more intensely on every potential front. We, preemptors, are the producers of your world. Get used to it. The War in Iraq was a success to the extent that it made the productivity of the preemptive "war on terror" a self-perpetuating movement—one that drones on, in altered form and under a different name, to this day (Scahill 2013).

Preemption is like deterrence in that it combines a proprietary epistemology with a unique ontology in such a way as to make present a future cause that sets a self-perpetuating movement into operation. Its differences from deterrence hinge on its taking objectively indeterminate or potential threat as its self-constitutive cause rather than fully formed and specified threat. It situates itself on the ground of ontogenetic potential. There, rather than deterring the feared effect, it actualizes the potential in a shape to which it hopes it can respond. It assumes a proliferation of potential threats, and mirrors that capacity in its own operation. It becomes proliferative. It assumes the objective imbalance of a far-from-equilibrium state as a permanent condition. Rather than trying to right the imbalance, it seizes it as an opportunity for itself. Preemption also sets a race in motion. But this is a race run on the edge of chaos. It is a race of movement-flushing, detection, perception, and affective actuation, run in irreparably chaotic or quasi-chaotic conditions. The race of preemption has any number of laps, each ending in the actual effecting of a threat. Each actualization of a threat triggers the next lap, as a continuation of the first in the same direction, or in another way in a different field.

## Operative Logic

Deterrence revolved around an objective cause. Preemption revolves around a proliferative effect. Both (unlike prevention) are operative logics. The operative logic of deterrence, however, remained causal even as it displaced its cause's effect. Preemption is an *effective operative logic* rather than a causal operative logic. Since its ground is potential, there is no actual cause for it to organize itself around. It compensates for the absence of an actual cause by producing a present effect in its place. This it makes the motor of its movement: it converts a future, *virtual cause* directly into a taking-actual-effect in the present. It does this affectively. It uses affect to effectively trigger a virtual causality.[15] *Preemption is when the futurity of unspecified threat is affectively held in the present in a perpetual state of potential emergence(y) so that a movement of actualization may be triggered that is not only self-propelling but also effectively, indefinitely, ontologically productive, because it works from a virtual cause whose potential no single actualization exhausts.*

Preemption's operational parameters mean that it is never univocal. It operates in the element of vagueness and objective uncertainty. Due to its proliferative nature, it cannot be monolithic. Its logic cannot close in around its self-causing as the logic deterrence does. It includes an essential openness in its productive logic.[16] It incites its adversary to take emergent form. It then strives to become as proteiform as its ever-emergent adversary can be. It is as shape-shifting as it is self-driving. It infiltrates across boundaries, sweeping up existing formations in its own transversal movement. Faced with gravity-bound formations too inertial for it to sweep up and carry off with its own operative logic, it contents itself with opening windows of opportunity to pass through. This is the case with the domestic legal and juridical structure in the United States. It can't sweep them away. But it can build into them escape holes for itself. Under Bush, these were most spectacularly enacted in formal provisions vastly expanding the power of the executive, in the person of the president in his role as commander in chief, to suspend the normal course of government in order to enable a continued flow of preemptive action. Under Obama, the assertion of such powers of exception has tended to take less avowed and more roundabout forms.[17]

Preemption stands for conflict unlimited: the potential for peace amended to become a perpetual state of undeclared war. This is the "permanent state of emergency" so presciently described by Walter Benjamin (2003, 392). In current Bush administration parlance, it came to be called the "Long War" replacing the Cold War: a preemptive war with an in-built tendency to be never-ending.

Deterrence produced asymmetrical conflict as a by-product. The MADly balanced East-West bipolarity spun off a North-South subpolarity. This was less a polarity than an axis of imbalance. The "South" was neither a second Western First nor another Eastern Second. It was an anomalous Third. In this chaotic "Third World," local conflicts prefiguring the present "imbalance of terror" proliferated. The phrase "the war on terror" was in fact first popularized by Richard Nixon in 1972 in response to the attack on Israeli athletes at the Munich Olympics when the Israeli-Palestinian conflict overspilled northward. Asymmetrical conflicts, however, were perceivable by the reigning logic of deterrence only as a reflection of itself. The dynamics of deterrence were overlaid upon them. Their heterogeneity was overcoded by the familiar U.S.-Soviet duality. Globally such conflicts figured only as opportunities to reproduce the worldwide balance of terror on a reduced scale. The strategy of "containment" adopted toward them was for the two sides in the dominant dyad to operate in each local theater through proxies in such a way that their influence, on the whole, balanced out. "I decided," Nixon said after Munich, "that we must maintain a balance" (Lardner 2002). He did not, as Bush did after 9/11, decide to skew things by unilaterally "going kinetic." The rhetoric of the "war on terror" fell into abeyance during the remainder of the 1970s, as Southern asymmetries tended to be overcoded as global rebalancings, and going kinetic was "contained" to the status of local anomaly.

The fall of the Soviet Union made containment a thing of the past. Its necessary condition of balancing polarity no longer obtains. Asymmetrical warfare has come out from under the overcoding of deterrence. After 9/11, anomaly is everywhere. The war on terror came back with a vengeance, thriving in an irreparably threat-o-genic environment. The Long War was off and running, in preemptive self-perpetuation.

It is in this context that the contemporaneous ascension of North Korea to nuclear-state status must be understood. It was precisely in that context that the unrepentant neoconservatives in the United States who were behind the Iraq invasion did in fact approach it. In November 2006 one of the main organs of neoconservative thought, the magazine *Commentary*, published a special issue on the current geopolitical situation. You would hardly know that North Korea's announcement of its nuclear capacity had taken place in the previous month. It is mentioned only in passing, and then only in order to justify a military attack on . . . Iran. Even though Iran was not yet a nuclear threat. The thinking was that North Korea would use its capabilities to proliferate the nuclear threat by assisting Iran in transforming its civilian nuclear program into a military one. North Korea could well become a breeding ground for nuclear terrorism. In the age of preemption, threat proliferates faster than weaponry.

Where have we heard that argument before? Could have, would have . . . we will have been right to bomb Iran. The neoconservative's main interest in the North Korean situation was indirect. What they are most interested in is using the issue of nuclear proliferation on the Korean peninsula as leverage for proliferating preemption elsewhere—for staying the overall strategic course even as tactical adjustments had to be made in Iraq. North Korea was hardly on their map, outside of this connection. That is because what is on their map is oil. The ultimate reason Iran must be attacked is because, nuclearly emboldened, it might well put a "choke hold" on the Strait of Hormuz in order to block oil deliveries to the West and thereby endanger the economy. This potential threat makes preemption right all over again. Regime change is once again conditionally "necessary" in the Middle East, to make the region safe for American capitalism (Herman 2006).

In the years since these discussions in 2006, an attack on Iran has not become the recursive truth of the situation. Neoconservative breast-beating on the issue has not stopped (nor have covert U.S. special operations). But under Obama, calls for direct intervention have lost their ring. As regards North Korea, traditional pressure tactics and diplomatic efforts have been revived. Preemption flows elsewhere, on the wings of a drone. None of this changes the global situation that in this brave new world of potential politics the operative logic of preemption renders only one thing certain: that the preemptive adventure has yet to run its course. Rest asymmetrically assured of the future affective fact that somewhere, at some scale, things will go proliferatingly kinetic again, by direct intervention or (Obama's preference) by proxy.

The self-perpetuating nature of the logic of preemption should be a subject of intense concern. The threat-o-genic climate in which situations like that of North Korea occur tend to feed a fast-moving operative war logic that is constitutively off-balance and thrives globally under far-from-equilibrium conditions in which threats proliferate faster not only than weapons, but than analysis and negotiation. Winging headlong into a warlike future on the threat-edge of chaos is a hard way to live the present. It is imperative to find a new operative logic capable of disarming preemption. Returning to old logics, prevention or deterrence, will not work. Voting a particular administration out of office is important, but has proven to be at best a palliative, and at worst an unintended steroid boost. The search for an alternative will have to come to grips with this radical assessment of the situation in which the world finds itself, penned by one of the inventors of the concept of asymmetrical warfare:

> Our understandings and definitions of 'war' are hopelessly out of date, and the same holds for 'peace'. The international law of war is basically irrelevant today, and I doubt it can become relevant again. . . . National security objectives will not be crystal clear, formulated in timely fashion, or fully underwritten by national will. (Barnett 2003, 135)

To quote another asymmetrical warrior:

> As people learn of the benefits of democracy, capitalism and the rule of law, they become fat and happy. . . . Until then, we all need to prepare for combat. (Berkowitz 2003, 221)

Given the preemptive "irrelevance" of international law and the exceptional escape hatches that have been bored into the governmental structures of the United States and many other countries, the rule of law seems to have fallen on hard times. Since the collective objectives pursued in such times as these will "not be fully underwritten by national will," democracy seems to be in a bit of tight spot as well. That only leaves capitalism. Are we "fat and happy" yet?

Until then . . .

## 2   National Enterprise Emergency

Steps toward an Ecology of Powers

*Of War and the Weather*

A leisurely three weeks after Hurricane Katrina, George W. Bush touched down in New Orleans, into the media swirl of a brief but lavishly staged son et lumière spectacular from the heart of the French Quarter. His nationally televised address struck the appropriate tone of urgency, in studied contrast to the languor of his practical response. Bush landed on the beachhead of natural disaster not as chief executive of the civilian bureaucracy but in his post-9/11 capacity as commander in chief. Help, he assured, was on the way "by land, by air, by sea" (Bush 2005b).[1] National Guard units recently returned from Iraq would spearhead the "armies of compassion" massing. They would be joined by the U.S. Army's 82nd Airborne Division, fresh from assignment in Afghanistan.

This transfer from an escalating war half a world away to a storm-beaten home front mid-America drew a link between war and the weather. Their respective theaters of conflict, geopolitical and socio-climatic, fell actively into line. The weather, exceptionally figuring as urban assault force, had taken a prominent place in the spectrum of threat. "This was not a normal hurricane," Bush reminded. "Nature is indiscriminate," a chorus of administration officials had repeated in the preceding days. What was this hurricane if not the full-force expression of nature's indiscriminateness, amplified to the status of a national emergency? Katrina was the meteorological equivalent of the improvised devices then exploding onto the scene of the U.S. effort in Iraq. This hurricane was to the weather what a terrorist insurgency is to "nation-building." Each bombing is a self-organized microevent punctually expressing endemic background conditions of instability. Like the fabled flap of the butterfly wing seeding popular accounts of chaos theory with an ebullition of proto-Katrinas, the agitations can bubble and build, resonating to crisis proportions. Background conditions of instability can feed up the scale, reaching the level where the security dikes are breached, channels of order are swamped, and bulwarks of stability erode and even collapse.

This is the figure of today's threat: the suddenly irrupting, locally self-organizing, systemically self-amplifying threat of large-scale disruption. This form of threat is not only indiscriminate, coming anywhere, as out of nowhere, at any time; it is also indiscriminable. Its continual microflapping in the background makes it indistinguishable from the general environment, now one with a restless climate of agitation. Between irruptions, it blends in with the chaotic background, subsiding into its own preamplified incipience, already active, still imperceptible. The figure of the environment shifts: from the harmony of a natural balance to a churning seedbed of crisis in the perpetual making. This hurricane may well have been abnormal. But it expressed nothing so much as the normality of a generalized crisis environment so encompassing in its endemic threat-form as to connect, across the spectrum, the polar extremes of war and the weather.

> *Questions*: Michel Foucault characterizes the dominant contemporary regime of power, coincident with the rise of neoliberalism, as "environmental": a "governmentality which will act on the environment and systematically modify its variables" (Foucault 2008, 271). Actions in this mode of power, he emphasizes, are not "standardizing" (2008, 261). The environment has stormed out of reach of normalization. It asserts its own normality, of crisis: the anywhere, anytime potential for the emergence of the abnormal. It has nothing but variables, perpetually churning. What is most relevant about them, from a power perspective, is their threatening tendency to defy the bell curve. Environmentality as a mode of power is left no choice but to make do with this abnormally productive "autonomy" (2008, 261). Given the indiscriminateness of the environment's autonomous activity, environmentality must systematically work through the "regulation of effects" rather than of causes. It must remain operationally "open to unknowns" (imperceptible stirrings) and catch "transversal phenomena" (nonlinear multiplier effects) before they amplify the stirrings to actual crisis proportions (2008, 261). What systematicity is this?

And: does power's becoming-environmental "mean that," politically, "we are dealing with natural subjects? [end of manuscript]" (2008, 261).

Where Foucault's question ends is where, today, we must begin, in light of how the recomposition of power whose dawning he glimpsed in 1979 has played out since. In the context of Foucault's theories of power the question amounts to asking, is this still biopolitics?

Foucault defined biopower as an inversion of sovereign power, whose formula was "to put to death (or let live)." Biopower's formula is to "make live (or let die)." (Foucault 1978, 135–138; Foucault, 2003, 239–242). It seeks to "optimize a state of life" by "maximizing and extracting forces." What it extracts forces from are "aleatory events." Biopower, "or the power to guarantee life," "intervenes at the level at which these phenomena are determined." (2003, 246, 253)

In their pre-neoliberal nineteenth-century beginnings, mechanisms of biopower construed the level at which aleatory events are determined as one of "generality." Generality was in turn understood in statistical terms, which is to say according to the laws of large numbers (2003, 246). Biopower's embrace of the aleatory was "massifying" (2003, 243). Although "aleatory and unpredictable when taken in themselves," the nineteenth-century assumption was that events, "at the collective level, display constants that are easy, or at least possible, to establish" (2003, 246). This made it conceivable that "regulatory mechanisms" could "compensate for variations within this aleatory field" of events to "establish an equilibrium" or "homeostasis" (2003, 246).

The field within which the aleatory events at issue took place was the population (Foucault 2007, 245–246). It was a matter, "in a word, of taking control of biological processes of man-as-species and of ensuring that they are not disciplined, but regularized" (2003, 247). What biopower sought to control were the relations between "human beings, insofar as they are a species, and their environment" (2003, 245). Biopower's regulatory mechanisms, although not themselves disciplinary, operated in reciprocity with disciplinary power. Disciplinary mechanisms followed an inverse path, starting from the species mass of humanity. They took charge of the human multiplicity in order to individualize it, in such a way to make the actions of the individual bodies composing the population conform to norms of conduct. It was the production of normed conduct on the part of individual bodies that made the possibility of establishing "constants" on the collective level conceivable, if not easy.

Biopower mechanisms would aim to make it easier by taking charge of the aleatory events that might hinder the extrapolation from normed conformity of the individual to mass-level constants. They would do this by regulating the life environment, within which disciplined bodies grew, at the "general" level on which those events were determined. The statistical characteristics of the events in question pertained to the biological processes of the population. Together, disciplinary power and biopower covered the continuum "that lies between the organic and the biological, between body and population." Their joint field of operation stretched between "the body as one pole and the population as the other" (2003, 253).

The balance was destined to shift. Biopower sought "not only [to] manage life but to make it proliferate" (2003, 253). From the time of the physiocrats, making life proliferate has meant making the economy grow. Guaranteeing the passage from individual conformity to collective constants could only limit the dynamism of the economy, which in the twentieth century came to be seen as predicated on innovation. "Innovation, that is to say, the discovery of new techniques, sources, and forms of productivity, and also the discovery of new markets or new resources of manpower" came to be "absolutely consubstantial with the functioning of capitalism" (2008, 231). To maximize innovation, the norms tended by disciplinary power had to loosen to admit a wider ambit of variation and a quicker turnover of conformities. This loosening was already in the works as biopower joined forces with disciplinary power. In fact, their conjoint operation changed the very nature of the norm. The norm would no longer be given as "intrinsic to any legal imperative" (2007, 56), or even moral imperative. It comes to be intrinsic to the biological processes of the human-species population and its innovatory evolution, consubstantial with the functioning of capitalism. Thus economized, "normal" is whatever appears as a statistical constant on the collective level. It is whatever proves to be consistent with generally livable economic conditions, factoring in that the conditions are of continual variation. Homeostasis is no longer a stasis. It becomes punctuated, moving from equilibrium to equilibrium, following the movement of the new. Which takes the "homeo" out of the (non-)stasis.

What we are left with, as the global dynamic of the power continuum between disciplinary power and biopower, is the emergent self-organization of punctuated equilibriums. Norms themselves emerge, as a consequence. Disciplinary power is no longer an imperative molding in conformity with an a priori moral or legal model. It becomes a correctional reuptake mechanism for emergent normative variation. This annexes disciplinary power wholesale to biopower's regulatory operation. The new tenor of discipline resulting from this Foucault names "normation," as opposed to "normalization" (2007, 57). When disciplinary power is annexed in this way to regulatory biopower, the mode of operation of the continuum of power as a whole assumes a new cast. Foucault calls this global mode of operation "governmentality."

It is at this point in his logic of interacting regimes of power that Foucault comes around to asking whether we are still dealing with natural subjects. Is an economized subject still a natural subject? In *The Birth of Biopolitics* (2008), Foucault's answer in many passages would on the face of it appear to be no. The neoliberal individual is not the sovereign subject, nor a moral subject, nor the subject of law. It is a "subject of interest," "heterogeneous" to these (2008, 274–276). The question of regulation is now as much about calculations of individual self-interest as it is about population-based biological processes. Calculation of interest, in a changing environment riddled with aleatory events, is a calculation of risks. The form of rationality involved in the calculation of risks is still bound to statistics. But as a "calculation" in the service of self-interest, it is at least as affective as it is rational (Massumi 2015a).

It is as much about pain, for example, as it is about competition and chances of success (Foucault, 2008, 271–277). Pain, in turn, is as much about empathy and antipathy as it is about probabilistic reason. What calculation is this?

Is it certain that the affective "calculation" will not destabilize rationalized regulation? Is it certain that the mode of operation of power will not tip from a rationality to an affectivity? Where now is the "bio" in biopolitics? Is its life environment still governable? Or is a shift taking place to another global mode of operation of power—still innovatively consubstantial with what is now neoliberal capitalism—that is beyond both biopower and governmentality? Is the power continuum tipping beyond even the provisional stability of punctuated equilibriums into irrevocably far-from-equilibrium conditions? What order is this? Does it still have the rationality of a system? Foucault's question about nature, as interpreted here, amounts to the question of what new concepts are necessary to grapple with this situation.

The counter-question from which this chapter departs is, how could the figure of a nonstandard environment, characterized by an ever-presence of indiscriminate threat, riddled with the anywhere-anytime potential for the proliferation of the abnormal, possessed of a threatening autonomy, which power must paradoxically respect in order to act on it, in a world that is in a permanently far-from-equilibrium critical condition—how could this *not* represent a major shift? To the question of what new concepts are necessary, Bush's Katrina speech gives the beginnings of an answer: a new concept of nature itself. This is the kind of answer that multiplies the question.

What is it with nature when the continuum of power no longer has the organic individual body and the species-being of the population as its poles but rather, in a stormy first approximation, war and the weather? What gives if the level at which the aleatory events characterizing the environment come incipiently to be determined is not general but as singular as the self-amplifying formation of a once-in-a-century hurricane? Would environmentality not move beyond even normation, and the biopolitical mechanisms of power associated with it? These counter-questions redouble the question of the subject of nature, with new urgency and changed valence.

The purpose of the following discussion will be to construct some of the conceptual tools necessary to follow the turbulent power vectors that "naturally" brought Bush to New Orleans in his capacity as commander in chief, and following whose arc the world has since threateningly moved along. In part, it is a preliminary exercise to approaching the issues just broached—of affectivity, rationality, and governmentality—working from Foucault after Foucault, as well as from Bush after Bush, through neoliberalism in connection with neoconservatism, and finally, dispiritingly, within an all-encompassing horizon of war.

## War Climate

In his address, Bush reinforced the war-weather continuum while at the same time strategically breaking its symmetry: "In a time of terror threats and weapons of mass destruction, the danger to our citizens reaches much wider than a flood plain" (Bush 2005b). The generic model of the indiscriminate threat remains, most broadly, the enemy in war. "Most broadly" here means most intensely: more insistently incipient, more everywhere, potentially. Weather conditions are unlikely be major formative factors in an IED (improvised explosive device) incident, but a large-scale weather-related disruption may well be enemy-agitated. Drought-induced fires in Greece in the summer of 2007 attracted investigation by counterterrorism agencies. Why? Because no one could say for sure that arson was not involved. Given that uncertainty, "we can say that this truly constitutes an asymmetric threat," said the minister of public order, "without elaborating" (Paphitis 2007).[2] Uncertainty truly determines a threat, prior to any elaboration, to be a potential national security concern.[3] In a crisis-prone environment, threat is endemic. Uncertainty is everywhere. A negative can never be proven. Positive military response must then be ever at the ready. The on-all-the-time, everywhere-on-the-ready of military response operatively annexes the civilian sphere to the conduct of war. Civilian life falls onto a continuum with war, permanently potentially pre-militarized, a pole on the spectrum. Any domain harboring threats with a potential to disrupt the rhythms of civilian life is similarly annexed, climate included.

The Bush administration formalized this operative annexation of the civilian sphere, in its chaotic interdependence with other self-organizing systemic environments such as the weather, with two reciprocal moves: on the one hand militarizing the National Guard, traditionally defined as a national police force for service in domestic crises, by extending its service overseas to Iraq; and on the other hand overturning the long-standing ban on the deployment of U.S. military forces on domestic soil, extending the military's reach in the inverse direction, toward active duty among its own civilians.[4] This mutual inverse extension of operations betokened the construction of a civilian-military continuum covering the full spectrum of indiscriminate threat. The operational continuum was laced with potential openings for outright military intervention at any point. The openings came in the form of arbitrarily invokable "exceptions" to such civil guarantees as habeas corpus and the right to privacy.

The aim was to make war response as ubiquitously irruptible as the indiscriminate threats it seeks to counter. The civil sphere would no longer stand outside the military sphere, defined as its opposite. It would become integrally paramilitary, in operative continuity with war powers, on a continuum with them, suffused with battle potential, even in peace.

The continuum, as it expresses itself on the amplified level of government administration, runs between two institutional poles. At one pole stand the many departments and compartments of the U.S. national defense establishment, and at the other pole stands that enduring monument of the Bush administration, the tentacular Department of Homeland Security.

## Natural Security

That the Obama administration would prove reluctant or unable to fundamentally reverse this full-spectrum recomposition of power was unintentionally foreshadowed before Obama actually took office. The announcement to the press of Obama's national security team contained a telling typo. "In this uncertain world," the statement read, the continued prosecution of the "war on terrorism" requires a "skillful integration" of American power in all its forms (read: on the full spectrum), enabling immediate response to any potential "catastrophe be it manmade or natural," as well as to "unconventional" (read: indiscriminate/indiscriminable) threats of any stripe. The public was assured that the future president had assembled the best possible team of "natural security" officers (New York Times 2008).

It is more than a slip of the keyboard to naturalize the continuum annexing the civilian sphere to the military. The "naturalization" at issue should not be understood in the social constructivist sense, in which the cultural comes to be taken for natural. The formula of the cultural "taken for" natural leaves the opposition between the two intact, attributing any blurring of the boundaries to mystification. Under indiscriminate threat, the opposition is no longer generally tenable and cannot be taken as a starting point. A base redefinition of nature is required outside any categorical opposition to the cultural, social, or artificial. The overall environment of life now appears as a complex, systemic threat environment, composed of subsystems that are not only complex in their own right but are complexly interconnected. They are all susceptible to self-amplifying irruptive disruption. Given the interconnections, a disruption in one subsystem may propagate into others, and even cascade across them all, reaching higher and wider levels of amplification, up to and including the planetary scale. The complexity of the interdependency among the changing climate system, the food supply system, the energy supply system, social systems, national governments, their respective legal systems, and military-security apparatuses is an increasingly preoccupying case in point.

Each subsystem harbors endemic threats specific to its operative domain. Each is also haunted by the exogenous threats represented by flow-over effects from neighboring subsystems. In spite of this diversity and variability, the relation of each subsystem to threat is isomorphic. This means that threat operates analogously regardless of the empirical characteristics of a given domain, the specificity of the domain's elements, and those elements' particular functional structuring in the workings of a given system.[5] This is as much a journalistic observation as a philosophical assertion. Let Newsweek speak. "Disease and Terror," screams a 2009 headline:

The similarities between the swine flu and biological terrorism are not coincidental. In recent years the world has changed in ways that have made the threats of natural and man-made epidemics more and more alike. As we deal with increasing prospects of a bioterrorist attack, we are also struggling with the challenge of emerging diseases. . . . The way these threats unfold—and the responses they call for—are becoming ever more similar. The central driver is the increasingly interconnected world we live in. . . . Diseases now . . . without warning, show up in far-flung towns and cities. . . . It's difficult to overstate the threat [of bioterrorist attack]. . . . It is virtually impossible to stop or interdict . . . organisms [that] would float as an invisible, odorless cloud, driven by breezes. (Henderson 2009)[6]

Threat is as ubiquitous as the wind, and its source as imperceptible. It just shows up. It breaks out. It irrupts without warning, coming from any direction following any path through the increasingly complex and interconnected world. The longer it has been that a threat has not materialized, the greater the prospects must be that it will: it is difficult to overstate an indiscriminate threat. It is impossible to stop. Absence makes the threat loom larger. Its form is a priori neither human nor natural. Its form is in the looming: as-yet undetermined potential to just suddenly show up and spread. Threat is self-organizing, self-amplifying, indiscriminate and indiscriminable, tirelessly agitating as a background condition, potentially ready to irrupt. The potential of threat is already, in the waiting, an incipient systemic disruption. The world did not wait for swine flu pandemic level five to disrupt daily routines, travel, and trade.

The etiology is always synergistic. In the web of highly interdependent subsystems, the moment a threat has amplified to noticeable proportions it is already fixing to propagate across the web of interconnections, its effects already prospectively felt. Complex nonlinear causation is the rule, between moments of the event (the outbreak already bringing a foretaste of the anticipated outcome) as between systems. The conditions of emergence of swine flu reside as much in the stress of industrial pork farming, the intensive human-pig commerce it necessitates, and the globalized capital market it feeds, as in the "natural" process of viral mutation. The "cause" of the pandemic is an ultimately untraceable nonlinear microflow that self-amplified and spread across the planet. The fateful interspecies connection between human and swine (with an avian contribution somewhere in the mix) occurred in a zone of indistinction between species, and between systems (genetics, animal behavior, economics).

Global warming is another prominent example. It is intensified by nonlinear feedback between a complex combination of factors. Hardly a day goes by without another "multiplier effect" being discovered. Even if contributing factors, taken separately, may be ascribable as either natural or man-made from the point of view of the classification scheme of a given system, in the synergistic process of their producing an effect they are integrally both and neither.[7] If indiscriminate threat could be categorized as natural as opposed to cultural or artificial it would not be indiscriminate.[8]

## Singular-Generic

Indiscriminate threat is generic threat, in a sense of "generic" that has nothing to do with "general." So far is indiscriminate threat from a generality that it deserves a name accentuating its difference: singular-generic.

The singular-generic of threat is the unstable holding-together of divergent possible ascriptions as to the form and identity of the threat in an inclusive disjunction. An inclusive disjunction is the either/or of a number of possible terms belonging to different genera copresenting themselves in such direct proximity as to stroboscope into what is effectively a both/and. The instantaneity of generic differences coming together is a singular event. More precisely, it is the just-beginning of an event, an eventfulness suddenly making itself felt. What is felt is more than the possibility of alternate ascriptions. It is the real potential for the coming to pass of eventualities answering to those ascriptions.

This incipience of an event as yet to be determined, overfull with really felt potential, carries an untenable tension. It strikes like a force. Its intensely problematic holding-together of what cannot actually come together is unbearable. The tension of this relation of nonrelation is unlivable. It must resolve itself. It is a life-problem that must play out. The both/and must shake down into one or the other. Foreign infiltrator or "homegrown" terrorist? Arson or climate change? Flu or bioterrorism? Accident or attack?

If at the moment of impact an assumption is made as to one or the other, any forthcoming response may well prove to have been misplaced by the event's subsequent unfolding. On the other hand, if at some point in that unfolding an ascription is not applied, if a determination is not made, systematic response will fail to develop.

The singular-generic is a compelling charge of felt potential striking with the full force of an indeterminacy that is not a simple lack of determination, but *a determination to be determined* of a coming event, welling into formation.[9]

The problem for systems triggering into operation to field the event is that the charge of indeterminacy which is the birthmark of the event carries across systemic determinations of it. It emerges out of the far side of the concerned systems' fielding, in the form of synergetic effects. The both/and returns. Arson encouraged and augmented by climate change: both/and. A copycat terrorist transposing the foreign onto the home front: both/and. Global warming intensified by feedback effects between human industrial activity and climate dynamics: both/and. In every case, there is the irruptive event of a threat just showing up, or noticeably crossing a threshold to another iteration. Each onset and transition hits with the force of an attack, and carries across into flow-over effects indistinguishable from one another ("the way these threats unfold and the responses they call for are becoming ever more similar"). What begins with an indeterminacy determined-to-be-determined ends by overspilling any system-specific definitions it may have been ascribed in the heat of the rapid response it necessarily calls for. What is born in indiscriminate potential, returns to it, out the far side of its assuming any determinate shape that may have been ascribed to it. The life cycle of a threat-event is a nonlinear looping, its "cause," complex and nonlocal. Any determination gained is pragmatic and provisional, relative to a particular systemic take on the event.

The accident is not one example among others. In today's environment, given the indeterminacy at impact, every event strikes with the self-overflowing attack-force of the accident. The accident is the general model of the singular-generic of threat. Or rather, since the singular-generic is by nature unamenable to any generality, it is less a model than the matrix.

### The Universal Accident

The singular-generic of indiscriminate threat must be as carefully distinguished from the notion of the a priori as from the general. Far from an a priori form of possible experience, it is the force of the formally unbearable, eventfully felt, to formative effect. It is less an ontological foundation than the matrixial strike of an ontogenetic event. Although not an a priori, the singular-generic is universal. It is immanent to all of the contributory operations of the system of systems that is the overall environment, at every point of its complexly differentiated space of operations, and at every moment of their multiple interlooping runtimes. It is on-all-the-time, everywhere-at-the-ready. Another name for its "problematic holding-together of what cannot actually come together" is the accident. The singular-generic of indiscriminate threat is the universal accident of the environment of life.

> At the root of what we know and what we are lies neither truth nor being, but the exteriority of the accident. (Foucault 1977b, 146)

The universal forcefulness of the accident is such that the tiniest local ingression of its indeterminacy actualizes the *conditions* of system-wide crisis. Whether the event of that conditioning amplifies into an actual crisis depends on a panoply of cofactors. The potential disruption that already makes itself felt with the strike of the accident may be absorbed into the system as a perturbation provoking a minor, readaptive iteration of a subset of system operations. In that case, the incipient disruption dissipates into a minor reordering that actually feeds the system's positive evolution. The force of the accident may, on the other hand, elude evolutionary capture and grow into a full-fledged systemic or even pansystemic disruption. It all depends on the cofactors with which it enters into complex resonation, within and between systems, as it feeds up in scale. It may amplify to crisis proportions, fall back into the immanence of the flapping agitation from which it breezily rose, or dissipate into a localized stir. It depends on intrasystemic response abilities and intersystem synergies. Whatever the case, it is always a case of complex co-conditioning.

### Antiaccident

Full-spectrum paramilitary power enters the co-conditioning fray with the mission to act as a synergy dampener: to stanch perturbatory amplification and its intersystem propagation. It continually toggles from one pole of its civil-military operational continuum toward the other, settling preferentially on a setting in between. It moves in lockstep with incursions of threat-potential, adopting forms as generically/singularly charged, and as proteiform in their eventual determinations, as those of threat itself. It aspires to the singular-generic. It aspires to supercharge itself with a force of indeterminacy determined to be eventfully determined, as a counter to the accident. Its vocation is to be the *antiaccident*.

The most visible form full-spectrum power takes in pursuit of its anti-accidental vocation is in the role of "first responder." This is power going out to meet the accident in rapid response, at the first flush of an eventfulness setting in. In this role, it takes many forms. The fabled first responder is the most visible figure of the hero in the "waging of peace" against indiscriminate threat.

### The Nature of Threat

Given the incipiently pansystemic reach of the slightest strike of threat-potential, it is clearly arbitrary to classify the indiscriminate threat as either natural or cultural in any final or stable way. It is just as unsatisfying, however, to say that it is a cultural phenomenon taken for natural, or again that it is a hybrid between the two. The singular-generic is logically and ontologically prior to discrete categories (which are presupposed by the notion of hybridity). An alternate strategy is to integrally redefine "nature" in such a way as to include in its potential the incipience of what comes to distinguish itself from it as "cultural": to begin with the mutual inclusion of the categories on the level of potential.[10]

Define nature as: the universal tendency for arising events to strike with a force of indeterminacy that is so determined-to-be-determined as to drive systemic evolution or breakdown. Nature is then a name for the immanent reality of the accident, as formative force.[11] It is the most singular-generic ascription to which this force is susceptible (bar God).[12] Defined in this way, the Obama team's accidental assimilation of "national security" to "natural security" makes perfect sense.

A consequence of this definition is that the more complexly differentiated and uncertain an environment, the more naturally charged it is. Nature's singular-genericness need in no way be reduced to threat. But in this epoch of the universe (to talk like Whitehead), from the lived perspective of earth's peak mammal, indiscriminate threat has become the bellwether of nature.

## Natures Natured and Naturing

It is important to note that this definition of nature does not make any force applied to counter the incipience that is the accident "cultural." Like the accident it counters, the antiaccident operates in a zone of indistinction logically and ontologically prior to the applicability of general-level classifications. Under pressure from formative forces, classifiable terms reemerge, with a difference. All are consequent distinctions, under variation.

To return to the example of global warming, what nature is for meteorology is palpably different since climate change has hit. The complexity of the interdependencies that naturally manifest themselves has vastly increased. Multiplier effects pop up everywhere. Mutual conditioning is the order of the day. Potential amplifications lurk in the slightest contributary factor and, perhaps even more worryingly, in applied counterforces (witness biofuels, which quickly about-faced from a celebrated global warming "solution" to a contributory factor, while simultaneously system-hopping into a major perturbation of the world food supply). Nature weathers far greater uncertainty, more widely fielded. The charge of indeterminacy carried in its each emergent event is intensified. Hurricanes wax "abnormal." What culture is in relation to its changed meteorological nature undergoes a correlative shift. The force and meaning of its past activity change, in back-projected synchrony with the uncertainty of its future prospects.

What nature is for meteorology is a *consequent nature*: nature as it appears for a particular system, consequent to that system's pragmatic take on its emergences. Nature comes in plurals. There are as many consequent natures as there are systems capable of wresting a serviceable nature-culture dichotomy from the zone of reemergent distinction that is nature in the universal singular-generic sense. Nature in the singular-generic is a supercharged *prototerritory* of distinctions rearising, of striking singular-generic indeterminacies coming to be particularly determined. Borrowing Spinozist terminology, the supercharged prototerritory of emergence may be termed "naturing nature," and the consequent natures distinctly wrestled with by particular systems "natured natures." Naturing nature is a prototerritory in the sense that the reiterative playing out of its formative forcing creates conditions for a plurality of extensive distinctions and their iterative regeneration. The reiteration is due to particular system's fielding successive emergences, that is emergencies, working them out and working them through, each in its own manner.

By "extensive" distinctions is meant a contrast between terms such that they can be effectively opposed to one another, as mutually external. This renders them juxtaposable, and in turn spatializable or territorializable. Each system internalizes the incursive force of naturing nature in the form of iterative variations on its own pattern of operations. The operative distinctions the system must make, to continue to make itself work, vary accordingly. This forced readaptive coupling, this folding together of a patterning of operations and an efficient system of extensive distinctions in codependent variation, constitutes a *territory*: a dedicated, internally differentiated, systemic environment. How "nature" figures for a territory, as opposed to "culture," is system-specific. System-specified nature is natured nature: naturing nature consequently coming to cultivation; formative force feeding in, working through, and being worked over.

Although consequent and cultivated, natured nature is real and effective. It really, effectively figures for the system as a given. The system's operations effectively assume it as a raw material, in passive opposition to what the system takes by contrast to be its own value-adding activity. The system-specific isolation of value-adding activity from passive nature defines what "culture" is for that environment.

A natured nature is produced *and* presupposed. It has the odd status of a produced presupposition, or cultivated givenness. This is the status Foucault attributes to the "object" of power. The emphasis on natured natures' operative reality and effective givenness distinguishes this concept from social constructivism's notion of naturalization. A natured nature is not "merely" constructed. It is both emergent and constructed, as presupposed as it is produced, given for the making and made a given. Its construction is a reemergent expression of naturing nature's determination-to-be-determined. Naturing nature is so determined-to-be-determined that it lends itself to consequent definition even at the price of bifurcating once again into an opposition between passive nature and active culture.

Such an opposition, however, holds sway only provisionally, and only on a derived level. It arises when a system's operations turn back over on themselves, in order to reference generally the particularities of the system's own process, in operative self-reflection. The appearance of a passive-nature/active-culture opposition is always a reflexive sign of a particular system's general self-referencing. It marks: a translation of the matrix of the singular-generic into a particular-general schema; a transduction of the inclusive-disjunctive intensity of an indeterminate, yet determinable, force of irruption, into a serviceable extensive distinction (serving as an ascriptive device); and a transposition of prototerritory into a territory. "Passive" nature is naturing nature natured, so as to stand, in a system's self-adapting, for its evolutionary outside. It is the systematic form in which the outside of the accident is unrefusably found, and reflexively kept, for systemic variation, in reiteration.

> *Discursus on Natures.* Foucault, in his account of governmental powers, generates a concept of "nature" answering to the criteria of what is here called "natured nature": "Nature is something that runs under, through, and in the exercise of governmentality. It is, if you like, its indispensable hypodermis. It is the other face of something whose visible face, visible for the governors, is their own action. . . . It is not a background, but a permanent correlative. Thus, the *économistes* explain, the movement of population to where wages are highest, for example, is a law of nature" (Foucault 2008, 16). Ascribable entities ("visibilities" in Foucault's terminology) are taken for visible markers of invisible laws of nature. The invisibility of the law of nature is the mode in which naturing natures's ontogenetic imperceptibility, its indiscriminability,

formally appears to the system as the correlate of its own functional operations. The laws of nature are the formal mirroring, for the system, of the system's own pattern of actions. They are the form in which the system internalizes the activity of its outside as its own.[13]

Although the distinction between natured nature and naturing nature is presented here in the context of the relation between systems normally taken for cultural and the environmental conditions within which they operate, the same distinction holds for what are normally considered "natural" systems pure and simple. A natured nature is found in "nature" in the conventional sense whenever the products of a set of operations settle together into a pattern of connection and succession (vibrations, rhythms, accumulations, articulations, reticulations) forming an emergent plane of mutual holding-together possessing a compositional consistency. A natured nature occurs in "nature" when the results of prior operations become available for reuptake into follow-on operations indexed to the plane they have composed. As taken back up, they figure as givens for the follow-on operations, whose deployment their givenness conditions. A simple example is a metamorphic rock taken up again by tectonic forces in a new composition forming a geological stratum (upon which additional specific territories may delimit themselves, in a further differentiation). Natured nature is "nature" as self-emergent and cumulatively self-conditioning. In a word, self-cultivating. The planes of natured "nature" correspond to the levels observed by the natural sciences (physical, chemical, geological, organic, etc.). Naturing nature, in relation to these levels, consists in the energetic conditions continually pumping their holding-together with eventness and transformation. In Deleuze and Guattari's account of natural composition these levels of natured nature figure as "strata" capturing energetic conditions of change and internalizing them as the motor of their own ongoing patterning (Deleuze and Guattari 1987, 39–73). Naturing nature figures as the unpredictable, change-bringing, singular-generic "Mechanosphere" running under, in, and through the strata, cutting into them and across them, sweeping them up in a continued movement of ontogenesis. Deleuze and Guattari's eventful concept of the Mechanosphere places the strata of "nature," in the natural sciences sense, on an occurrent continuum with what are conventionally considered "cultural" strata. "There is no biosphere or noosphere, but everywhere the same Mechanosphere. . . . There is no fixed order. . . . The apparent order can be reversed, with cultural or technical phenomena providing a fertile soil . . . for the development of insects, bacteria, germs, or even particles. . . . It's even worse nowadays: you can't tell in advance which stratum is going to communicate with which other, or in what direction. . . . There is no lesser, no higher or lower, organization" (Deleuze and Guattari 1987, 69). There is no realm of nature "pure and simple." There are no "laws of nature," except in Foucault's sense of the formal self-mirroring of specific systems of operation in a holding pattern on constitutionally mixed strata of the sort conventionally deemed "cultural." The concept of a "nature-culture" continuum is developed at length throughout *Anti-Oedipus* (Deleuze and Guattari, 1983) as well as *A Thousand Plateaus* (Deleuze and Guattari, 1987).

## Force of Time

The proto-"territory" of naturing nature is, in its own activity, more insistently temporal than distinctly spatial. Its everywhereness forecuts any possibility of it having a specifiable territory of its own. It occupies an intensive "zone" of spatial indistinction. Having no territory of its own, naturing nature can only "give" of itself, to various territories' systemic self-organizing. What it gives is a charge of indeterminacy to-be-determined, which strikes with driving force. Its ubiquitous "zone" of indistinction is the universal "before" of a coming to emerge. Its prototerritory is the force of time, just making itself formatively felt. The force is only determinately felt in the consequent form of its effects. The native tense of the force of time is a universal will-have-been: a will-have-been felt, for the forming (followed by a will-have-been formed for synergized on-flow and overspill, tending toward a limit of pancatastrophe).[14]

*Ontopower*

When threat becomes ubiquitously generic, and the generic makes itself singularly felt, with effectively indeterminate formative force, toward an irruptive impulsion that is immanently conditioning, driving potentially pansystemic disruption and reordering, it becomes the bellwether of naturing nature for the complex, crisis-incubating environment of life. Preemptive power directly follows.

An antiaccidental exercise of power, at whatever setting on its operational continuum, can only counter the event-driving force of the accident if it catches it in the before of incipience. To do this, it must move into that prototerritory. It must move as the accident moves, to where it may irrupt, catching it "before it actually emerges" (as the Bush doctrine of preemption instructs). It must come as "naturally" as the enemy. It must give of itself just as insistently. It must mimic the accident, in operative anticipation of the actual playing out of its potential effects. It must preempt.

Dampening accident-amplification is not enough. An alternate growth pattern must be planted on the prototerritory. Full-spectrum power preempts threat by counterproducing its own systemic effects in its stead, in a supplanting of incipience. Its business is to induce potentially systemic countereffects through an alter-emergent incursion of change-conditioning force of nature. Preemptive power is the cuckoo in the nest of naturing nature.

Preemptive power is environmental power. It alters the life environment's conditions of emergence. It is not, however, a "biopower" strictly speaking. Biopower's "field of application" according to Foucault, is a territory, grasped from the angle of its actually providing livable conditions for an existing biological being. Biopower normatively regulates the life conditions obtaining in the territory. Preemptive power operates on a prototerritory tensed with a compelling excess of potential which renders it strictly *unlivable*. It turns on an incursive surcharge from which life's iterations are obliged to wrench their reemergent formation. It targets an unlivability impelling a potential more of life to come. It does not correlate to the normative species-being of a population. It correlates to its singular reemergence. In his post-Katrina speech Bush indicated as much. He did not say, as might have been expected, that his emergency measures were aimed at bringing life back to *normal*. He said that they were aimed at "bringing life *back*."

An environmental power that returns to life's unlivable conditions of emergence in order to bring life back, redirecting its incipience to alter-emergent effect, is an *ontopower*. Ontopowers rejoin naturing nature's force of emergence, in order to ride it out, and even hijack it. Full-spectrum preemptive power is a mode of ontopower that hijacks naturing nature's force of emergence by counter-mimicking the accident.

In more familiar political vocabulary, a term that can be used for full-spectrum preemptive power is neoconservatism. This word usage is itself a supplanting. For what is meant by neoconservatism used in this sense is not a historically specific group of individuals advancing a particular political project. In this context, it refers to more than Dick Cheney and Donald Rumsfeld and their allies, working to realign U.S. foreign policy on full-spectrum preemptive power, starting in the Ford administration, continuing through the Reagan presidency, into the Project for a New American Century at the cusp of the millennium, and on to the George W. Bush administration. It refers to the tendency their actions expressed. It refers to the momentum impelling the tendency beyond this particular cast of its carriers' exit from the scene. Understood in this way, neoconservatism is a *process* carrying the force of naturing nature through history in a certain mode defined by the dynamic of the antiaccident. Each particular expression of this tendency in an explicit political project will suggest, in consequence of its playing out, extensive nature-culture distinctions for territorialization (it will produce a natured nature). The tendency itself, however, is a powerful rejoining of nature on its own naturing prototerritory. Neoconservatism, understood in this way, is an intensification of the *nature* of power.

## Process

A "process," in the terminology suggested here, is different from a system. It takes as its field of application ("where it implants itself and produces its real effects"; Foucault 2003, 28), not the ground of territory but the accidental groundlessness of the prototerritory. It does not settle into guarded and reproduced extensive distinctions. It starts in the striking simplicity of inclusive-disjunction, passing eventfully through system definition, only to overspill any and all acquired determinations ascribed it, in the end complexly rejoining its inclusive-disjunctive conditions of emergence, with an added difference (consequent to this actually-having-come-to-pass). Process refers to this life cycle of potential, from its incursion, or what Whitehead calls its "ingression," to its "satisfaction" in an actually effected transformation (Whitehead 1978, 26). The coherence of a process is that of tendency, feeding back on itself in such a way as to generate always another difference. A process is fluctual. It is essentially unstable.

A system, on the other hand, is an emergent, provisional stability arising at the crossroads of processual tendencies whose formative force it siphons into its own self-organizing. A system feeds back on itself in order to settle things for itself: in order to settle a territory. Its mode of coherence is self-reproductive. Its operations feed back on themselves in the interests of their own conservation. A system is effectively self-referencing in virtue of its operations self-guardedly turning back over on themselves. Certain system operations may take other operations of the same system as their objects. There may emerge from this operative self-referencing a second-order self-organization, figuring in a pilot capacity on a derived level of functional self-reflection.

Both process and system are reiterative. Processual reiterations, however, are difference-referenced. They are alter-referenced. The tendency is directed toward an effectively added variation. A system's reiterations, by contrast, are self-referenced.[15] The systemic tendency is toward regaining or preserving a provisional stability. Variation is again the rule, but it arises as a by-product of self-preservation. It is adaptive. The adaptability of the system depends on the evolution of a second-order self-referencing (which, once it arises, is operationally inseparable from first-order operations, or those considering themselves to act upon an object).

A system is not the opposite of a process. System is a mode of expression of process. It is a self-stabilizing expression of ingressive potential's determination-to-be-determined. A system embodies a processual tendency toward self-preservation (adaptive self-reproduction). Both process and system involve positive feedback. Thus neither a process nor a system can be accounted for without accounting for the nonlinearity of its causality.

If a system is territorializing, a process is deterritorializing—starting from and returning to the exteriority of the universal accident.

There are many systems, as many as there are natured natures. There is, however, but one process. That one process, which is naturing nature, holds the multiplicity of reemergent tendencies in inclusive disjunction. In view of this immanent multiplicity, it is admissible to speak of "a" process among others when referring to the life cycle of a tendency, bearing in mind that no one tendency ever expresses in isolation. An incursion of processually formative force always brings more than one tendency into incipient expression. It is this coming-together that must eventfully play itself out.

In the playing out of the tension of what cannot hold together, having come together, tendencies compete with each other. One may dominate another. A given tendency may end up monopolizing the production of difference. Many tendencies will fail to fully express. More creatively, a new capacity for actually holding together may emerge from the playing out. A symbiosis has been invented, immanent to process's unfolding. Systems also vie and mutually adapt, in their own ways. The complexity of the playing out of processual tendencies and their systemic expressions, in the eventfulness that is the overall environment of life, demands an ecological approach. All the more so as there is a tension and interplay between systems and process, exponentially raising the degree of ecological complexity.[16]

## Infra-Colonization

Neoconservatism is the process whereby naturing nature comes to be militarized, along the full spectrum. Emergence is militarized at the same time as the military is politicized, making civilian life a degree on the continuum of war. War is no longer the continuation of politics by other means. Politics is an intensity setting on the continuum of war. Neoconservatism, as the term is used here, is the nonlinear onrush toward dominance of this processual tendency to monopolize naturing nature for battle potential.

The neoconservative power of the antiaccident occupies the prototerritory immanent to all life's extensions. It is infra-vital. Incoming, extending upward, through, and outward. Its immanence to life is also, indiscriminately, the imminence of death: the threatening actualization, everywhere and at all times, of the conditions of emergence of life crisis.

The prototerritory occupied by the antiaccident is at life's operative limit. It is where life rebeginning loops into such short-circuited proximity to its end that the back-and-forth stroboscopes into a both/and so rhythmically taut, so compellingly tense, so indiscriminably intense, as to strike with undetermined force. The antiaccident coming—like that of the accident it preempts—carries a singular-generic imperative: reactivate or die.

## Bare Activity

Activation is a word for the leading edge of incoming event at this intensive limit of life. Bare activity is another word for it. "Bare" not as in stripped-down, but as in "barely": barely there. Activation is the just barely-there of a generically life-challenging event singularly stirring, as yet unextended and already overfull, carrying any consequent extension and all extended qualities, in welling potential. It is the barely-there of a compelling "any-and-all" at the impelling edge of incursion, to be eventfully determined.[17]

This is not Agamben's "bare life," the life without qualities. Bare life for Agamben is that life station consisting in its stripping down to the animal minimum, excluded by nature from culture and politics. It is life radically emptied, dequalified, in implosive indifference, held eventlessly in suspension. Death in life: potential stillborn. Bare activity is the taut suspense of a dynamic indeterminacy agitating the field of life's emergence. It is the already imperceptibly astir, readying toward an imperative move into another pulse of life carrying risk of death. It is the unlivable, impelling life potential (actively including that of death).

Bare activity is naturing nature's own ontopower. It is what neoconservative power preemptively infra-colonizes. The preemptive tendency is to supplant life's emergence, to antiaccidental altereffect.

> *Discursus on Bare Life.* For Agamben, bare life pertains to the "simple fact of being alive." It is foundationally excluded from poli-

tics. It is the life of the animal body (*zoe*) as against the life of the polis (*bios*). Corresponding to the voice before language, it is outside the sociocultural sphere that Agamben takes to be coextensive with the logos of language. Paradoxically, the "inclusive exclusion" of bare life forms the "original nucleus" of political sovereignty. Although Agamben ascribes the logical status of the "singular" to this exceptional state of inclusive exclusion, his concept of bare life remains tethered to the traditional classificatory logic of genus and species. What is singular about bare life is that it marks the starkness of the difference between the human and the animal, as species of the genus of living things. The bare life of the inhabitant of the camp is a human life animalized by being reduced to nothing more than the simple fact of being alive in stark contrast with impending death. The state of exception of bare life replays the specific distinction between the human and the animal ("presenting it without representing it"). At the same time, bare life's foundational inclusion, as radically excluded, relegates it to a "zone of undifferentiation" between the two. The proximity of zoe and bios in the zone of undifferentiation of the original nucleus constitutes a dialectic without synthesis (Agamben 1998, 1–10, 24).[18]

In the present account, a different ensemble of concepts is mobilized: the "singular-generic" (as a force of becoming *productive* of classif*iable* differences for the unfolding, rather than presenting a foundational replay of predetermined classifications); an active "zone of indeterminacy determined-to-be-determined" of life rearising, even at the risk of death (versus a zone of undifferentiation reduced to the passivity of pure proximity with death); "inclusive disjunction" as an effective overcharge of multiplicitous tendency (the paradoxically productive logic of mutual inclusion versus the depotentializing of the paradox of excluded inclusion); and a positively formative force of eventfulness (versus the aporia of dialectic without synthesis). These concepts are designed to displace the discussion onto an ontogenetic prototerritory that does not take such oppositions as body/culture, animal/human, natural/political, private home sphere/public sphere as in any sense foundational, and that suggests a logic of self-organizing complexity rather than one of generic-specific classificatory difference and aporia. Here the proximity of life to death is better conceptualized along the lines of Foucault's discussion of Xavier Bichat, as interpreted by Deleuze:

> The informal outside is a battle, a turbulent hurricane zone where singular points and the relations of force between them stir in agitation . . . [a] domain of uncertain doubles and partial deaths, where things continually emerge and fade . . . this is micropolitics. (Deleuze 1988, 121; trans. modified)

The stirrings in this micropolitical zone of emergence are "collected and solidified" into strata, or what in this chapter are called territories and systems. This collection and solidification involve a step-up to higher-level, macro systems operating extensive distinctions while remaining in vital touch with the singular-generic zone of their emergence, whose event energies they capture and transduce into their own driving force, in the form of self-adaptive modulations in their operations. A crucial point here is that the strata, in Deleuze's words, are fundamentally "unstable *physical* systems in perpetual disequilibrium" whose constitutive operations are "distinct from any combinatorics" (Deleuze 1988, 35–36; trans. modified; emphasis added). The strata achieve provisional stability under conditions of instability, wresting an operative order from the storm of accidental incursions. They are provisionally self-equilibrating expressions of process. Their provisional equilibrium is perpetually disturbed by incursions, and must be iteratively regained. They are re-self-organizing, in serial becoming. For Agamben, on the other hand, constituted domains of "politics" and "culture" are defined by normative systems of operations analogous to the signifying system as described by structuralism, for which the model of the linguistic combinatoric is fundamental (Agamben 2005, 36–37). A combinatorics holds the possibility of the generation of permutations in endless series, but is itself invariant. It is defined as a synchronic matrix, which is to say that its definition excludes becoming. It is by definition nondynamic. The status of an unbecoming, nondynamic matrix is purely *logical* (in the normal sense, not in the sense of an operative logic). The conditions it defines are merely *logical conditions of possibility*. Agamben's appeal to the structuralist combinatoric, coupled with the foundational exclusion of the animality of bare life, brackets the physicality of systems, and with it the real, potential-charged, naturing-natural event of their emergence. In a word, it brackets their incipience in occurrent bare *activity*. This bracketing of bare activity separates systems from their *real conditions of emergence*. In other words, it separates them from process, as defined here.

The effective role of the concept of bare life in Agamben's work is thus to consign vitality to conditions of possibility, which are then struck by the aporia of inclusive exclusion. This yields a self-defeating logic purified of the ontologic—better, the ontopower—of the universal accident as singular-generic formative force. Potential's signature expression is then construed to be the "power not-to": potential's aporetic self-suspension. This separates potential, at its highest expression, from the ingressive force of the singular, paradoxically making it generic by physical default (leaving it only logically singular, in an aporetic way). Potential's highest degree is then a degree zero of suspended intensity, as opposed to an $n$th degree of intensity in suspense, as it is held to be in the present account. Potential becomes stolidly self-recursive (Agamben's Bartleby). It loses its aleatory incursive edge, as the bare-active cutting-in of a coming ontogenetic event.

The concept of force is, it is true, central for Agamben. But in keeping with the purely logical status he attributes to the singular, the generative force the singular plays on is purely *formal*. It is entirely bound to the concept of the law. The issue is no longer the force of time, but the force-of-law. The force-of-law is "separate" from its "applicability." As applied, the law gives rise to normative effects in the empirical field. The force-of-law is the "indeterminate element" immanent to every effective juridical act by virtue of which the act is endowed with the "capacity to command." The force-of-law is nothing other than the "formal essence" of the law. The effectively generative political event is the imperative indwelling, in the norm-producing act, of the essence of the law. Faced with this generative reciprocity between "normation" and the law, what is singular about the state of exception is that it opens an "anomic space" where the applicability of law is separated from its force. This amounts to "radically separating . . . potential and act." This is a "fiction," but an effective fiction foundational to politics (Agamben 2005, 35–39). Any act of counter-singularity must assume this anomic space. Its act consists in occupying the anomie so as to "show" the fiction. It does this by "exposing itself" and only itself, as a "pure means" of expression which, like the state of exception whose singularity it counter-matches, is without empirical referent. It is a pure act of self-reference, in Emile Benveniste's structural-linguistics sense (Agamben 2005, 87–88). It is a language act. For Agamben, that act is synonymous with life, outside and against the norm. Life, for Agamben, is anomie against normation. Everything in his political thinking plays between the norm and the law, and between their politically foundational reciprocal presupposition and "life" as equated with language. Once again, physicality is suspended. The animal is excluded from "life" (if not from biopolitics, which for Agamben is the effective playing out of animality's excluded-inclusion in the political and cultural spheres). The result is an exceptionalism of the language-endowed, which can itself be placed in suspension (when speaking being enters a zone of undifferentiation with the nonspeaking animal) but never worked around or overcome. Protestations to the contrary, this amounts to a de jure supremacy of the language-endowed human over the animal (as in Heidegger).

The perspective developed here refuses to exclude the animal from politics and life, even "inclusively," or to separate in any way human expression from the animality of its body.[19] It refuses to take the law as in any way foundational, or to box life into an alternative between normation and anomie. It resituates life, rearising as bare activity, in a philosophy of creative nature: nature effectively creative of difference, in an imperative playing out not of the force-of-law but of the force-of-time. By this account, there is no "essential" participation of the law in generative process. There is no *the* law. There are laws, always on the consequent level of natured nature. The ultimate concepts are *activity and pro-*

*cess*, rather than law and language. Active process is a universal *animatedness*. The classificatory opposition between the human and the animal is no way pertinent to its concept, even though this animatedness must be counted as physical. The physicality of active process cannot be reduced to animality in the usual sense, for it is inseparable from the immateriality of eventness, tendency, and the lived quality of animatedness that is affect. "Physicality" must be understood in terms of Foucault's "incorporeal materialism" (Foucault 1982, 231).[20] Laws, norms, languages must all be re-derived from naturing nature's physical animation. For laws to take generative effect, they must cycle back through nature's active process, thence to recollect and resolidify in strata, recaptured by self-organizing systems. The only thing "essential" about them is their derivative status to the accident. The resubmitting of the law to the "exteriority" of the generative accident is necessary to separate (the deleuzo-nietzschean) Foucault from Agamben's (structuro-heideggerianizing) embrace, around issues of life and politics, and toward a rethinking of biopolitics in its relation to, and in contradistinction from, ontopower. The project is for an atheological political philosophy of nature affirmative of the positive potential of generative force, as against the negative theology of an aporetic foundationalism of the law. The philosophy most explicitly articulated on the concepts of activity and process is that of Whitehead. However distant Whitehead's political thinking may seem from Foucault's, for an ecology of powers their meeting is only natural (as is the role of Deleuze as go-between).

## National Enterprise Emergency

The supplanting of emergence by the antiaccident of full-spectrum preemptive power sows the ontogenetic seed for a Bush-like "bringing life back" with a difference. But if in order to do so preemptive power must mimic the accident it aims to counter, what prevents the antiaccident from becoming its own enemy? What prevents its counteractions from themselves amplifying into a systemic disruption? This is a real danger that neoconservative power faces by nature, and often succumbs to.

Bush's May 2003 declaration of preemptive "victory" in Iraq announced nothing so much as a protracted, self-amplifying geopolitical crisis that was to propagate to Afghanistan, then to Pakistan, then back to Iraq, and is still many years and countless lost lives from having played itself out, in spite of the change in U.S. administrations.

If the danger of "success" is so far-reaching, why risk it? Because the stakes are equally high. Neoconservative power's process does not move alone. It is one half of an ontogenetic couplet. In addition to delivering to territorial systems incipient countereffects potentially feeding those system's evolution, it cooperates with another process for which it similarly serves as an ontogenetic delivery system. It entrusts this other process with the job of amplifying its counteragitations into adaptive modulations of a more or less sustainable large-scale life system. When the feedforward succeeds, the ubiquity of indiscriminate threat is transduced into an emergent global order. A "successful" military intervention is just the first flap of a higher order fanfare. It is worth risking large-scale crisis, losing lives along the way, because the stakes are as far-reaching as they come: nothing less than global. Preemptive power infra-colonizes the environment of life toward the emergence of a macroprocess as ubiquitous, as indefinite in reach, and as tendentially monopolistic as preemptive power is itself.

If there is any doubt as to what process makes the relay, Bush once again makes it clear in his post-Katrina address. Rather than referring to the storm as a natural disaster, or a national emergency, he dubbed it a "national *enterprise* emergency." Neoconservatism's naturalization of national security activity is one half of a double movement. As power moves into the bare-active realm of emergence to bring life back, life's induced return is met by an economic expansionism that wraps life's rearising into its own global unfolding.

Preemptive power is a positive power, in the sense of delivering the potential for intersystem enhancement effects. These are maximized when its interventions kick-start amplificatory movements whose nonlinear synergies come in the form of economic multiplier effects. The enterprise aspect of Bush's Katrina response was represented by his strategy of replacing government assistance with outsourcing to the private sector and shunning the shelter of government-planned and -regulated redevelopment for the gale winds of enterprising investment following eagerly upon those of Katrina. The aim was less security-assuring than productivity-boosting. It was less a return to the perceived stability of a preperturbed normality than a fast-forward into a brave new neoliberal world of unleashed capitalist enterprise.[21] The same impulse was formalized in post-invasion Iraq by a far-reaching series of unilateral decrees issued by Coalition Provisional Authority administrator Paul Bremer starting immediately after Bush's declaration of victory, which radically reorganized the Iraqi economy along neoliberal dream-lines following the International Monetary Fund's (IMF) familiar blueprint.[22]

Neoliberalism is a sister process to neoconservatism. As it operates in this epoch, it is predisposed toward a symbiotic relaying of incursions of preempted naturing nature into the economic value-creation. It is amenable to relaying unfoldings of formative force of all tendencies. But it is most adventitiously predisposed to the neoconservative sort, flowing into the generation of profit. Or more precisely, of economic surplus-value: investment capital feeding back into its own process to produce multiplier effects driving not just growth, but in theory at least, an accelerating rate of growth. Neoliberalism, as the term will be used here, is the capitalist process turned ontopowerful, in symbiosis with neoconservatism (but also in its own right, for example, through technological supplantings of life's incipiency driven by purely capitalist concerns, as in the biotechnology industry). The symbiosis between neoliberalism and neoconservatism is not without tensions. Although adventitiously predisposed toward symbiosis, they both rejoin the prototerritory of life, in relay, but also each in its own way. The prototerritory, lacking determinate extension, knows no bounds. Thus both processes entertain monopolistic tendencies, once again each in its own way. Since they share the same unboundedness in different monopolistic modes, the two processes are in potential conflict by nature.

## Beyond Security

Neoliberalism, as a process, does not presume stability. It does not prioritize a stable-state vision of security. In a white paper extolling the virtues of globalized deregulation published not long before his ascension in Iraq, Paul Bremer cites a poll of American business executives finding that 68 percent believe that neoliberal policies increase their risks (Bremer 2001). Support for those policies was correspondingly high.

Neoliberalism wrestles with the complexity of an uncertain, neoconservatizing environment in which risk is not only endemic but inexpungible and ultimately unknowable. Far from operating in a securely closed field, it operates in what Michel Foucault calls "an indefinite field of immanence" in which life falls under the "dependence" of a "series of accidents" (Foucault 2008, 277). The interests of an individual human inhabitant of this environment, Foucault continues, will depend upon "an infinite number of things," "accidents of nature about which he can do nothing and which he cannot foresee . . . linked to a course of the world that outstrips him and eludes him in every respect." The enterprising individual of neoliberalism is at the perturbing mercy of incursions from an "uncontrollable, unspecified whole": naturing nature. Nonetheless, from this "apparent chaos" there spontaneously arise "positive effects" of convergent order. This spontaneous self-organization is owing to synergies between productive activities of the individual lives unfolding in the universal risk environment. Individual activities automatically and mutually readjust to create a "directly multiplying" mechanism "without any transcendence" (2008, 277–278). Neoliberalism operates in a field of immanence whose bare activity, fed forward and transduced into enterprise activity, amplifies into a self-expanding pattern of economic multiplier effects cresting into an emergent order. That order, which never transcends its environmental conditions of emergence, is the neoliberal economy as globalizing process. The neoliberal economy is commonly called a global "system." In terms of the present vocabulary, however, this is a misnomer. Neoliberal capitalism values its own exuberantly irrational momentum (to paraphrase Alan Greenspan) over any particular systemic holding pattern. It values "creative destruction" (Joseph Schumpeter) over self-preservation. To mark the difference of the volatile self-ordering of the capitalist process from a system, as it is defined here, Deleuze and Guattari borrow the notion of the "axiomatic" to describe it (Deleuze and Guattari 1987, 460–473).

The neoliberal economy is in a state of enterprise emergency by nature, at every complexly interconnected level, from the local through the national to the global. And it embraces that condition. Its mechanism is

to ride waves of metastability through the turbulence of a permanently uncertain environment. A metastability is not so much a provisional stability as a wave patterning. Neoliberalism's metastable order explicitly operates under the uncontrollable dependence of the unspecified accident
(and antiaccident). It does not try systematically to shelter itself from the
storm. It spontaneously self-organizes following the turbulence of a far-
from-equilibrium environment whose immanent agitation never ceases to
haunt it with the specter of its wave-convergent synergies suddenly fork-
ing into crisis. Faced with the specter of catastrophe, it does not turn self-
protectively inward. It fully assumes the risks of its ontogenetic outside.
A metastable order positively embodies instability. Rather than turning
back on itself, it flees forward. It lives out its instability. It is emergent order
on the edge, riding the wave crest of everywhere-apparent chaos. It is not
its business to pause to self-reflect. It self-references only as a technical
mechanism to boost its momentum (such is the purpose of market indexes). To self-reflect in the systematic sense is to adaptively self-regulate.
Neoliberalism is by naturing nature deregulatory. This makes it adaptively
challenged—and all the processually stronger for it.

## Exception Incorporated

For an edge system born and fed on instability, the perturbation of an "abnormal" accident, even of the magnitude of Katrina, can actually offer a
supersized opportunity. A once-in-a-century hurricane is just a "natural"
instance of the far-from-equilibrium creative destruction that is the driving force of neoliberal capitalism. For that matter, what accident is not
abnormal? It is of the very nature of the accident to confound the normal
course of things. Under neoliberalism, normativity ceases to be a foundational concern, or even a constitutive factor. The neoliberal tendency
is not to mold to the norm, as do systems characterized by Foucault as
disciplinary powers. Rather, neoliberalism's tendency is to capture the exception and incorporate it (in both senses of the word).

Neoconservative power actively concurs. It realigns its own process
along the axis of exception, in dogged pursuit of operative outs from instituted limitations on arbitrary exercises of full-spectrum force. It does
not incorporate the exception in its own right so much as it precipitates

through openings perforating the fabric of the state and governmental powers. By "state powers" is meant the interplay of the executive branch of the state with legislative systems and their associated systems of jurisprudence (constitutional, civil code, or common law). "Governmental powers" is taken in Foucault's extended sense of regulatory systems, whether or not they are formally a part of the administrative apparatus of the state, which aim to provisionally stabilize and ostensibly secure the environment of life by "rationalizing" how its teeming population of territoried systems interrelate. The neoconservative outs from state and governmental powers enable antiaccidental strikes to cut in. Neoconservatism's dedication to preemptive power puts it in a posture of pronounced processual cynicism toward forms of power that delude themselves into operating according to the principle that the overall environment of life, at the mercy as it is of indiscriminate threat, can be effectively rationalized. Neoconservative power's propensity to take every out it can from the limitations of state and governmental powers also deviates it from regulated disciplinary powers, such as the prison system, for which unregulated "black sites" are substituted. This is only natural, given how closely preemptive power embraces the "abnormality" of the accident.

> *Discursus on State Power.* Foucault defines neoliberal governmentality as an "environmental type of intervention" in which "action is brought to bear on the rules of the game rather than the players" (2008, 260). It is associated with "an optimization of systems of difference, in which the field is left open to fluctuating process" (259). The distinction between self-organizing *systems* determining of differences and fluctual *process* to which they are constitutively open is integral to Foucault's definition of present-day governmentality. That governmental action bears on the "environmental" rules of the game evokes an ecological theory of power. Attention is focused less on individual human actors than on the interactions between natural-cultural systems inhabiting an open field of accident-prone covariation. This shift in the modus operandi of power corresponds to a "massive withdrawal with regard to the normative-disciplinary system" (260) renegotiating how disciplinary power cooperates on the continuum of powers. "State

NATIONAL ENTERPRISE EMERGENCY 55

powers" as used here involves a mix of regimes of power, unique in the case of each actually existing state, between Foucault's "sovereign power" (the power "to put to death or let live"), "disciplinary" power (the normative production of the individual by a collective apparatus operating in self-enclosure),[23] and "governmentality" (regulation of production in an open "transactional" field following the formula "make live or let die").[24] Governmentality overlaps with state power but is not reducible to it: it "is both external and internal to the state, since it is the tactics of government that allow the continual definition of what should or should not fall within the state's competence" (Foucault 2007, 109). Governmentality's extending beyond and encompassing of the state exerts a defining pressure on state power, pushing it massively away from disciplinary power and at the same time placing it in tension with the arbitrariness of sovereign power. The counter-pull of sovereign and disciplinary powers in response to this centrifugal pressure gives rise to a continual movement of reciprocal reintegration and regathering (and at times mutual limitation). This movement of reciprocal reintegration of regimes of power, in its interplay with preemptive and capitalist process, is what defines the contemporary state as a system.

A typology of state powers would be based on an evaluation of the tendencies moving through particular actually existing states' signature movements of self-reintegration, as incursively modulated by the formative forces of process. This is an ecological evaluation of evolutionary tendency. It is not a description of a structure, especially not in terms of its statistically average functioning. Whenever process is included in the picture, conceptualization must link any functional description of existing formations to tendency. That is: averaged-out being (functional) must be linked to singular rebecoming; the ascriptive "what" (and "what for?") to the formative "how" (as in "come again?"). The arbitrary outs from state power that preemptive power cuts-in reinvent sovereign power, in a manner tendentially unsubordinated to the reason of state which traditionally moderated it.[25]

*Ontogenetic Couplet*

The coupling of neoliberalism with neoconservatism's assertion of the primacy of preemptive power, operating on a full-spectrum paramilitary continuum telescoping war into peace, is largely of mutual benefit to the two intertwining processes. Preemptive power, already an onto-power, gains the cachet of contributing more extensively and metastably to life-productivity. Neoliberalism for its part gains both in intensity and in extension. It gains in intensity by following closely in the wake of preemptive ontopower as it tracks the accident into the immanence of its natural environment. Neoliberalism's incorporation of the emergent effects, accidental and antiaccidental—a distinction that is ultimately impossible to sustain given the effective mimicry of one by the other—gives it a proprietary hold on life's emergence. The neoliberal economy becomes ontopowerful in operative relay with war-in-peace at every setting, from the hardest of the "hard" of all-out invasion to softest of the "soft" of data mining and surveillance. As alluded to earlier, the neoliberal economy already has its own proprietary ontopower in relay with another, in this case technoscientific, system of operations. Following the intensive investment vector of biotechnology, the economy has a direct plug-in to the variational field of life's emergence, from a specifically infra-biological angle.[26] Piggybacked on preemption, its ontopowers boost into earth orbit. As its intensification extends globally, technoscience infra-opens life to its forces of capital-value creation.

The traditional model of imperialist colonialism is not adequate to describe the ontopowerful co-operation of the neoliberal economy and neoconservative power. That view often casts the apparatus of war as a consciously applied device for capitalist expansion. This underestimates contemporary war, reducing it to the status of a passive tool. It also overestimates the knowability and manageability of capitalism. It treats the capitalist process as if it were a self-reflective system piloted by a second-order level that folds back on its operations self-referentially in such a way as to fulfill hierarchical control functions.

Both the neoliberal economy and neoconservative war power are processes. They are neither integrally self-referencing nor given to hierarchical control. It is not illegitimate to describe them as complex "open systems" if the term system is used advisedly. They are perturbatory and amplificatory. As a nonlinear consequence, they are both indefinitely complex, each within its own ambit and even more so in operative relay. Preemptive power is only apparently territorialized in the systematic operations of the military establishment. Its reach, by nature, spills over from that territory toward the civil pole of the continuum. In doing so, its operations extend ubiquitously into the prototerritory of indiscriminate threat. This is a realm that is unviable for the sustenance of any particular system, or organization. Preemption's ontopowerful countereffects cut away from rationalized state and governmental limitations, to sew themselves into the prototerritorial field of emergence. Supplanting effects then percolate back up through the organized-system levels of state, civil, and other systems. These receiving systems are forced to modulate their operations around the incursive force of the event. The only hope they have of effectively adapting is if they find a way of responding to the temporal force of the prototerritory. They respond with urgency. The state of emergency is the form in which the singular-generic, formative force of time systemically appears.

Preemptive power's umbilical link into the prototerritory of emergence gives its process uncontainable, trans-systemic scope. This dynamic uncontainment produces tensions with the military establishment which is war power's rationally assigned territory. Systematic attempts are made to rein it in. But it always outflanks them. The state of emergency is, after all, a condition of exception. And as Walter Benjamin foresaw, if anything is normal now, it is the state of exception. The state of emergency, turned everyday life condition, affords ample exceptional outs from such process encumberments as the international laws of war, internationally instituted human rights, and domestic civil liberties.

The exercise of neoconservative power follows its own rhythm. It forms its own preferential relays. It reiteratively varies its processing. It forwards its own momentum. It becomes increasingly self-driving. The on-all-the-time ubiquity of its potential deliveries to territorial systems gives it such plasticity that its drive lacks, overall, an ascribable organizational form of its own. It lives up to its vocation to be as indiscriminate, and indiscriminable, as threat. As naturingly natural, process is possessed of an operative autonomy overspilling any containable system of operations. A process abhors closure. A process achieves horizon-expanding liftoff from the institutional territories purporting to contain it. They are its launching pad. They are conditioning of its trajectory but not, of themselves, determining of it. Preemptive power lives out its nature as process, full-spectrum.

The neoliberal economy, predicated as it is on a constitutive openness to the accident, has the same tendential complexity and self-organizing drive. It similarly achieves liftoff from the territories conditioning, without containing, its emergent axiomatic order. These territorialities include national and international regulatory institutions; protectionist legislative measures expressing a nationalist dynamic in tension with capitalism's drive toward the global; moralizing formations in ecumenical competition with neoliberalism's globalism, and fundamentally uncomfortable with the processual embrace of the abnormality of the accident it shares with preemptive power; local and regional particularisms threatened by its deterritorializing momentum; and stability-seeking tendencies reacting to its unstoppable exuberance by recoiling into individual-, family-, or community-based fortresses of self-protection.[27] The neoliberal economy is a master at finding ways of using these countertendencies as a launching pad for its own process (a prime example, in relation to moralizing formations, is the rise of "prosperity churches" in the United States). At every liftoff, the neoliberal economic process frees itself to further its own process, and to renew its preferential alliance with preemptive power.

The constitutive openness of these two processes to each other is a match made in nature. There is, however, nothing ordained about their interlooping. Their connection is adventitious, a marriage of historical convenience between two processual autonomies that have happened to form, in this epoch, a mutually reinforcing ontogenetic couplet. This is not to be confused with a structural coupling. This is a processual relay, occurring at a fortuitous intersection of self-driving tendencies.

There is nothing in principle preventing the processes from decoupling, except the bonds of reciprocal strengthening born of their spontaneous convergence. Still, that reciprocity is a mighty force. Its staying power in the face of organized opposition is not to be underestimated. But it is not a destiny. The form of the processual relay naturally readjusts to some degree from one organized transition to another, as can be seen in the transition from the Bush to the Obama administrations. The Obama administration's extension of the Bush-era rules of exception in many of their forms, which came as a cruel surprise to many hopers, indicates a trans-administration tendency to hold the potential for preemption and its economic coupling in ready reserve (see afterword). Certain legal and regulatory limitations have been applied to them, it is true, and certain wedges inserted between them to loosen their mutual embrace. But these measures should be (and have been) greeted with considerable skepticism. The odds are that the neoconservative/neoliberal ontogenetic power confect is not going away anytime soon. Hope aside, it has many accidental adventures, and adventurous antiaccidents, ahead of it.

# PART TWO

# Powers of Perception

# 3 Perception Attack

## The Force to Own Time

### Syncopating Politics

"We remember what we do not see."

This is how Governor George Pataki of New York, standing pious before unseen towers, inaugurated the 2004 Republican Party Convention that was to carry George W. Bush to a second term in office, riding the surf of 9/11 and the "war on terror" one last time before the swell subsided (Associated Press 2004). Standing in the ebb, years later, far from Ground Zero, a reminder may be in order that the swell was more like a tidal wave. It burst levees, eroded embankments, and laid down sediment, leaving the political landforms over which it swept reshaped. The governor's dictum might capture something more of the altered landscape than it might first appear from its proffering as a rhetorical flourish. It locates the flourishing of the political between memory and perception. This would be familiar ground, were the relation between the two presented as one of continuity: we remember now what once we saw (the towers); or, now we see what we shall henceforth remember (the towers' reduction to ruins). Pataki, however, telescopes the moments of memory and perception into a single present tense. Memory and perception share the moment, entering into immediate proximity to each other, while remaining strangers. Their disjointed immediacy syncopates the instant from within. We do not see now what we can never have seen, even as we watched: the enormity of the *event*. The present tense where memory and perception come disjunctively together is the time of the event that is like a lost between of the towers and their ruins, an interval in which life was suspended for an instantaneous duration that was more like a stilled eternity than a passing present, comprehending reflection gone AWOL. In this time of the event, perception and memory fall out of step together, jointly retaining the syncopated power to affect. The offbeat time of the event disallows any one-to-one correlation between perception and memory. This makes the ground fall out from under the notion of representation as applied to politics. It also makes time a directly political issue: the present's relation to the past—or for that matter, to itself—is politically operationalized.

Kierkegaard famously distinguished two regimes of memory. "What is recollected has been, is repeated backward, whereas repetition is recollected forward" (Kierkegaard 1983, 131). Whereas memory as normally understood is a recollection of what has been, repetition is a recollection of what has not yet come—a memory of the future. This is not so hard to grasp if we think of repetition as self-contracting, on the model of habit. Habit moves us to the other pole of the event: from the enormity of the once-in-a-lifetime macro-event to the micro-events that are the stuff of everyday life. We say we have a habit, but we all know that it is really the habit that has us. It is an automatism that has taken hold and inhabits us. It is of its nature as an automatism to pass under the radar of awareness. We are only ever aware of a habitual action *having* occurred. What we consciously perceive are its next effects. Otherwise we would catch it in the act and decide to execute the action or not, in which case it will not have acted as a habit. A habit is self-deciding. It is a self-effecting force from the past that acts in a present that appears only in a next-effect. The present of the force's actual operation is elided. This is a kind of syncopation of time itself, where the skipped beat is the operative present, the present of the operation. This active present is expressed only in the nextness that comes of it. It actively disappears into its forward expression. We normally think of habit as bare repetition, and of repetition as barren by nature. In Kierkegaard, as in Nietzsche and Deleuze, repetition is a positive force carrying the past forward into a next expression. It is a positively organizing, even creative, force of time. This implies that it may be captured and put to use. The elision of the operative moment may be operationalized.

The U.S. military knows this, judging by the currents in war theory on which it has nourished itself since the fall of the Soviet Union and the sustained priorities of its research wing, the Defense Advanced Research Projects Agency (DARPA). In its future repetition of war, the military has been an off-step or two ahead of Governor Pataki. Like him, it knows that we habitually remember what we do not see. It also knows that this is a political-time issue critical to the "war on terror" so loudly trumpeted by the Bush administration, and with which the policies of the Obama administration have quietly remained in continuity in so many respects, despite its intermittent abnegation of the phrase.[1] But it goes further, to the philosophical realization that there is a positive power to repetition, which means that it is not barren and that even so humdrum a species of it as habit partakes of the creative force of time, the same force expressing itself dramatically in events at the macro-scale.

We need only think of attention. Attention is the base-state habit of perception. Every awareness begins in a shift. We think of ourselves as directing the shifts in our attention. But if you pay attention to paying attention, you quickly sense that rather than you directing your attention, your attention is directing you. It pulls you into your coming perception, which dawns on you as attention's next-effect. Attention is the perceptual automatism that consists in tagging a change in the perceptual field as new and potentially important and building awareness on that change, for the very good reason that it may signal a necessity of a response or an opportunity for action. The next perception into which you are pulled is already a convocation to action-reaction. According to contemporary perception studies, in a confirmation of attention's habitual nature, this happens in the elided present of repetition.

> *Nonconscious Aside:* The gap between consciously registered shifts in attention is called "attentional blink" in the experimental psychology literature. It refers to a fraction-of-a-second blanking out of conscious awareness that occurs between successive changes in the perceptual field. The gap in awareness corresponds to a latency period in perceptual processing during which the coming perception is undergoing "potentiation." The gap in awareness during the potentiation of emerging perception was first brought to general attention by Benjamin Libet, in a series of now-famous experiments in the 1970s (Libet 2005). The term attentional blink was introduced in 1992. Since that time, attentional blink and associated issues in nonconscious perception have been the object of a steadily expanding and diversifying field of specialization within experimental psychology.[2]

Much of the research energy has been dedicated to studying nonconscious perceptual processes occurring in the attentional gap in awareness during which a next conscious perception is informing, in potential. It has been found, for example, that conscious shifts in attention are pre-rehearsed on the nonconscious level in the form of emergent patterns forming amid the largely random autonomic micro eye movements (or saccades) that coincide with the blink in attention. Tendential saccadic movements toward the focus of coming attention are detectable. A major area of research has been the phenomenon of "priming." This refers to the capacity of micro-events occurring in the attentional gap to modulate the coming perception. The modalities of priming are numberless. All involve what—were they not occurring nonconsciously—would be considered "higher" cognitive functions (face, object and word recognition, situational understanding of images that pass by too fast to enter conscious awareness, generalizations concerning, for example, cultural difference, gender, and race, and even decisional cost-benefit analysis).

What distinguishes priming from the outmoded concept of subliminal influence is that priming does not imply a straightforward stimulus-response operating by linear causality, akin to a reflex. Priming *conditions* emergent awareness (creatively modulates its formation) rather that *causing* a response (reproducing a preexisting model). It implies complex thought-like processes occurring as a nonconscious dimension of emergent perception, too rapidly for thought actually to have been performed. The implications of priming for the philosophy of perception, consciousness, and decision have barely begun to be plumbed. A. N. Whitehead's concept of "nonsensuous perception" (Whitehead 1967a, 180–183; Massumi 2014b) and C. S. Peirce's concepts of "perceptual judgment" and "abduction" are far better starting points for this task than either the archaic behaviorist model informing theories of subliminal influence or the neuronal reductionism informing much of today's experimental psychology (Peirce 1997, 199–201; Peirce 1998, 155, 191–195, 204–211, 226–242; Massumi 2015a, 44–53).

The DARPA program concerned with attention and related perceptual issues is the Augmented Cognition Program. The program's purpose is to develop wearable technology enabling real-time brain and physiological monitoring of states of awareness, lapses in attention, and the nonconscious perceptual processes occurring in the gaps. The monitoring technology is designed to be networkable in such a way as to enable tactical coordination aimed at diagnosing and overcoming limitations in battlefield performance related to deficits in attention, reaction time, and memory-formation capacity, either inherent in the human perceptual apparatus or induced by fear, stress, fatigue, and the "fog of war." The program also has a positive aim: it is proposed that the technology be used in training to help soldiers develop perceptual techniques to increase their "cognitive load" capacities beyond average parameters. These techniques include ways of increasing vigilance by diffusing attentiveness across the perceptual field ("continuous partial attention") or by distributing focused attention ("multitasking"). The strategy of increasing vigilance by diffusing attention is particularly relevant here, in that it amounts to an operationalization of what is discussed below in terms of the "in-bracing" of "bare activity" understood as incipient action-ability. Chapter 4 treats at length the most radical lines of attack in the U.S. military's post–Soviet Union project of operationalizing the "blink" in perception and cognition through techniques of attention, habit, and priming integrated systemically into informational networks.[3]

## The Proto-Epistemology of War

The possibility, evoked by Pataki's statement, of operationalizing the elided present of attention at political ground zero must be understood against the backdrop of the realignment of military doctrine over the last twenty years on "full-spectrum force." Full-spectrum force is the extension of military affairs to "grey areas involving non-traditional Operations Other Than War (OOTW)," in the words of Harlan Ullman and James Wade, the authors of *Shock and Awe*, one of the classic statements of the doctrine (Ullman and Wade 1996, 18). This expansion of the compass of military operation beyond the classical battlefield to areas formerly considered the exclusive purview of civil institutions is a response to the blurring of boundaries characterizing contemporary war, in which the archetype of the enemy is no longer the uniformed soldier but the "terrorist." The assumed organization of the adversary, as another contemporary classic drives home (Arquilla and Ronfeldt's *Networks and Netwars*, 2001), is then no longer the identifiable regular army and its centralized state scaffolding but the diffuseness of the network. On this, even the second-term Obama, on the eve of the U.S. drawdown in Afghanistan, remained in syncopated lockstep with his predecessor in the White House: "For the foreseeable future the most direct threat to America at home and abroad remains terrorism. . . . We have to develop a strategy that matches this diffuse threat . . . to more effectively partner with countries where terrorist networks seek a foothold" (Obama 2014a).

The network is diffuse because recessive. It melts into the population. It is pervasive, "unbounded and expanding" (Arquilla and Ronfeldt 2001, 10). It insinuates itself across the technological and communicational nerve paths of society. The attacks it enables irrupt without warning. They rise up from within an unbounded field, rather than striking out in a determinable direction from a locatable base. The infiltrating reach of "netwar" is potentially coextensive with social and cultural space. This irrevocably blurs the boundaries between the civil and military spheres. Other boundaries blur as a consequence, for example, that between offense and defense (Arquilla and Ronfeldt 2001, 13).

When the civil is no longer clearly demarcated from the military, nor offense from defense, it becomes impossible to say where the exercise of force begins and ends. Military affairs bleed across the spectrum. They span a continuum stretched between two poles or extremes. At one end lies the traditional application of "force on force" (Ullman and Wade 1996, xxiii, 21–22). This is the pole of traditional engagement on the model of the battle, siege, or occupation. At the other pole lies "soft power" (Arquilla and Ronfeldt 2001, 2). As a first approximation, soft power can be understood as the military use of information and disinformation, and of "psyops" or what used to be called psychological warfare. Arquilla and Ronfeldt characterize soft power as "epistemological" warfare because its business is what people know or think they know.

Of course, epistemological warfare is nothing new. But the paradigm has significantly shifted. Traditionally, what is now called soft power was a helper to hard power. It was secondary to force-on-force, whose effectiveness it was meant to boost. It was an additive, like leavening. Now on the other hand, according to Arquilla and Ronfeldt, all conflict is by nature epistemological. Soft power, rather than an additive or booster, is a baseline state. This is a necessary consequence of the full-spectrum situation. War is no longer punctual, like a battle. It's on low boil all the time. It is no longer localized, like an occupation. The heat is everywhere. The definition of action underpinning the force-on-force of hard power is fundamentally that of friction: matter on matter, metal on metal, projectile against shielding, metal in flesh, flesh splayed, splashed on hard surfaces. Force of attack against opposing force of resistance. The overall aim of force-against-force is attrition (Ullman and Wade 1996, xxiii, xxviii). It meets the enemy head-on and wears down his capabilities across an extensive series of frictional engagements. Its aims and means are painfully tangible.

In the current field of conflict, this kind of punctual engagement has lost its centrality. It has been replaced by waiting. Being in the thick of war has been watered down and drawn out into an endless waiting, both sides poised for action. The baseline state is now this always-on of low-boil poising for action. One is always in the thin of it. When a strike of force-against-force comes, it stands out against the background continuity of this thin condition, which Paul Virilio presciently called the "nonbattle" years before it became the obsessive concern of leaders both military and civilian (Virilio 1975). When it comes, the irruption of action is an ebullition, a momentary boiling-over in this low-intensity broth of the always-on conflict of the nonbattle. In the nonbattle, the relation between action and waiting has been inverted. Waiting no longer stretches between actions. Action breaks into waiting.

Soft power is how you act militarily in waiting, when you are not yet tangibly acting. It is a way of preventing the wait itself from being an attrition, or even a way of turning it to advantage. In the condition of nonbattle, when you have nothing on which to act tangibly, there is still one thing you can do: act on that condition. Act to change the conditions in which you wait. After all, it is from these same conditions that any action to come will have emerged. By acting on the wait-time conditions in the intervals between boilings-over, you may well be able to reduce the potential of an eventual attack, moderate its powers of attrition if it comes, or even better, induce it to take tangible shape when and where you are ready for it. That way you have a chance of disabling it before it reaches its full magnitude, or even in the case where it bursts forth at full strength, you can be reasonably confident that you will be able to respond to it with rapid and overwhelming counterforce.

Thus you take as your military field of operation the environmental conditions in which both combatants and the noncombatant population live, or what Ullman and Wade call the "total situation" (1996, 9). The only way to act on the total situation is to act on the conditions of emergence of the battle, prior to its occurrence. These conditions concern threats that in the parlance of the doctrine of preemption, which has come to define the present era of conflict as integrally as deterrence did the Cold War, are "not yet fully formed" (see chapter 1). What is not yet fully formed is still in potential. It may already be brewing like a recipe for disaster, or ominously looming like an unclear, almost-present threat. It carries an irreducible degree of indeterminacy. That measure of indeterminacy makes it as intangible as it is ominous. It's a tall order: you must act "totally" on the intangibles of the situation's conditioning. The ultimate boundary blurred is between the tangible and the intangible, the corporeal and the incorporeal. Because to act on the former you have to act on the latter.

There are two ways to act totally and intangibly on a situation. The first is by transposing your action from the spatial axis of the battle, siege, or occupation to come, onto a time axis. You operate in and on the *interval* in which what is not yet fully formed is already imperceptibly brewing. You can act on that *almost-present* in order to influence the active form of its next-awaited emergence. Preemption is proaction: action on the conditions of action, prior to its actually taking shape. The second way to act totally and intangibly on a situation is to act on perception. It is perception which prepares a body for action and reaction. By modulating perception, you can *already* modulate subsequent action-reaction. This in fact makes perception a royal road to the almost-present. The two ways of acting intangibly with a view to the total situation are convergent.

It was perception's powers of proaction that motivated Arquilla and Ronfeldt's characterization of contemporary war as epistemological. But it is a mistake to take too cognitive an approach. The move into perception is accompanied in the contemporary theater of war with a correlative move toward the "capabilities-centered" approach much touted by Donald Rumsfeld and his fellow neocons (Rumsfeld 2002b). In this approach, you move into perception in order to operate not at the level at which actions are deliberatively decided, but at the level at which the very capacity for action is forming. Operating on the level at which decisions have been *made* focuses on the properly cognitive aspect of knowledge: its informational contents, their availability, reliability and manipulability, their actual usability. Operating on the level at which the capacity for action is *in the making* is a very different proposition. It focuses on a pre-decision process occurring in an interval of emergence antecedent to both informed knowing and deliberative action. This is a point before know-ability and action-ability have differentiated from one another. At that point, a modulation of perception is directly and immediately a change in the parameters of what a body can do, both in terms of how it can act and what it will know. This antecedent level of capacitation or potentialization is *proto*-epistemological—and already ontological, in that it concerns changes in the body's degree and mode of enablement in and toward its total situation or life environment.

Any application of force at this level is an *ontopower*: a power through which being becomes. An ontopower is not a force against life, as any force-against-force must inevitably be at its point of application. It is a positive force. It is positively productive of the particular form a life will take next. It conditions life's nextness. It is a force *of* life.

## The Force to Own Time

Ullman and Wade are unambiguous about the fact that operating on this level is indeed an exercise of force, even though its object is intangible. It is not a lesser force, even though it is exerted in the thinness of nonbattle. It is, they say, "*more* than an application of force"—a surplus of force (Ullman and Wade 1996, xxvii). It exceeds the parameters of tangible applications of battle-force and of the known contents of life upon which those applications bear and to which they add a hard permutation through their action of attrition. The productive force of the nonbattle returns to the level of conditioning at which the parameters for attritional force are set. There is always a follow-up action-reaction to an exercise of force-against-force. There is a second-next enveloped in the next, and a third in that. What is conditioned is a forward series of potential repetitions. There is a power of potential continuation, a power of a continuum, wrapped up in each exercise of force-against-force. The power of the continuum is an *excess* over any next, immanent in each one. Nonbattle force takes this excess as its field. This is what makes an exercise of ontopower a surplus of force—or a *surplus-value* of force. The relation of nonbattle force to the force-against-force is analogous to the relation discovered by Marx between money as a means of payment and money as capital.

Capital is the driving force of the series of payment exchanges: money in the making; money beyond money. At each payment, a punctual return is made to capital. Profit is fed back into investment, replenishing the forward-driving force of capital. Money loops from its punctual exercise as means of payment into a feeding of the conditions of its own continuing. This excess of forward-driving force over any given payment-engagement is surplus-value, as distinguished from profit. Surplus-value is not the amount fed back. That is profit. Surplus-value is different from profit. It is not quantitative. It is processual. It is the processual quality from which quantities of money are generated in forward-driving fashion. It is the ever-nextness of proliferating quantities of economic value. Surplus-value is realized punctually in the explicit act of exchange, in such a way as to cyclically exceed any such exchange. Value beyond value, immeasurably on the make.[4]

"Nations make war the same way they make wealth" (Cebrowski and Garstka 1998).[5]

Like capital, nonbattle force is at the same time forward-driving and cyclic. At each frictional engagement, it feeds back into itself toward the conditioning of what will come next. It is the ever-nextness of actual military value as realized punctually in explicit acts of war. *Force-beyond-force*, intangibly on the make. The force-beyond-force is the processual quality of conflict from which tangible military outcomes are generated.

Ullman and Wade do not hesitate to link the force-beyond-force, as processual quality of war, to time.[6] This is not, they say, a force to overcome resistance. Rather, it is the force "to own time" (Ullman and Wade 1996, xxvii, 53). Recent military thinking has revolved around the concept of rapid dominance. " 'Rapid' means the ability to move quickly before an adversary can react" (xxv). The *force-to-own-time* operates in an interval smaller than the smallest perceivable. "The target is perception," always and at every band along the full spectrum (28). Even in the thick of things, when conflict boils over and force-against-force is to be engaged, the force-to-own-time must still operate. It must squeeze into an interval smaller than the smallest perceivable between actions, so as to condition the enemy's reaction. This is the "shock" of shock and awe. The exercise of force-against-force is qualitatively different from the force-to-own-time, but if its exercise is separated from the force-to-own-time it rapidly loses its effectiveness. The force-to-own-time is *infra-level* force. It is infra-active because it occurs in a smaller-than-smallest interval between actions. It is infra-perceptual because this same interval is also smaller than the smallest perceivable. And it is infra-temporal because, being imperceptible, the interval of its exercise is an offbeat of time, a missed step in the cadence of actions and reactions, an elided present between one moment and the next.

In the thin of things, at the nonbattle end of the spectrum, the force-to-own-time still operates to infra-condition action by "controlling the enemy's perception" in the interests of "total situation control" (Ullman and Wade 1996, 9, 54). In the absence of dramatic action spiking punctually from the baseline of the nonbattle, the conditioning of the environment by the force-to-own-time appears continuous. But this is only so because we are not paying attention to paying attention. The offbeat is still there. The baseline habit of perception has not ceased contracting itself in us. It still inhabits us. The pull of attention has not ceased to take hold of us. It still directs us to a next perception, and through it to next action-reaction. The baseline of war has accordioned into the baseline of perception. At the infra-level where the two baselines converge, war at the macroscale of the battle, siege, and occupation falls into absolute processual proximity with war at the microscale of everyday civilian life.

## The Life Bare-Active

The infra-interval is where perception itself is in absolute processual proximity with the body. This raises the military (and political) stakes inestimably.

The automatism that attention possesses by virtue of its sharing a nature with habit means that its operation rejoins the reflex workings of body matter. It is our bodies that contract habits, which are acquired reflexes. The operation of attention occurs at a point of indistinction between emergent perceptual experience and the autonomic mechanisms of the brain and nervous system. To a certain degree you can bypass the shielding or immunizing effects of preoperative cultural conditioning as well as of personal histories, dispositions, and allegiances, by plugging into the nervous system and approaching attention from that autonomic angle. It is possible to find tangible handles to leverage the intangible dimensions of the life of the body. It is possible, within limits, to machine experience.

The limits are due to the fact that the system of perception, like capital, essentially involves feedback and is thus, like an economy, nonlinear. By definition, in a nonlinear system you cannot guarantee a one-to-one correspondence between a given punctual input and an outcome. You do not *cause* an effect. You effect a *modulation*. You can create resonance and interference effects at the emergent level. The smaller-than-smallest interval of the force-to-own-time vibrates with infra-level agitation. The innervated body poises, in vital commotion. It reacts: habits are primed. It proacts: its reacting is already a tensing and a tending to the future. The body is attending in the instant to the immediacy of life's unfolding. Everything hangs in the balance. Except, far from equilibrium, the balance is off. Everything hangs in the off-balance of the instant. The nature and duration of the agitation formatively filling the instant inflects what follows.

The object of full-spectrum power's force-to-own-time is not "bare life." It is not human life re-animalized, stripped of its human content, its vitality reduced to the physical minimum, in absolute proximity with death. It is *bare activity*.[7] This is human life in the instant's offbeat. In that instant, a life is *barely* there, recoiled, bodily consumed in its infra-relation to itself. It is a life without determinate content. In that imperceptible instant, what its content will be next is in the making. A life is *formatively* barely there, tensely poised for what comes next. In that measureless instant, a life is intensely barely there, regathering in an immediacy of its capabilities. This is not vitality reduced to the minimum; this is *life primed*. This is also war. The life primed may indeed be in proximity to death. Yet the body is already arcing toward a next vital exercise of its capacity to act. Not re-animalization: re-*animation*: a stoking for the next step. This is a far cry from a life reduced to brute matter. It is the embodied event of a life regathering in recoil. This is life self-enfolding in *affective* vitality.

The object of full-spectrum power is the affective body regathering in its capacities across a stepped interval of change. Which is to say that full-spectrum power does not actually have an object. Rather than having an object, it finds a fulcrum—if a fulcrum can be said to leverage time. It leverages the future, in the bare activity of action dawning.

Shock, in the next instant, spills over into action. Infra-agitation amplifies, issuing in a macro-move. The actual resulting action does not exhaust the commotion of bare activity preceding it. That infra-activity coincides with a recapacitation of the body poising it for any number of potential outcomes, only one of which eventuates. The unacted remainder of capacitation constitutes a background modulation of the operational parameters of the field of potential action. It is by virtue of this reconditioning of the pragmatic field that the outcome is always in some degree nonlinear. The conditioning interval of shock does not simply issue an ensuing action. It sets that next actual action against an unexhausted background of potential actions, many of which are in actuality mutually exclusive. The outcome overall is a changed *relation* between the action that has actually resulted and the newly modulated experiential field from which it emerged. It is "ecological."[8] The field of potential action vibrates with the resonances and interferences of poisings unperformed, unsatisfied in action. This ecological remainder of actionability accompanies the ensuing action, retensing it even as it happens.

## Shock

The ecological relation between the action and its dynamic background colors the action's affective tonality. The bare-active poising is embodied in a *posture*, which, like a posture in the everyday sense, complicates the action with the vaguely felt accompaniment of what has been left unacted and will inflect further actions coming after. It is through posture that the agitation of shock and its poising commotion feeds forward through the line of actual actions. Posture holds the arc of the action-line for the present. It is the dynamic form of infra-agitation's presently passing down the line: a dynamic holding pattern of inflection's on-flow; a carrying-on of continuously modulated action capacity; a *carriage* of pragmatic potential.[9] Less decisive than an action, more insistent than a state of rest, posture is not exactly active or passive. More moving than passivity, less momentous than activity, it registers the bare activity of an action, in infra-accompaniment to it. Posture as carriage is the dynamic sign of bare activity uncoiling from the infra-interval into action, and carrying the intensity of that passage across actions, under variation.

Posture, as a sign, is indicative of a continued ecological conditioning of the pragmatic field. Carried with the conditioning is a continuing uncertainty. The resonating and interfering remainder of capacitation flowing down the line is as apt to remodulate on the fly as to follow the arc. A field once inflected may reinflect.

This poses a problem for the military exercise of force-beyond-force. As a force-to-own-time, its avocation is to leverage futurity by altering action's conditions of emergence. The fact that the outcome of shock it administers toward this end is complex—a dynamic relation between a punctual action and its continuously modulated background conditioning—means that the future it inflects retains a significant degree of uncertainty. Force-beyond-force must concern itself with managing uncertainty, not only that associated with preexisting field conditions into which it intervenes, but with its own future success.[10] Strategies must be put in place to manage the arc of the action-line to prevent it from drifting too far afield or reaching a sudden turning point where it bifurcates unexpectedly. A kind of shock therapy becomes necessary. Military strategy crucially assumes the task of shock management as a central feature of its ontopowerful perceptual conduct of proto-epistemological warfare.[11]

The strategies are many. All involve the use of force-against-force. The future is accessed by addressing perception, perception is accessed by a call to attention, and the call to attention is by nature an administration of shock—especially considering that what qualifies a call to attention as military is that ignoring it is not an option. It is forced. However "softly" administered, it does violence. It administers an affective jolt. The ontopower of the force-to-own-time is an added value, a surplus-value effect, of hard power's violence. It is force-against-force which gives ontopower purchase. Battle and nonbattle go hand in fulcrum. Force-against-force is the "realization" of soft power, just as the economic act of purchase is the "realization" of capital. Force-against-force and force-beyond-force, battle and nonbattle, are processually wed. They are reciprocal functions. It is only at the far ends of the spectrum of force that they seem to separate out.

At the far end of the spectrum, at the furthest extreme of the force-to-own-time, lies soft power at its softest: the simple call to attention, administered by an emission of signs, without explicit violent action. The call to attention *suspends*. It interrupts habitual or conventional entraining of actions, if only for an imperceptible affective interval, in order to inflect their direction. At its softest, soft power exerts a deflecting force of interruption. It reorients action potential. It suspends to divert, and diverts as a smaller-than-smallest step toward ecosystemic "total situation control." The diversion may involve traditional techniques designed to "deceive, disguise, or misinform" (Ullman and Wade 1996, xxix). In this form, it is "info-war" understood in the traditional sense of propaganda war (a subset of "psyops").

The notion of propaganda, and even of info-war, is inadequate for understanding the perceptual deployment of full-spectrum force. It misses two crucial points. First, the administration of shock addresses infra-instantaneous recomposition of the pragmatic field. This means that it is addressing *potential* actions. The meaning value or informational content of the intervention is in affective suspense. In that instant, it is indeterminate. Soft power's fulcrum is the vital affective dimension of bare activity. At the heart of its exercise it is life processual, not informational or communicational. Cognition, understood according to the currently dominant model of information processing, and communication understood as mediated information transmission, may well enter into the planning of the intervention and will rejig into retrospective operation in the aftermath. This does not change that fact that the leverage point is purely affective: a suspensive jolt. An exercise of soft power, even at the soft extreme, can forgo information manipulation. It can limit itself to a bare technique of attention, whose every little shift is a suspenseful micro-shock to the infra-system. This leads to the second reason against the notion of propaganda war: there are circumstances in which the military effect of soft power can be enhanced by a conscious awareness that an infra-hit has taken place. This is a *felt* awareness, without determinate cognitive or communicational content: a conscious perception of being imperceptibly affected, lines of action and analysis momentarily interrupted, in able embodied suspense.

## Awe

This felt awareness is in *awe* of the force-to-own-time. Awe is the conscious registering of shock. It is the cognitive aftershock of a perception attack on bare activity. The military effect of an administration of hard power in particular can be awe-fully enhanced. What is specific to full-spectrum power is not its use of (mis/dis)information. What is specific to it is that, from one end of the spectrum to another, cognition is systematically, dynamically, bodily remanded to an affective event-dimension addressed by direct perceptual means, to awe-full effect. At the heart of the force-to-own-time lies the perception attack. At that fulcrum, signs function in all immediacy as performatives: event catalyzers.

As Deleuze and Guattari point out, a performative sign only requires a minimal grammatical difference, presenting just enough semantic contrast to catapult the body into an affective posture of poised participation in a changing pragmatic field, of whose potential the sign effects a direct inflection. The minimal grammatical difference between "Fire!" and "Fore!" inflects a world of pragmatic difference. More than informing the mind, the call to attention differentially "insigns" the body: it immediately inserts the body into a field of potential under imminent transformation, the marked suddenness of which calls the body to abruptest attention, forcing it to assume an adaptive posture without first pausing to cogitate. The suspended interval is not of informed reflection, but of bare-active bracing. It is an integral absorption in the coming event. It is a consuming of the life of the body with its own readiness-potential, self in-bracing. This sign-triggered self-consuming of the body's potential for readiness is a direct exercise of power. It is an *induction* (in its military sense as well as in the sense of "to induce"). "A grammatical rule is a marker of power before it is a syntactical marker" or a conveyor of semantic content as such (Deleuze and Guattari 1987, 75–76).

## Shock and Awe

The shock and awe of war is less a question of psyops in the sense of info-war or propaganda war than it is of "signature management" (Ullman and Wade 1996, 2, 6). *Signature management* in this context is the performative signposting of militarily changing life conditions.[12] Its aim is to stretch the modulation of the pragmatic potential of postured bodies into a serial repetition extended over time. What is managed is the rhythm of shock's passing suspensefully into awe and issuing in actions that may lend themselves retrospectively to reflection along lines desired by the shock administrators. What is managed is the syncopation between the infra-instant of affect and macro-time action-line.

The management of this rhythm can almost be thought of as a "signature" in the musical sense. Its aim is to set the beat for emergent experience in the field of war. The time signature of the serial perception attacks may leave an empty beat for reflective cognition—or not. When it does, info-war in the traditional propaganda sense may fill the beat. The conduct of info-war, syncopated by repeated and varied perception attack, will nevertheless tend to be discursively challenged. The possibilities for meaningful development of a sustained discursive logic will be undermined by the cyclic interruptive return of the re-bracing offbeat of shock. Under these conditions, the general result of propaganda is more likely to be an affectively fueled speculative run on whatever minimal information survives the offbeat, than it is to be a settling into a transmitted ideological position. Affectively fueled runaway information takes the form of rumor. Runaway rumor in turn fuels conspiracy thinking. When it comes to information, signature management is less oriented toward meaningful persuasion or ideological inculcation than it is preoccupied with controlling the rumor-producing process it sets in motion itself.

The incitement of rumor is in many ways a positive thing for the military strategist because it heightens the awe. The heightening can go to the point of inducing skips in the beat of action, effectively prolonging the shock-effect and bumping it up to the macro-level where its suspension of potential action translates into actual passivity. Passifying enemy bodies is of course a most useful tool of war. But it may not be strategically desirable in all phases of an operation. It is not an advantage, for example, when the modulation of the pragmatic field is meant to issue at some subsequent step into "nation-building" lines of action, as was ostensibly the case in the Bush administration's invasions of Iraq and Afghanistan. The heightening of awe may also backfire, particularly when it is overextended. Fear and uncertainty fatigue may set in, causing awe to fade into resentment, evoking a reactive posture more likely to result in resistance. Bodies then must be called powerfully back to attention. A next perception attack will have to be administered in the hopes of shocking them back into a more "pragmatic" posture.

## Time-Based Terra-Forming

Signature management invariably involves linguistic signs, from pamphlets to proclamations to news conferences. For maximum performative effect, however, it must make frequent use of nonlinguistic signs. In the case of an invasion, these may involve, among many other things: displays of weaponry demonstrative of the capacity for further intervention; the removal of flags, portraits, monuments, and other countersigns of the old regime; the striating of the territory with marked no-go zones, special function areas, and checkpoints regulating the flow of the everyday; varying patterns of movement as troops, military police, military contract workers, and both civilian officials and military officers selectively show themselves, deploying and redeploying in ways that may be frightening or comforting but always demand attention; and signals conveying a capacity for sudden, unmarked intervention, for example, through random stops and searches or intermittent rapid attacks liable to occur anywhere at any time, so as to render ever-present the threat of violence. Given the fraughtness of any war situation, even interventions carrying linguistic content will pack an illocutionary force of variable character and magnitude depending on the delivery. For example, a mass airdrop of pamphlets following an intensive bombing campaign, a tactic used early in the Iraq invasion, is a very different "proposition" than the same pamphlet hand delivered by occupying forces on patrol.

The advantage of nonlinguistic sign action is that it performatively effects a kind of terra-forming. The interventions touch ground. When they do, they spatialize what is an essentially temporal form of power, the force-to-own-time, in what amounts to a processual phase-shift analogous to the transition from water to ice. The phase-shift enables military force to toggle to more classical tactics, such as occupation and zone-clearing, as needed. But the spatialization is never complete. It cannot be allowed to become frozen completely in place. Full-spectrum force implies a peculiar mode of occupation in which the territory is held without actually being occupied (Deleuze and Guattari 1987, 352–354, 363–364, 368).[13] Control of the territory depends much more on the ability to rapidly redeploy than on an implanted spatialized presence rigidified into a war of position. Time remains the overriding operational parameter. Military theory and strategic manuals become and remain speed-obsessed. Territorial control becomes less a traditional taking and holding of space than a time-effect. Time-based interventions take place more in the form of redrawable on-the-ground zonings and on-the-fly spatial differentiations than enduring structurings of the territory.

The lay of the conflictual land is the spatial form in which a time-based power process effectively appears, in much the same way that the color of an afterimage is the optical form in which a time-based visual process, in itself imperceptible, effectively manifests itself. Under pressure of a temporal power, the territory takes on characteristics of flow. It becomes meltable and malleable, unsettlable and resettlable. The potentialized flexibility of a capabilities-based approach coupled with rapid response submit the territory to repeated destructurings and adaptive restructurings. What is at stake is less a definitive striation of the terrain than a management of patterns of movement, in all of their operational, performative, and affective dimensions. All parties, friend and enemy, military and civilian, are swept up in overall ground conditions of flux. The ground of war is a surfacing, on the macro-perceptual scale, of recurrent background conditionings occurring in the suspensive interval of the infra-instant.

The territory is the surface form extruded by the life-priming of bare activity. It is the effective form of expression of what Deleuze and Guattari would call a cutting edge of deterritorialization (1987, 88 109, 587), understood as the processual suspension of prior griddings remitted to the formative commotion from which they emerged. The perception attack is the edge of that edge: the cut. The ground of war floats and tosses on a commotional abyss incised by the force-to-own-time. The territorial striations of the surface are the functional traces of generative fault lines racking the embodied potential of a population.[14]

The fact that what the force-to-own-time most directly manipulates are signs does not make it pacific. Even at the far end of the spectrum, at the softest signature-managing degrees of soft power, its performative semiotic force does violence. In the arena of war, every sign emitted by an adversary is a sign of potential danger. It is a threat. Threats command attention. They rivet. They plug directly into the nervous system. They shock the body into infra-agitation. They tangibly stir the body, so as to intangibly modulate its life potential across a bracing interval of suspense. This is a bodily violence, committed immaterially, performatively, in a hit of perception.

Soft power does not in the end, even at the extreme end of the spectrum, separate itself out from violence. It *immaterializes violence*.[15] It suspends the physical friction and ups the perceptual quotient. What varies across the full spectrum of power is the ratio in the equation of violence of frictional acting-out to perceptual in-action, of attrition to in-bracing. What seems to be a separating out at opposite ends of the spectrum, violence at one extreme, soft persuasion at the other, is nothing of the sort. The relation of violence to persuasion is not binary, on-off, zero-one. The spectrum is exactly that: a spectrum, a continuum. The two terms are imbricated, enfolded in each in mutual processual implication. What varies as the cutting edge of operational engagement cursors from one setting on the continuum to another is the ratio of their commixing. When the setting changes, qualitative variations occur across the spectrum. Persuasion slides between infra-perceptual conditioning on the one hand to macro-perceptual cognition and conscious reflection on the other.

In its infra-perceptual exercise persuasion exerts nonconscious influence in the form of priming. As explained earlier, although often discussed in cognitive terms as an orienting of "implicit knowledge," priming occurs at an emergent level where cognition is in the making. Its consequent nature is precisely what is at issue. Priming can be contained within psychology only if the embodied psychological dropout state of the bare-active offbeat of coming experience is conveniently bracketed. It is not "subliminal" if by that is meant an experience describable in the same cognitive terms as conscious experience but occurring below a threshold of manifest awareness. It differs qualitatively from conscious experience.

The scale of violence, for its part, goes from the entropic materiality of attritional-frictional battle-force at one end to the immaterial violence of non-battle-force at the other. Because it stretches between the material and the immaterial, the continuum of violence radiates problems that can only be characterized as metaphysical.[16] The most basic of these is of course the very difference between the material and the immaterial, and the manner of their co-implication in each other across their difference. In the field of war this question translates into the nagging question of how to assess and address the "intangibles" so intimately entangled in the constitution of every situation. In that guise, it infiltrates other issues. It is central to the question of force and persuasion, or the difference between and co-implication of war and peace. It extends to action and perception, perception-in-action and cognition, the body and its performatively stoked potential, time and its phase-shifting into spaces, the discreteness of the act and the continuity of the experiential spectrum, emergent order and the edge of chaos. All of these problematic knots rehearse the distinction between the tangible and the intangible, reformulating each its own way the question of the materiality and immateriality of conflict. These constant recapitulations carry metaphysical concerns into the very heart of the theory and practice of war. For all these reasons, "metaphysical" serves as a better qualifier for contemporary conflict than "epistemological."

## War Music

As war doctrine underwent renovation and reorientation through the 1990s into the 2000s, a great deal of the ferment has focused precisely on this question of how militarily to address the "intangibles" of conflictual life occupying the "soft" end of the spectrum (Ullman and Wade 1996, 1, 3). The failure of the most high-profile military campaigns to come out of this Revolution in Military Affairs (RMA), the 2001 U.S. invasion of Afghanistan, the 2003 U.S. invasion of Iraq, and the 2006 Israeli invasion of

Lebanon, is commonly attributed to their fumbling the intangibles. This has led to calls to retheorize contemporary war with renewed emphasis on what, quite wrongly, is being called the "human terrain."[17] The intangible terrain of war is anything but human. If everything comes to hinge on the infra-instant, that is where the intangibles most palpably reside. The fulcrum of war power is now at the level at which the emergence and reemergence of the human are modulated. War is no longer a power of the human but a power productive of it in novel configurations: an ontopower. Ontopowers of the human are themselves infra-human.

Soft power and hard power are imbricated in the same continuum. They are spectrally co-involved. What holds them together is threat. The threat is of deadly force. The ever-presence, in the pragmatic field of potential, of the menace of lethal violence makes hard power operative, in some intangible way, at every setting. It is always at least bare-actively operative. It is always at least "insigned," for in war signs of danger are liable to drop anywhere, all the time.

Violence, although always insigned, cannot ever *only* be insigned. Force-against-force is a necessary complement and follow-up to hits of soft power. The use of physical violence is required to maintain territorial griddings within certain functional parameters between intervals of modulation, and to hold modulations within certain bandwidths of functional variation when they do occur. A checkpoint does not work as an exercise of movement-patterning soft power without a shoot-to-kill policy intermittently triggered into action in a flash. It also does not always work to have checkpoints in continuous operation or set permanently in place. Similarly, as technology has developed attempts to control "diffuse" threats on the ground without actually occupying it have increasingly come to rely on flash attacks and occasional in-and-out special-ops incursions, supplementing more continuous, softer power operations such as military advising, police and military training of indigenous proxy forces, surveillance and intelligence networking, and "nation-building" exercises such as school construction.

Soft power needs hard power, to operate as its local spigot or voltage control. Hard power needs soft power, to give it span by stretching it across the whole spectrum of force. In each act of war, they co-occur as processual reciprocals, coactive in varying degrees of mixture producing a ratio of force-against-force to the force-to-own-time, frictional attrition to surplus-value war-process lubrication. In each act, one or the other will dominate. The dominant will give the act an overall felt quality leaning toward one end of the spectrum or the other. A soft power dominant can give hard power deniability (it's "only" a threat). A hard power dominant can make soft power a relief. Toggled together, in varying mixtures and degrees, their coactivity expands the active scope of war. The invasions of Afghanistan and Iraq have oil-spotted into a seeping expansion of the geographical, as well as operational, spectrum of active U.S. military intervention to previously unseen extents (between 2000 and 2014, U.S. military personnel are known to have been deployed for operations of varying natures not only in Iraq and Afghanistan, but also in Sierra Leone, Côte d'Ivoire, Nigeria, Liberia, Chad, Mali, Uganda, Libya, Somalia, Pakistan, Yemen, Bosnia, Georgia, East Timor, the Philippines, and Haiti; for a full count up to 2004, see Grimmett 2004).

Signature management involves alternating the dominant from one act to the next, producing a complex rhythm of punctual macro-acts set against a continuously modulated background of field potential. The rhythm has four compositional beats: the reconditioning interruption of shock; the prolongation of shock into a state of awe carrying the shock-effect to and through the next action; the actual execution of a next action; then a repeat shock, itself conditioned by the carryover awe, as it was modulated by the intervening action. The beats do not necessarily correspond to a chronological order. They may be reordered, remixed, or selectively skipped. There is a rhythmic composition to war involving a complex play between battle and nonbattle, the punctual and the continuous, the step-by-step of the line of action and its arc, which literally gives war a musical character. In the new art of war, according to Cebrowski and Garstka,

> combat at the operational level is reduced to a step function. . . . After the initial engagement, there is an operational pause, and the cycle repeats. . . . The step function becomes a smooth curve, and combat moves to a high-speed continuum. . . . Each element of the force has a unique operating rhythm. . . . The results that follow are the rapid

foreclosure of enemy courses of action and the shock of closely coupled events. This disrupts the enemy's strategy and, it is hoped, stops something before it starts. (1998)

Stops something before it starts: the composition is as essentially *preemptive* as it is *productive* of a next pulse of reconditioned life (see chapter 1 on the productive nature of preemption). Military force rhythmically returns to the level at which actions emerge in order to stop what could have happened from happening as it otherwise would have, while priming the territory for other lines of emergent action (on the conditional as the signature mode of preemptive power, see chapters 1 and 7). The conduct of war overall consists in a preemptive modulation of action potential. What is "revolutionary" in contemporary military affairs is not only the operationalization of ontopower, the addressing by military force of powers of emergence, but also the priority of the perception attack, performed with a pronounced preemptive lilt. According to Donald Rumsfeld:

> The situation is this: We are going to address fixed targets as we find them. We are going to address emerging targets as we find them. Things will not be necessarily continuous. The fact that they are something other than perfectly continuous ought not to be characterized as a pause. There will be some things that people will see. There will be some things that people won't see. And life goes on. (Rumsfeld 2001)

Action alternates between macro-perceptual targets that are actually found on the ground, and emerging targets as yet only in potential. Things will therefore not be continuous. And yet they will be. There will be intervals, but the intervals will not be pauses. They will be nonbattles. They will be filled with action of an unseen nature. Not everything that happens will be perceptible. Perception is on the blink, and precisely because it is, it will be centrally at stake at every moment. Life, at any rate, will go on, marching to a staggered military beat of perceptibility and imperceptibility, on-the-ground step-functions and field-repotentializing interruptions, friction against things fixed and the insigning of a smooth abyssal curve of fluctual refix.

## Metaphysics of Violence

Physical violence itself is rhythmed and ratioed. An application of physical force is a material sign of a greater degree of unapplied force. Part of what is felt with a blow is the holding back of a harder blow: this time it's the bludgeon, next time it'll be a bullet. Physical violence always presents a ratio of actualized and potential force. This is even true of physical violence at the lethal extreme: that time it was him; next time it will be you. The actual physical strike is explosive and dissipative, but it operates simultaneously on another processual dimension on which it is retentive. Violence is its own sign. Its occurrence signs its own potential. Violence performs its own threat. That too is felt, immaterially yet unmistakably, in immediate accompaniment to the actual sensation of the blow. What is immaterially felt is a retained remainder of force. This is a quantum of awe, indexing the shock-value of the quantum of force actually applied.

Physical violence also plays to a scale. Each punctual exercise holds within itself a continuum of varying degrees. Each degree holds within itself a qualitative difference. That difference is a bracing in mutual relation of material and immaterial processes. An act of violence is never reducible to the punctual physical act. Violence continuously overspills the discreteness of the empirical, in the classical positivist sense. The music of war orchestrates a metaphysics of violence. Violence is superempirical.[18]

Physical violence, in its superempirical dimension, saturates the space between bodies. A witness to violence will be nonsensuously struck by the performed remainder of force as certainly as the recipient of the blow (if with a different valence). Somebody hearing about the violence secondhand will also be affected. In its immaterial dimension of threat, violence propagates nonsensuously from body to body. It crosses the actual intervals separating them, in affective contagion, at a velocity faster than the fist. It can step from the deed to perception to the word, and back, faster than a bullet. It ricochets in the interval, incorporeally affecting what bodies feel themselves enabled to do. In the bodily between it resonates, interfering with what doing would otherwise have been.

An act of violence exfoliates a field of performed threat-effect engulfing a multiplicity of bodies. It saturates bodies' shared field of potential action, changing their relation to that field, and through it their relation to each other. This surplus-value of violence operates at an infra-collective level, in the sense that it modulates the pragmatic field subtending the interrelational action-potential of a bodily multiplicity. It could as well be called infra-individual, in that it modulates that relational field by affecting individual bodies en masse at nonsensuous altitude. Its performative taking-effect flies beneath the cognitive radar of the implicated individuals, caught unawares in affective contagion. The effect comes less from its giving grist for reflection—in information content it is minimalist to a sometimes dangerous extreme—than from packing an illocutionary force. In language employed performatively words can strike with bodily force, without the actual violence. Conversely, bodily force can strike with the communicative force of language, without the actual articulation.

The strike of violence suspends what bodies can do, at once individually and collectively. There will be a bare-active pause, spilling between. In the commotion, there will be some things people see, and there will be some things people don't see. Sensuously or nonsensuously, all this is felt. Life at any rate will continue, on a different footing. Altered pragmatic ground conditions will now be in force. Bodies' relation to their shared field of potential action will have recomposed. They will have collectively reindividuated, in violence-steeped infra-relation to each other.[19]

## Blowback

The surplus-value that violence packs makes it an incomparable tool for modulating the life-potential not only of those it physically strikes but of entire populations at a stroke. It was seen earlier that the force-to-own the formative time of life carries a risk of reactive backlash even at the soft end of the spectrum. That risk is even greater at the hard end, due to the inarticulate communicability of the forcing leveraged by physical violence. The intensity of the unacted remainder of potential may mount as it spreads. It may come to ground as a waxing pressure of geologic proportions that sooner or later erupts into physically violent reaction. This is a form of what in CIA talk is termed "blowback." Blowback reactions are difficult to plot or predict because the level on which they incubate, governed as it is by a nonlinear causality, is not fully articulable. Because the affective logic they follow is more strongly coupled to a transmission of nonlinguistic forces than to semantically formed discourses, it cannot easily be mapped into recognizable ideological positionings. The large-scale use of violence is an incomparable tool for interventionist "total situation control," but it is also incomparably risky. It requires meticulous orchestration and compositional follow-up, or it may blow up in the face of the perpetrator.

This, of course, is exactly what happened in Iraq and Afghanistan.[20] Blowback first came onto the scene in Iraq in the form of the "improvised explosive device." The unpredictably of the placing and timing of IED attack undermined the U.S. military's terra-forming for "nation-building." The IED mimics, by other means, the anywhere-at-any-moment ubiquity-effect of U.S. rapid-response capabilities (as does suicide bombing). It answers the high-tech threat of just-in-time delivery of lethal force with improvisation and clandestinity—just what the rapid-response capabilities were designed to preempt. The IED's unpredictable punctuation of the everyday with physical violence produces through low-tech means a continuous, countervailing threat environment comparable in degree of saturation and contagiousness to that of the invading forces'. By this device an "asymmetrical" equivalent of the perception attack is fielded, in a kind of asymmetric mimetic rivalry. Its most significant effect militarily is not the individual body count. It is the body count's unquantifiable field-effect on overall enemy morale. The IED struck tangible blows to the intangibles of the total situation.

In theory, it was not meant to be that way. The 2003 U.S. invasion of Iraq was ostensibly designed to follow in its general outlines the "shock and awe" strategy developed in the 1990s. As authored by Ullman and Wade, a shock-and-awe attack begins the beat of war on the crescendo. An overwhelming exercise of air power against military and civilian targets prepares the ground for the entry of troops. This inaugural "Deep Strike" (Ullman and Wade 1996, 128–129) must be extensive enough and swift enough "to render the adversary impotent. . . . Physical and psychological effects must be obtained" (xxiv). The goal is to "so overload an adversary's perceptions and understanding of events that the enemy will be incapable of resistance . . . rendered totally impotent and vulnerable to our actions. . . . This incomprehension produces a state of awe" (xxv). For this to succeed, hard military targets must be physically taken out with rapidity and decisiveness. More important for the ultimate success of the operation, however, is the way in which the physical strike double-functions as a perception attack. The extremity of the violence and its proportionate threat-effect bombs the population into inaction and incomprehension. The relay between perception, reflection, and considered action is broken. People are "paralyzed." They are remanded to a precognitive level of affective agitation from which there seems to be no possible issue in deliberate action. They are commotionally overloaded. They are in shared bare-active suspense. Even if they escape physically unscathed, they are still affected. The rhythm of attack is planned in such a way as to extend the interval of suspense as much as possible. Shock stretches into prolonged awe. By the time the paralysis wears off, it's already all over. The invading troops have entered the capital, and are busy insigning new life conditions by such performative feats as tipping oversized statues. When the action-potential of the populace shifts back into gear, it will be in joyful cognizance of the changed life conditions. The budding terra-forming of the future client state will have already blossomed into a springtime shower of bouquets raining upon the triumphant troops, in a flowering of full-spectrum force. This, at any rate, was Donald Rumsfeld's original vision of speedy success in Iraq, echoed by the fantasy expectations of the United States regarding the Iraqi population's response.

However deep the strike and overpowering the show of force, the ultimate goal is to alter the intangibles of the situation. "The issue is how to determine what demonstrative use of force will affect the perceptions of the intended target in line with overall political aims" (Ullman and Wade 1996, 30). A "rapid application of force to intimidate" may "convince the majority that resistance is futile by targeting and harming the few" (27). The "principal targets" are "the *fundamental values and lives*" of the population (27; emphasis added). The force-to-own-time which lies at the heart of full-spectrum force dips ontopowerfully into bare activity in order to "bring life back" on a new footing (see chapter 2). It is biopolitical *in effect*: resuscitory. The aim is nothing less than a *revaluation* of collective life.

There is not occupation of territory, on the one hand, and independence of persons on the other. It is the country as a whole, its history, its daily pulsation that are contested, disfigured. . . . Under these conditions, the individual's breathing is an observed breathing. It is a combat breathing. (Frantz Fanon 1965, 65; cited in Perera and Pugliese 2011, 1)

## Counter-Value Attack

A tactic applied toward the revaluation of the life of the population is what Ullman and Wade call the *counter-value* attack. The counter-value attack is an operation against civilian targets that erases the physical markers of what is perceived to unify the population by insigning national and/or civilizational pride and belonging. The U.S. military's decision to stand by while the National Museum of Iraq was ransacked can only be interpreted as a deliberate counter-value attack. It cannot have been a mistake. It was entirely consistent with a strategic goal of creating the conditions for an integral revaluation of life. Although not a mistake, it was certainly a "misfire"—like so many of the decisions made in the continuing "war on terror."

Ullman and Wade are clear: shock and awe can indeed backfire. "The classic misfire is that the adversary is not impressed and, instead, is further provoked to action" (Ullman and Wade 1996, 27). Within months in Iraq, the paralysis of the Deep Strike's awe gave way to active blowback. The window for terra-forming closed. The population failed to assume the posture. The U.S. occupation administration seriously fumbled the segue into "nation-building." This was due in part to the Department of Defense under Rumsfeld misunderestimating, as Bush might say, the number of ground troops necessary for the complex and exacting labor of territorial flow patterning and ongoing signature management. Full-spectrum war is designed to minimize the number of "boots on the ground." But the necessary minimum is relative, with many variables entering into the equation, many of them in the intangibles column. Coupled with this force-on-force miscalculation were spectacular "human terrain" misfires such as "de-Baathification" and the creation of conditions for large-scale inefficiency and fraud in the rebuilding program (through the replacement of military personnel with profit-motivated civilian contractors working with legal immunity and no effective oversight). It was not until late 2007, more than four years after the commander in chief's battleship-deck declaration of the "cessation of major hostilities," that the U.S. intervention could point to any positive indicators whatsoever. By that time, the war of perception was being lost on the domestic front as well, as a majority of live American bodies were counted as opposing the war for the first time.

The war-flowers of invasive spring had withered on the counter-value branch. The buzz of drones was already humming on the horizon, eager to claim their spot in the diffuse sun of the autumn of the Long War's invasions. The coming Obama generation of high-tech, low-footprint pollinators of preemption was readying to take wing.

## 4 Power to the Edge

### Making Information Pointy

*Thought (As We Barely Know It)*

Key military theory texts of the late 1990s and early 2000s called for a far-reaching reorganization of the military around augmented network intelligence with a focus on the operationalization of the infra-instant of bare activity discussed in chapter 3. "It became clear to me and many others," writes General Stanley McChrystal, commander of U.S. forces in Afghanistan under Obama, "that to defeat a networked enemy we had to become a network ourselves." For this to succeed, he continues, the military has to learn how to move in the " 'blinks'—time delays and missed junctures where information was lost." This in turn requires creating "a shared consciousness" (McChrystal 2011). Once again, the complex knot of time (off its hinges), perception (ajar), and action (potential) asserts itself as the central problem of war. But a new element comes to the fore: in this brave new network-centric world of war, when you blink, your eyes must open onto *collective* consciousness. That consciousness must be, in all immediacy, an effective, and effectively collective, *will* to fight. This project immediately encounters an obstacle: the very complexity it is meant to marshal.

*The Fog of Info-War*

The point of departure for the contemporary theory and practice of war can be summed up in a phrase: the world is an increasingly complex place full of unpredictable and proliferating threats. The military must be reorganized to bring it up to the task of responding to these threats whatever form they take, whenever they arise, and wherever they fall. The reason regularly cited for the increase in complexity is the globalization of the deregulated economy and the accelerated circulation of goods, information, and people upon which it is predicated. These premises are shared by virtually all of the major texts in military theory of this period. They all take this uncertain ground as a given.

In a way, the appeal to globalization may understate the problem, if it is taken to imply that complexity sets in at the global level due to the sheer number of interactions its system subsumes, assuming that the local components are simple and that their definition poses no problem when they are taken separately on their own level. A global field of complexity, however, is not composed of simple units, with the complexity only a result of the quantity of their higher-level interactions. The local components are complex subsystems in their own right. The local miring of global U.S. strategy in Iraq (not to mention Afghanistan and Pakistan, each in its own way) is evidence enough that complexity, and the uncertainty accompanying it, "goes all the way down" (Stengers 1997). How much more complex and fundamentally uncertain is the situation when it is acknowledged that the ground is groundless, and even when you go "all the way down" there is always more to go! Or worse: when on the way down you may suddenly find yourself back at the top, as through an Alice in Wonderland rabbit hole in reverse. Feedback between levels, including between the highest and the lowest, is a defining characteristic of a complex system. A complex system, grounded in groundlessness, bootstraps itself on the nonlinear playing out of its own complexity. General McChrystal voices the consensus when he equates the challenge of reinventing the military for the network age with rendering the "linear" chain of command obsolete, as a way of dealing with the "blink" that twists action and perception into a knot of consciousness (McChrystal 2011).

In classical theory, of course, uncertainty was already acknowledged as a constant of war. "The great uncertainty of all data in war is a peculiar difficulty," Carl von Clausewitz wrote in his classic text *On War*, "because all action must, to a certain extent, be planned in a mere twilight" or as in a "fog." The "fog of war" has since become a household term. The difference is that for Clausewitz it came in the middle as a caveat (1946, vol. 1, bk.1, ch. 7). It now comes in the preface as mantra.

For Clausewitz, war was by nature intelligible. It can be fully comprehended if one "consider[s] first the single elements" then "advance[s] from the simple to the complex" (1946, vol. 1, bk.1, ch. 7). For him, the fog of war was but a "peculiarity" of perception, like an imperfection on a camera lens. It could be dissipated by the personal battle experience and "extraordinary mental power" of the general. "*If we have seen* War, all becomes intelligible. . . . Everything is very simple in War, but the simplest thing is difficult." The difficulty is due to the "friction" of "petty circumstance" (Clausewitz 1946, vol. 1, bk. 1, ch. 71 emphasis added). At bottom circumstantial, the friction can be overcome by the well-oiled will and honed intelligence of the general. By the mid-twentieth century, however, it is taken for granted that *we have not seen*. Walter Lippmann saw this unseeing coming already in the First World War: "Most people seem to believe that, when they meet a war correspondent or a special writer from the Peace Conference, they have seen a man who has seen the things he wrote about. Far from it. Nobody, for example, saw this war. Neither the men in the trenches nor the commanding general. The men saw their trenches, their billets, sometimes they saw an enemy trench, but nobody . . . saw a battle" (Lippmann 1920, 43–44; cited in Trudel 2013, 199).

Already true of twentieth-century conventional war, how much more true it is of today's asymmetric warfare. In today's war, as Pataki drove home, we always have not seen (chapter 3). Not only is perception syncopated, its ground is indeterminate. These two conditions are intrinsically linked: it is the ground of indeterminacy's heaving rhythmically into view that suspends perception mid-making. We remember what we do not see. But this is not the memory of conscious reflection. It is not the kind that nourishes a character-building accumulation of personal wisdom and a strengthening of rational will for well-considered control.

The crux of the matter, in the words of a more recent war theorist, is that "we must appreciate that we cannot hope to control what we cannot see, hear or understand" (Szafranski 1994, 52). David S. Alberts, the main architect of the concept of network-centric war, concurs. Even if under certain circumstances it is possible to reduce the fog of war, under no circumstances can it be eliminated (Alberts et al. 2000, 11, 71–72). The fog of war no longer appears circumstantial, but essential and undissipatable. It is not only of the very nature of war, but of human perception itself: "Consciousness flickers; and even at its brightest, there is a small focal region of clear illumination, and a large penumbral region of experience which tells of intense experience in dim apprehension" (Whitehead 1978, 267). The field of war cannot be fully comprehended even by the experienced general, so much less so the first-tour trooper on the fog-befuddled ground. Not to mention the "first responder" on crisis-ridden civil soil. Personal intelligence and individual will never suffice. Across the spectrum, in war and security, there is an ineradicable margin of unknowability. It follows that there is an equally unavoidable degree of strategic undecidability in any operation wherever it may lie on the spectrum.

What's a network-centric warrior to do? How is shared consciousness to be conjured up out of unknowability? And how, from the flickering of this emergent consciousness, can a unitary will issue in decisive action?

## The Topology of Power

Short answer: the complexity must be "relocated" in the military network itself (Alberts et al. 2000, 65). What is at stake, in other words, is the "*topology of power*" (Alberts and Hayes 2003, 165, 203).

The first step toward a decisively effective topology of power is to build enhanced operational responsiveness into the machinery of war. Tactics on the ground must be fluidly adaptable. There must be channels for the adaptions to feed instantaneously up the chain of strategic command in order to make the machinery of war self-correcting, giving it a built-in capacity to evolve. The evolutionary adaptions must then be able to feed back down to the lowest level "battlespace entity" (as the terminology goes), each and every one wherever they are stationed. Considering that time is now of the essence of war, the evolutionary feedback must operate in as close to real time as possible, the up and down feedback occurring with such lightning speed as to make the military hierarchy the topological equivalent of the horizontality of the network. Of course, this instant information diffusion requires enhanced networking using the latest in communication technology. Hence the obsessive concern in recent war theory, particularly in the shadow of the failure of the U.S. intervention in Iraq, for the deployment of new information and communicational technologies designed to revolutionize command and control, summed up in the watchword of "augmented intelligence."

It would be to seriously miss the operational point of this renewed focus on intelligence to interpret it as a simple return to an information-processing model within the traditional horizon of mediated human communication. It is difficult to communicate what one does not "hear, see, or understand." Augmenting intelligence is not about making space in war for informed reflection based on complete information. If the fog of war is not merely circumstantial, information is and will remain lacunary. Improved networking cannot change that fact of complexity. The stubborn epistemological fact of asymmetrical warfare is that there will be gaps in intelligence, essentially and necessarily. It is not about making space in war for reflection. It is about remaking the space of war, in absence of complete information and the leisure to reflect on it, in the pressure cooker of the time of threat.

This epistemological incompleteness theorem at the basis of network-centric war is an expression of an ontological condition: the "real time" of war is now the formative infra-instant of suspended perception. What are normally taken to be cognitive functions must telescope into that nonconscious interval. What would otherwise be cognition must zoom into the "blink" between consciously registered perceptions—and in the same movement zoom instantly out into a new form of awarenesss, a new collective consciousness (see chapter 3 on "attentional blink"). Augmented perception attack: its nonoptional battlefield is the embodied terrain of priming. Its ultimate weapon is the modulation of readiness potential, the productive power to effect what may come next. Increasingly, this proto-territorial terrain is the crux of decision. In the bare-active blink, thought enters a new alliance with coming action, and action with perception in-the-making, each of the terms fusing with the others such that all become something else together, and together overspill the terrain of the human as we think we have known it, returning, militarily, to what has always lain emergently, evolutionarily, at the heart of it: the more-than-human of becoming (Manning 2013; Massumi 2014a, 92–94).

The ultimate goal of improved networking, practiced as a topology of power, is thus not to augment human intelligence as we know it, by better informing it. It is to integrally transform it, in lockstep with the machinery of war. The point of practicing a new topology of power is to alter the place of the human: to redefine the very meaning of the "human terrain"; to displace it, in a blink. This involves creating a military machinery capable of dipping into the infra-conscious action-potentials of bare activity in order to extract from it a surplus-value of force, emergently expressing itself as a self-deciding military *will*: one that performs itself in real time, distributed across a self-adapting network of action-perceptions fused into operational solidaritiy through complex relations of mutual feedback. The networking is less for distributing information than it is for this self-deciding of action-potential. The complexity is less cognized without (gaining a better perspective on the military system's environment) than it is *enacted* within (immanently, full-spectrum, emergently *constitutive* of the system). The reorganization of the military that the strategists advocate is not just aimed at transforming it. It is aimed at making it self-transforming. Self-constituting and self-transforming: integrally, infra-lly, ontopowerful.

The following section gives a sketch of how this might work, based on a synthetic reading of two key policy texts in military doctrine post–*Shock and Awe* (Ullman and Wade 1996). Both answer to the need, widely perceived among military analysts of the 1990s, for a Revolution in Military Affairs to bring into the military orbit what in the business-management and public-press discourse of the time was called the "Information Revolution." The first text, *Network Centric Warfare: Developing and Leveraging Information Superiority* (NCW), by David S. Alberts, John J. Garstka, and Frederick P. Stein, was originally published in 1999. It fleshes out for the military establishment the concept of "netwar," advanced by RAND think tankers John Arquilla and David Ronfeldt in the early 1990s. This concept, under the more sedate moniker "network-centric warfare," was to be adopted as official U.S. military doctrine in the summer of 2001, on the basis of a report to Congress, and was integrated into the official *Army Field Manual* that same year. This came just in time to orient the full-spectrum U.S. approach to the "war on terror" declared by President Bush in the wake of the attack on 9/11, and network thinking has been central to U.S. military strategy ever since. The second text, *Power to the Edge: Command and Control in the Information Age* (PE), by David S. Alberts and Richard E. Hayes, dates from just before the invasion of Iraq in 2003. It works out a vision of the "revolutionary" restructuring of the military necessary to make network-centric war capabilities an organizational reality. A stated aim of this restructuring is to chart out a "business model" for the military (on the confluence of contemporary modes of power and neoliberal capitalism, see chapter 2). Just as the first, early 1990s flush of Revolution in Military Affairs theorizing drew on the corporate management models of that period (Total Quality Management and Reengineering), Albert and Hayes' approach mirrors subsequent private sector organizational strategies developed in response to the globalized information economy and the uncertainties of the far-from-equilibrium geopolitical environment in which it operates.

On the surface, the call for far-reaching reorganization of the military establishment articulated in these texts is dedicated to enhancing the military's ability to fight across the spectrum and prevail by enriching its ability to gather and effectively process high-quality information. The texts pay lip service to this easily digestible image of the agenda. But under pressure from the infra-instant, they go further. It does not take much scratching under the "info-structure" surface to see that the operative logic of these closely allied texts represents a radical departure from the conventional model of optimizing intelligence by enhancing the quantity and quality of information. If information is understood as conveying factually precise and semantically rich content, information is not what is at stake.

What is at stake is the place of human thought and perception in the coming evolution of the topology of power. Advancing its evolution involves a topological projection transforming the arena of power from a conventionally centered "battlespace" into a cutting "edge" carving its own operational space in time: the just-in-time of infra real-time. The edge is the wedge for making hierarchy as good as horizontal. Its full spectrum is the space-time continuum on which individual intelligence becomes collective, network-distributed cognition gets bare-lively embodied, such that what is produced is not knowledge but power: immediately, self-augmentingly, decisively. Where once was human cognition, now whirs the machinery of a full-spectrum *will to power*: knowledge-power (without the actual knowledge).

It is not about information. It is about taking information to the edge. It is about making it "pointy": a direct weapon of war (PE 173).

## Power to the Edge

It goes something like this, in thirteen not so easy steps (augmented with increasingly lengthy, and loopy, theoretical detours):

1. Capture chance.
2. Mass effects not forces.

3. Positively preempt.

4. Economize.

5. Suboptimize.

6. Perform forward, so as to know backward.

7. Prime for nonrecognition.

8. Sample the future.

9. Capacity-pack the past.

10. Command to prime.

11. Make information pointy.

12. Self-synchronize and differ.

13. Take it to the edge.

## 1. Capture Chance

Even in simplest processes, reliable prediction is impossible. The future cannot be modeled (NCW 163; PE 225). All the more so in the new asymmetrical field of war, a "threat-based" environment bubbling with a chaos of emergent situations (NCW 70; PE 1–3, 226). This threat-environment exhibits all the hallmarks of a complex system whose behavior is nonlinear (NCW 20, 60, 162; PE 206). It is a turbulent "ecosystem" (NCW 22) affording no possibility of plotting a straight line from an identifiable cause to an isolatable effect. All one is given to know are effects (PE 76), and they are not isolated. Rather than following from causes in orderly fashion, effects "cascade" into each other (PE 89–90). Everything happens from one complexity effect to the next, effects crashing into effects, begetting still more effects, in such a swirl that the only causation is what this turbulent stir activates in itself. Restricted to relations between effects, causation is so nonlinear as to be indistinguishable from chance.

The only thing certain is that unforeseen situations will effectively emerge. The lay of the land in an environment of emergence is shrouded in a "fog." One again, this is not Clausewitz's fog of petty circumstance. It's the fog of potential (NCW 11, 71–72, 80; PE 8, 108). Potential is "unknowable," not by mere circumstance but by nature (PE 76). Or rather, it is unknowable by nature because force of circumstance is all there is to serve for causation. There is nothing "mere" or "petty" about it. The force of circumstance is not just something occurring outside the logical frame of a presiding order. It is a disorder of potential. It is excessive, enveloping multiple prospective orders. The cascade of effects, swirling into complex relation, gives any number of competing logics and alternative presidings a chance. Force of circumstance is chance, in the sense that it is given. It is of the nature of the accident (chapter 2). Which means that when it is given to order, order must emerge from it. The order will be post hoc: second-order; a consequent order-out-of-force-of-circumstance. Any knowledge garnered will be of that order. That is: equally second-order. Any presiding-over earned with that knowledge will be the rarest of gifts: a second chance.

In times of turbulence you cannot count on second chances. Circumstance is forcefully astir, seething with accident. The only viable option is to learn how to "capture chance" while it is still in first swirl, at the cusp of its taking effect (PE 213). Snatch chance in potential. Don't wait for the gift of optimal conditions, *take* the chance. Counter-stir the turbulence, and see what gives. Never forget that although potential is unknowable, "power is an expression of potential" (PE 213).

### 2. Mass Effects Not Forces

Don't go chasing after lost causes. Adopt "effects-based operations" (NCW 62; PE 2, 102–104, 132, 143, 148, 206). This means finding "levers of control" (PE 206) at the emergent level. This is not a science. It requires a fair amount of groping in the dark. It is an experimental practice of trial and error (PE 227–230). Gaining control does not mean inserting one's own linear causal influence into the field of war to straighten out the situation once and for all. It involves just the opposite: injecting one's own strategic dose of randomness (PE 150). Leveraging control means tweaking the nonlinearity of the situation so that the cascade of outcomes remains (it is hoped) within certain "bounds" of variation (PE 207). The goal is to reset the parameters of emergence so as to redistribute the probabilities of the range of potential outcomes (PE 145). Reprobabilizing is as close as "control" ever comes to certainty.[1] Uncertainty can be kept within bounds, but never eliminated.

No one intervention will do the trick. Trial, error, trial, error . . . control is open-endedly iterative (NCW 69, 74; PE 16). A cascade of effects is induced, and immediately thereafter a re-tweaking is necessary. If the turnover is fast enough, the curve of events can be modulated on the fly. The motto is "minimize planning, maximize real-time modification" in an evolving ecosystemic field of tweaked potential (NCW 159). Another way of saying this is: "mass effects not forces" (NCW 7, 90, 173–174; PE 104). Operationalize the generative force of circumstance, the force-to-own-time, rather than accumulating force-against-force in the form of heavy equipment and lumbering infrastructure.

### 3. Positively Preempt

When you capture chance, you have not simply deterred a threat. You have "dissolved" an emergent situation and replaced it with another (PE 2). You have "foreclosed or countered" some eventualities while "shifting seamlessly to other alternatives" (PE 143). You have productively preempted. You have positively "created new effects" whose emergence has short-circuited that of other effects not of your tweaking (NCW 68). You have counter-effected. In the best-case scenario, for example, in a large-scale "shock and awe" campaign in which the massing of effects is instantaneous, the enemy's capacity to act suffers "strategic lockout" (NCW 165). Paralysis. Or in a less dramatic scenario, a small modulation that gives the enemy momentary pause, a vanishingly thin suspensive interval into which your next action may move. If you iterate actions fast enough, you will eventually gain the advantage in modulating the parameters of the field of war, in this case through a cumulative massing of effects. You will have widened the "bandwidth" of your potential actions while narrowing your enemy's (PE 185). Either way, instantaneous or incremental, the control lever is in your counter-effective hands.

### 4. Economize

What use is a lever if not for gaining "leverage" (PE xvi, 2–4, 173, 186, 215; NCW 6, 13, 21 and passim)? Force-against-force has the advantage of producing dramatic local effects. Its impact is direct and visible. Aside from the danger of blowback, its disadvantage is that it is fundamentally "frictional." It is attritional not only in relation to the enemy but for one's own operations, since each blow requires an unrecoverable expenditure of resources. Even holding force-against-force in reserve for future use is attritional since it involves constant upkeep and upgrade. Force-against-force is leadened by the added cost of attrition. In an uncertain field, where targeting often goes amiss, the cost-to-benefit equation can be marginal. The greatest yield is obtained from attacks that mass effects beyond their immediate impact. What really pays are actions, violent or not, that produce cascades of effects that resonate beyond the local point of application in such a way as to reset the parameters of the global field of potential. "Synergies" (positive feedback effects) multiply the returns. The return may then be significantly larger than the input (PE 149; NCW 184).

Synergies yield "added value" (PE 2–3; NCW 18, 205). Surplus-value. An action that produces field-wide synergies is an investment. Why spend when you can invest? The field of war is not just experimental, it is speculative. The rule of thumb is to economize mere expenditure of force in favor of "leveraging your capacities" (PE 173, 186; NCW 75) through effects-based added-value operations. In the globalized economy, abstract speculative instruments like derivatives, futures, and credit default swaps are where the surplus-value really flows. These are effects-based economic instruments (they capitalize on trends, emerging situations as yet uncertainly determined by unknowably complex systemic interdependencies, to whose momentum they themselves contribute and whose eventual course they modulate). Physical plant is frictional. It is the economic equivalent of force-against-force. In war as in capital, the "intangibles" are where the real action is (PE 172). This is no wonder. The global economy is also an uncertain threat-environment, haunted by the specter of crisis, whose behavior is resolutely nonlinear. Like the field of war, it is a complex ecosystem (NCW 36–37, 53).

Not only is the economy a complex threat-environment like war—it is the *same* complex ecosystem. War and the economy are not only interlinked, in the obvious sense that since the rise of capitalism control of resources and market share has always been one of the prime stakes in war. Not only are they interlinked, they are processual twins (however dissimilar in content and function they remain; see chapter 2). In view of this, what any successful military needs these days is less a brilliant strategic plan than an appropriate "business model" (PE 83). As discussed in the opening sections of this chapter, the days of the Clausewitzian "heroic commander" are over (PE 203). The trademark of Paul Bremer, head of allied operations in post-invasion Iraq, was a business suit bottoming out in combat boots.

## 5. Suboptimize

It is a romantic fiction of bygone capitalism that economic prowess is about optimizing production. Economic prowess is less about efficiencies in the frictional domain than it is about playing the speculative field to good added-value effect. So too in war. Physical prowess and valor in the face of hardship are commendable. But what is crucial is how "efficiencies" beyond force-against-force generate a nonlocal surplus-value of violence. Counterintuitively, in order to maximize added value creation on the level of force-beyond-force you have to "suboptimize" on the combat level. The "fixation on optimality" betrays a centralist organizational bias that is hopelessly outdated (PE 62). It fails to realize that in war things now "move so fast that it is difficult to optimize anything" (PE 68). "Reality conspires against us and we rarely, if ever, are able to centralize collection and decisionmaking" to the point of achieving anything approaching the optimum (NCW 107). "In reality, optimization is not even an option" (PE 207).

Acting suboptimally is the necessary price to be paid for real-timeliness. What should be sought is not optimality but simultaneity (PE 68). The equation for eventual success is "agility" plus "adaptability" (PE 83–84). A self-correcting series of less-than-optimal actions can add up to a victory. If, that is, discrete actions "combine to form effects greater than those they would achieve individually" (PE 149). In other words, taken in aggregate, suboptimal steps can produce a surplus-value of action. When this added-value accumulates it alters the overall field conditions to positively preemptive effect. Once again, the goal is "to keep a situation within bounds, rather than seeking an optimal solution" (PE 207). Suboptimal actions are able to produce this surplus-value of action because the lack of centrally imposed planning and hierarchical micromanagement leaves room for innovation (PE 217). Added-value success rests on creativity in action, not correctness in analysis. If you expect to be adequately informed before having to act, that's where you're really mistaken. If you think you can specifically plan for contingencies, think again, differently. Victory against fast-moving asymmetrical enemies who are themselves agile, adaptable, and innovative in their own suboptimized, IEDish way requires a different approach that capitalizes on real-time creative response. For that, the impulse to optimize is a positive impediment.

## 6. Perform Forward, So as to Know Backward

Take for example the case of the shrinking family (PE 67–68). It was not a combat situation that could have been foreseen and specifically planned for. To begin with, the first problem was that it was not a combat situation. In typical full-spectrum fashion, U.S. troops serving in Haiti find themselves in nonbattle. The local political establishment has fled, leaving U.S. foot soldiers to fill the role of surrogate civil authority. An agitated woman has approached the unit's corporal, screaming that neighbors have placed a curse on her family that is causing it to shrink. Without missing a beat, the officer pulls out an envelope, sprinkles a brown powder over the woman, and pronounces the curse lifted. The woman returns to her home praising the American intervention in the highest terms to all who will listen. The village is won over. The powder, by the way, was coffee. This is an example of the "flexibility, innovation, and adaptability" required in contemporary war (PE 66). It leveraged a surplus of goodwill-effect from a mere dusting of frictional force. The corporal's action was suboptimal by any normal operating standards. Your typical field manual would not include lifting curses on the list of military tactics, and since there was neither a linear relation nor proportionality between the means and the result, the result cannot be counted as reliably forecastable. Only a creatively improvised performative action is able to negotiate an unforecastable qualitative and quantitative gulf of this magnitude between action input and leveraged effect.

Added-value, it seems, can be had not only in aggregate but, in propitious conditions, from a single performative act. When it is achieved in aggregate, it is because each step has performed modestly, and the performance-effects cohered and accumulated. In either case, and at whatever end of the full spectrum, combat performance requires an equally full-spectrum "situation awareness" factoring in the "cognitive and social" intangibles (PE 68).

The cognitive and social domains are among the most crucial of military domains. The way they are differentially embedded in each situation ties that situation integrally to every other situation composing a given field of combat. This locally embedded nonlocality, this integrable differential, provides an immaterial fulcrum force that a clever hand on the right lever at the right time can use to bump a local effect up a level. This is the combat equivalent of chaos theory's butterfly effect, in which a microbeat is amplified by the complex system of the weather into a macroeffect. The cognitive is a beat in the weather of war. Its place is not in lofty oversight, not in general foresight, neither hovering over the action, nor coming before it in commanding fashion. It comes, instead, close upon the ground, in the lowdown of action, in absolute proximity to that messiest of military things, the social.

Once again "cognitive" must be used advisedly, nowhere more so than on the social terrain. Just as the insect wing beat is only "weather" when considered from the wider and retrospective vantage point of its amplified effect, so too the just-in-time improvised combat performance of the foot soldier at coffee-powder level is "cognitive" only retrospectively, as amplified and in effect. Had the curse-reversing soldier been truly informed, briefed in counterinsurgency anthropology as certain recent approaches to military intangibles management have recommended, he would have known all of the reasons why his action was more likely not to work. In the daily course of normal everyday life, the "felicity" of a performative requires that a certain set of generally applicable, conventional conditions be in place (Austin 1975). In the exceptional and unfelicitous situation of a foreign occupying force supplanting previously prevailing conditions and re-terra-forming the field of potential by the very fact of its on-the-ground presence, it is highly uncertain that such conditions will apply.[2] In the face of this uncertainty, the informed actor would be well advised not to try any stunts. Good judgment will advise that a coffee curse-lifting performance not be hazarded. Whether or not such a performance would have worked would then never be known, since a hazard-conditions performative of this kind is not prevalidated by convention. It is validated only retroactively by its effect. In an uncertain and complex environment—which all environments are by nature—putting the cognitive above and before positively undermines the production of knowledge.

Underlining the cognitive indeterminacy of the situation need in no way foster a posture of skepticism. To the contrary, it recommends a thoroughgoing *pragmatism*. As William James, a founder of pragmatism,

argued, all cognition is trial and error and retrospective in just this manner. "Knowledge . . . comes to life inside the tissue of experience. It is
*made*; and made by relations that unroll themselves in time. . . . The terminus of the chain of intermediaires *creates* the function" (James 1996a,
57). Whatever perception terminates the chain of unfolding retrospectively validates the starting-point as having been cognitive of the outcome,
correctly or in error (felicitously or as an experimental misfire). The
cognitive function is recursively self-creating. Cognition is only ever will-
have-been. Effective knowledge is always and by nature "effects-based."
If you isolate the inaugural act that sets going the unfolding, it can be as
yet only a germinal or potential cognition, a "virtual" knowing (James
1996a, 67; Massumi 2011, 29–38).

The recursive nature of cognition means that at its starting-point it is
essentially a "remembering forward" performatively dawning in an incipient line of action pragmatically processing toward a consciously assess-
able end-perception that will retrospectively determine the nature of the
originating function. The starting point is infra-cognitive: still cognitively
undetermined, yet immanent to what will prove to have been a determinate cognitive process. Until the end-effect of the line is reached, the
cognitive nature of the starting point is in suspense. It is in-braced in the
interval, out of which it can only be performed. It cannot be consciously
thought out. It must be dynamically unfolded: experimentally and innovatively acted out. In the interval, cognition is as yet indistinct from creative
action. At the same time, it features as a dimension of memory. It is not
only action and perception that are bound together in bare activity, but a
futuristic Kierkegaardian form of memory as well.

### 7. Prime for Nonrecognition

If you were to operationalize Kierkegaardian memory, priming is how you
would do it. Priming is memorial. It is the making active in the present
of an inheritance from the past, brought forward in the habitual form of
a reflex or a learned response. Priming occurs in the bare-active blink of
nonconsciousness. It *is not perceived*. In the interval, it inflects an action
whose execution is formative of a next perception.

Take for example a bicycle commuter. Her trajectory out the door on the
way to work undergoes a brief detour to the shelf where the safety helmet

is kept. By the time she mounts the bicycle, it is on her head. It is only then, when she pauses briefly to take stock before pedaling, that she consciously registers the presence of the helmet. The act of commuting has been inflected with an accent of security. The detour to the donning of the helmet was triggered by a cue, for example, reaching a certain turn in the hallway, which itself went unperceived. The commute's safety inflection was signed-in to action by the cue. This is priming: an invisible insigning that comes into action through what would have been a perception had it been perceived, but in actuality is only contained in perception consequently, as an accomplished modulation of a line of action registered retrospectively.

One might be tempted to say that the cue triggering the modulation has "informed" the body of an acquired capacity for self-protection. It would be more precise to say that it has "in-formed" the coming *action* and its issuance into a self-protected perception: it has affected the action-perception's formation from within. It was effectively an internal factor contributing to the production of the experience. Specifically, it contributed to determining which lived qualities (such as safety) this line of action (preparing to go out) would pass on to the next (biking). Priming is an immanent creative factor contributing to coming experience a qualitative difference in constitution.

The comingness of its contribution forbids equating priming with memory—that is, if memory is equated with recall. The cue is as much a call to the future as it is a recall of the past. It is as much a call for the future to be qualitatively different from the present as it is a recalling of the present into conformity with actions past. It may be memorial, but it is also futuristic. What is memory *for* if not the future? To remember is to have anticipated an immediate future in which something of the past returns. Nailing memory to functions of sameness under such categories as recognition and repetition, even in its most automatic and unreflective modes such as ingrained habit, is to neglect its essential futurism. If the cue were merely recognized, and the action triggered a simple repetition, its functioning would be dangerously maladaptive.

Consider the inhabitual day our bicycle commuter rented a car. After a full day of driving on errands around the city, she pulls up into a filling station. Alerted to something amiss by the quizzical look in the station attendant's face, she realizes that she has been driving without her seat belt on—and with a bicycle helmet on her head.[3] Her priming that day erred on the side of sameness. It leaned too heavily toward the memorial, and in doing so contributed to that day's line of actions a heady memorial to habitual misfire. If soldiers in the field were primed for recognition, their acquired competencies would equally misfire, leading to the kind of memorial they would attend in a box. The more uncertain the operational environment, the more habit must be for the future and the variation that it brings, to the relative detriment of the memorial. In an asymmetrical war environment, combat training meant to ingrain in recruit bodies habits of agile and adaptive soldierly response cannot merely ingrain habits of recall. It must ingrain the future in the habit of recall, and make recall pass into action unperceived. In today's war, it is crucial that real-time decision making *not* be "recognition-primed or naturalistic" (PE 144).[4] To prime for an unpredictable future, you have no choice but to prime for nonrecognition.

What must be "recognized" is change, the more rapidly the better (PE 147). You can't afford to trundle along the lanes of war wearing a bicycle helmet. But what does it mean to recognize change? Change is what hasn't happened before. It fits no type. There is no category for it yet. It is unrecognizable as it happens. "Recognizing" change is thus the same as priming for nonrecognition. Take the car-driving bicyclist again. The change in the transport situation settled in too late. The problem began at the outset. Or rather, the problem was that it didn't begin at the outset. The cue took effect unproblematically, as if the situation were the same and the coming action called for simple repetition when what it was really calling for was a variation on the lived theme of self-protecting for transportation. The helmet-donning proved to have been recognition-primed, when what it needed to do was "recognize" a change.

The double nature of priming as memorial and futuristic can be figured dynamically as two vectors moving in opposite directions, each looping back to its point of departure, the cue, in an instant smaller than the smallest perceivable. One vector moves in the direction of the past and brings back to the cue an already mastered action, with whose onset the cue now coincides. This movement in the smaller-than-smallest interval makes the just-beginning of an established form of past action coincide with the first flush of a presently forming experience.

Since the beginning of the line of action is already unfolding on cue, the completion of the triggered action sequence is pushed forward from the cue-point into the future. The second vector boosts the past's future-push with a prospective pull toward its terminus, drawing the action further out of the past. The action is already on the roll. Its habitual form of completion beckons its rolling momentum. The terminus of the line of action operates for the action, flush with its just-beginning, as a self-attractive dynamic force toward its own renewed satisfaction. The two inverse movements meet in the smaller-than-smallest interval, where they join forces for the unfolding present. This is the birth of James's *specious present*. It is not the present of linear time, figured as a mathematical point without thickness. This a present tightly woven out of a dynamic line of pastness energetically entwined with a thread of futurity, in the incipiency of an event just launching. This is a present primed—to play itself out as a duration. At the precise point where the past and future vectors meet lies the strike of the cue. Here, the specious present's coming duration is compressed into a smaller interval than the smallest perceivable. It has not yet actually lived out its duration toward renewed experience. Its duration is absorbed in its own bare-active potential.

The cue, or prime, coincides with that absorption: the intensity of the here-and-now. The priming coincides with the unfolding from that strike, for the duration: the specious present.[5] In chapter 3, it was said that there were three kinds of memory: three modes of the presence of the past. Now, it eventuates that there is more than one mode of the present as well. The durational specious present is one mode. It is conscious (or can be, when attended to). The other mode is by nature imperceptible. The here-and-now of the cue cannot presently be perceived because it is the point at which the present's unfolding is incipiently consumed in its own push-pull, future-past potential. The cue can only operate if it falls out of actual experience, in the interests of the coming durational experience it presently catalyzes. The cue as such is nonconscious by nature. If anything about the present is like a mathematical point, lacking any actual thickness of experience, it is the cue, this prime. It occurs, but not for itself, only for the coming experience. The cue is infinitely thin, effectively infra-thin, like the blade of an insubstantial knife opening a microscopic fissure in the fabric of experience, just enough for a new stitch of time to tie potentially into the weave of life.

The cue is the unperceived cut of life's perceptual advance. It disappears into its own act of triggering into operation a self-propelling future-past force of action-perception on the make. The prime is self-effacing. It is the trigger of another process's self-production, a release of potential for an activity whose unfolding and form of completion lie beyond it. It is a catalyst. It is only felt, insubstantially, in its effects. It registers in the coming action as a qualitative difference in *how* that action will actually unfold, compared to how it might otherwise have ended (unhelmeted).

In the bicycle example, the push of the habitual past and the attractor pull of the future helmet-donning call to each other and call on each other. They work in concert. It is the same action sequence whose onset is pushed forward by the past and whose terminus pulls back on it from the future. The call-and-response of pastness and futurity echo and amplify each other in the no-time of the interval, concertedly exerting in the gap a time pressure toward the present expression of a life-effect. The pressure is toward an existential modulation of the unfolding situation that will imbue it with an emergent quality like an immaterial birthmark (safety or danger). The concertation proposes for the coming action a *commanding form*: an intensive rhythm to the push-pull that paces the action's unrolling through a stepwise sequencing toward its renewed achievement.[6] After the fact, the commanding form may be retained as the time signature of that accomplished occasion, whose felt duration as a drop of experience is the specious present.

Every occasion has its uniqueness. The commanding form of the coming action will force its unfolding across a number of variations native to this iteration. Each specious present has its own emergent quality. Every occasion is an action motif, at the same time belonging to a series and asserting its uniqueness as a variation on it. If the habitual terminus, in this case of helmeting, is reached it is not because the occasion was exactly the same as the last. There is always a difference. It is because the difference did not make enough of one. The occasion's native variations were not strong enough to jam the commanding form's self-accomplishment. No dissonance occurred jarring enough to make the action's phrasing stumble on its own steps. The action rolled over the rough spots and smoothed them over with its own onward momentum, acknowledging them, if at all, with a slight inflection in its dynamic form and an unperceived variance in its experiential quality. The result is a new production of a repetition across variation, and possibly with a variation, but not of the ambit to exceed the bounds of the recognizable. The repetition is the product of a creative differential: between pastness and futurity, and between each and their cue-induced coming-together in the complex life of the situated body. The actual recognition that had been primed came last, quizzically capping the formation of a life-sequence. The line of action was differentially re-produced. How different the re-production actually had been in this example was not apparent until the embarrassing finale.

The world is astir with cues. Every situation swarms with primes. A situation is made of primes, nothing but primes. Its every eventually-discriminable perceptual trait is a potential prime. There is always a multiplicity, in principle infinite, of unexpressed primes. They mutely populate the background of action. The vast majority do not register in catalytic effect because they were overlaid by cues with more pressing commanding forms. For example, a potential counter-helmet prime such as the jangle of car keys in a coat pocket may well have rung unheeded. Had the ringing registered, it would have given the coming action pause by folding into the same interval a competing unfolding. This would have posed a problem for the coming action. A nonconscious commotion would have resulted, as two mutually exclusive lines of action noisily interfered with each other's future-pastness. This dissonance might have had its own effect, forcing an awareness of the glitch. It might have demanded attention. It might have induced a conscious feeling of nonrecognition, a felt awareness of an unresolved differential between commanding forms. This would give the body under the combined time-pressure of both forms a momentary pause, in a becoming-conscious of the life-priming interval. This registering of the nonconscious shock of the cue times two would be felt as a tiny dose of everyday "awe," mini-awe for the situational differences it is life's own habit to serve up. As it happened, the inertia of the transport body's habitual posture, the persistence of its customary carriage out the door, rolled over the irregularity. The cue-induced commotion remained

nonconsciously backgrounded, to helmeted effect. The priming for recognition won out.

There is a lesson for the conduct of war in this everyday mini-drama.
If the body is recognition-primed it is primed to under-experience the
constitutional complexity of its situations. In war, particularly in the
full-spectrum uncertainty of asymmetrical war, the occasions when one
can roll on through a missed experiential difference with minor effect
are far outnumbered by times when the consequences will be dire. The
problem with recognition-primed action is that it presupposes, until commotionally proven otherwise, that the developing situation is unproblem-
atic. But as we have just seen, even the most habitual and banal situation
is constitutively problematic, if only mutedly. Its action-line begins with
a differential: a disparity between a pastness and a futurity, exerting a
time-pressure which can only resolve itself in the active working-out of
an experiential effect due to both dimensions jointly. This experientializing differential is embedded in another: the contrast between the mul-
titude of backgrounded primes and the dynamic foregrounding of the
action sequence. This second, spatializing differential is created by the
working-out of the first, at the same time it provides the setting for it.
The less pressing primes recede and meld together to form an only apparently uniform background against which the catalyzed action dynamically
stands out. This back-setting of the primes produces the perceptual environment, or associated milieu, for the existential salience of the action's
unfolding.[7]

There is really no such thing as recognition-primed action, if by that
is meant an action cognitively triggered by the recognition of a cue. Every
action is difference-primed, born nonconsciously of a cued micro-cut in
the continuity of experience. There is no such thing as the same situation. There are only situations in which an experience of sameness is produced against an only apparently uniform background. There may be no
recognition-primed action, but there is priming *for* recognition: priming
for the production of recognition. Since soldiers will be operating in what
is presupposed to be an always and uncertainly changing world, their
training must prime them for nonrecognition. They must be trained to
"recognize" change, that is to say to perceive it, so as to be poised to live
out its problematic difference.

Not that change is ever actually perceived. Only the effects of change are actually perceived. Change is the living out of its own generative difference, the working-out of a differential in the field-conditions productive of actual perception. Change takes effect at the strike of a prime, which by its very operation falls out of the experience it catalyzes. Change is infra to the experience registering it. It does not feature as such in the experience, nor in its environment. Change is experientializing, not experienced. Neither is it pre-spatialized. It comes, as Deleuze would say, from an outside more distant than any mere exterior (Deleuze 1988, 96–97). When it comes on cue, it time-presses the unfolding of an action-perception. The time-pressure it releases in-forms the coming action sequence while producing the experiential space of its salience (its co-emergent associated milieu). Change registers perceptually at the terminal phase of the unfolding, as a qualitative variation that has folded into the action's unfolding. When, on the other hand, change comes with interference between cues, so that no particular action is immediately forthcoming, it registers as an extended interval giving the body pause. It hits as a prime commotion of bare-active shock, and registers in awe. This is a confused perception, in dissonance stillborn. Change is normally only experienced either retrospectively as a perceived *quality of action*, or in suspense as a confused feeling of *activation*. It is always a scansion of action, a beat in the rhythm of life's dynamic phrasing: *animation* (Sheets-Johnstone 2009a).

What is at stake in "perceiving change" and "priming for nonrecognition" is proto-perceptual and proactive. The inculcation must occur at perception's generative level, on a level with life's infra-experiential well-spring, in the proto-active irritability of the bare-active body. What must be inculcated is an extra-normal sensitivity to prime interference. This is not a matter of acquiring a positive skill. The needed sensitivity is for the hit of difference, at a level prior to the consequent determination of experience in the terminally loopy course of its unfolding. It is at this level that an emerging event may be most ontopowerfully modulated. What must be trained-in is a posture of openness. Priming for nonrecognition means posturing the body for *exposure* to the incipient arrival of a not yet effectively determined event: an openness to being open-endedly affected; contentlessly, but all the more complexly for that; differentially, by the problematic strike of more than one priming around each single hit. Then it means carrying this openness into the emerging experience, across the most minimal pause possible, as speed and agility. This is less the acquiring of a particular skill in life than it is the in-bracing of an affective orientation *toward* life: the in-training of an adaptive tendency. It is about a tendential intensification of bare activity.

Intensifying bare activity consists in leaving an opening for multiple terminal attractors to pack into the catalytic onset of life's next iteration, without habitually pre-resolving the problem this poses. The principle is: the more intense the problem, the more creative the response. The more commanding forms there are in bare-active competition, the less beholden is the experience-in-the-making to any one in particular. The principle is: the more commanding forms, the freer is the ensuing action from command. The more registrable primes, the more potential unfoldings. Project: in-train the habit of suspending the triggering of habit, for an extended interval. Operationalize the problematic offbeat of experience. Without waiting for the dawning of reflective consciousness from the unresolved differential between commanding forms. The human lag of conscious consideration could prove fatal. Action must arise from the interval *as if* conscious reflection had telescoped into the unextended interval; as if the interval itself had become conscious; as if action arising were thought's already having occurred in an interval smaller than the smallest perceivable, in a no-time infra to any detectably human moment.

Had our car-driving bicycle commuter been in a posture to "perceive change," the inteference between the car-cue and the helmeting reflex would have worked itself out nonconsciously. The suspension occasioned by the interference would have remained within an unnoticeably extended micro-interval. It would not have drawn out into a dawning conscious awareness taking experiential time. The commanding form associated with car keys would have imperceptibly muscled out the bicycle priming to modulate the coming line of action with all the nonconscious fluency of habit, while introducing a novelty. Conscious awareness of the barely missed misfire may never have fully dawned. The micro-drama that had played out would never have extended past the micro-pause. After all, there is nothing remarkable about wearing a seat belt in a car. It is taken for granted. In this scenario, the unfolding of the seat belt priming does not reach conscious awareness. But that does not mean its specious present was nonconscious, as what agitates the here-and-now of the infra-instant will always remain. On the contrary, the belting is an accomplished fact that will indefinitely remain available for retrospection. Rather than nonconscious, it is *preconscious*: lying dormant for reflection. It can easily be reconstituted, should it ever be deemed important to do so. The cut of the cue is by nature nonconscious. But the priming-effect that unfolds from it, the specious present of its playing out, is cognizable. It is accessible for reflection.

This is "implicit knowledge": knowledge that has already been effectively produced but remains bound up in the lived fact of its production. All it needs is to be isolated from the action of its production. All it needs is an act of conscious recollection to extract it from the past, to make it a presentable content in a body of acquired knowledge. Implicit knowledge attaches to memory in the non-Kierkegaardian sense of the conscious retrieval of an aspect of the past as a content of present cognition. Implicit knowledge is possible content. It is cognitive content, ready and waiting for conscious realization. All it needs is attention. The fact that its emergent *potential* played out in the lived past is what makes it available for *possible* conscious replay in the cognizant future. What was once integrally bound up in the lived quality of a dynamically in-formed unfolding, is now externally presentable as an isolated bit of information.[8]

The point is that in the nonrecognition-primed action required in the field of contemporary war, knowledge production can be taken for granted. Knowledge may safely remain implicit unless and until ulterior circumstances make it important for it to be brought into retrospective relief. What counts first and foremost is the real-time modulation of action-perception as it effectively unfolds from potential. This is effectively unknowing. The possibility of knowledge is always secondary to and derivative of this effective unknowing energizing the event, for the modulating. Knowledge is extractable from this intensive, infra-thin of experience on an as-needed basis, post facto to the action. We effectively remember forward, for knowing backward.[9]

### 8. Sample the Future

In nonrecognition primed action-perception, "the very logic that relates problems to solutions changes" (PE 89). Response ability must be adapted to an uncertain "threat-based" environment. This involves making prob-

lem-solving "scenario-independent" (PE 124). Response agility "is mani-
fested over a space (a range of values, a family of scenarios, a spectrum of
missions) rather than being associated with a point in space (a specific
circumstance, a given mission)" (PE 124). The responding body must go
"beyond what is happening" (PE 102). It must look past the actual circumstances to a "space" of potential cases of solution. What is seen in the present are enemy "capacities" for future action (PE 124) and corresponding
capacities for action on "our" side. A multiplicity of potential future engagements and outcomes is mirrored back into present perception. This
fractures the spatial and physical unity of the present. The present is cut
into by a co-presence of futures. This amounts to temporalizing the space
of present experience, now crammed with futurity. Reciprocally and in-
versely, the future is proto-spatialized into divergent pathways.

It is as if the impact of futurity on the solidity of the present created an
immaterial friction exploding into a shower of future sparks, only one of
which will actually strike tinder and take. Each spark is a future path of action. Like every path, it implies a stepwise unfolding against the dedicated
background of an emergent action-environment. What distinguishes this
potential unfolding from a sensorimotor schema (see note 8) is that at
this commotional level of bare activity, steps are only vaguely indicated,
mutually included with each other, and with eventual variations on themselves. Struck as it is with the imperative to perceive chance, the potential
unfolding must be pregnant with the potential for improvised variations
on itself. It must be effectively vague, of the kind of vagueness that is
not simply the absence of clearness and distinctness, but an energized
overfullness with a positive determination to be improvisationally determined. Each such future spark is a space-like time-unit (a commanding form) presenting an integrated package co-implicating a potential
action-line with the potential spatiality of its time-pressured unfolding, all for the modulating. Each space-like time-integral is monadic: a
monad of modulatory potential.

Only one such integral will actually return to the future from which
the company of commanding forms came together. The future sparks are
collectively present from the angle of their prospective separation from
each other. They are discordant, present as a necessary divergence from
co-presence, but still fundamentally belonging to each other. They belong

to the same "family" as divergent dynamic evolutions in competition for actuality in the coming event. They belong to each other not because they bear a family resemblance, but because they share a genealogy that requires them actually to differ.

The germ of their future divergence is in the same "going beyond what is happening," or seeing past of actual circumstances, whose immaterial time-pressed friction sparked them into co-presence. Their co-presence is a motley topography of emergent action-environments. Each is like a region of a more extensive landscape of potential. Except that they do not fit together at the edges. Each relates, monad-wise, only to its own potential unfolding (which in a certain sense includes all the others precisely by holding them in disjunction from itself).[10] They are in a relation of nonrelation.

Although they are space-like, no spatial logic can contain these regions of potential. They only cohere in the excessive time-logic of a future-crammed present on the dynamic edge of emergence. They are co-present as a puzzle whose pieces cannot fit together.

"Solving" the puzzle means drawing out the consequences of this incompatibility. This cannot be done by consciously puzzling out the situation, surveying its topography, apprehending the lay of the potential land, and then choosing a well-informed path. This cognitive option is not available. No amount of reflection will solve the puzzle in the sense of fitting the pieces together in a way that logically resolves the problem of what action to take, because the landscape in question is simply not available to perception. It can only be seen-past. This is because its presence is fractured by time. It is "spatial" precisely by virtue of presenting, under time-pressure, the spatial paradox of regions that cannot combine into a logical order of actual juxtaposition.

The only way to solve the puzzle and resolve the problem posed by the circumstances is to overcome the presented disparity dynamically—which is to say, to *act it out*. The solution must be performed. The logic must be enactive, *producing* its own conclusion. An action must be executed that plays the potential futures against each other, tipping the competitive balance in one direction or another. Any action taken will modulate the terms under which the futures came into co-presence by altering the sparking circumstances. Given the volatility of the situation, any action is apt to give tender for an effective, divergent unfolding of one of the action-lines against the background of its correlative action-environment at the expense of the others. The unlit sparks will languish in the past eternally, forever futures of a cut of a present left behind. This catalyzing of a potential take is called "sampling" the future (PE 124).

The trigger-action is not a decision, if by that is meant an implemented conclusion. It is more like a cue given to a future to unfold itself, while enfolding a modulation consequent to its having been cued. It is the future itself, not reflection, that processes the decision. Here decision is a performative forwarding. It belongs to the immediate future, whose immediate past it will no sooner have been. It belongs to the future-past of action, operating in the cut of the fractured present, jumping over any possibility of a cognitively full present of conscious reflection.

Decision in action is not in time. There is no time of decision—for the simple reason that in the ever-accelerating thick of action there simply is no time (NCW 65). There is only cut, and as the cut, a cue. Decision doesn't take time, it makes time. It gives a body more time: if the decision was "right," the soldier will still be alive and kicking. Any decision that leaves a body alive and kicking was the right decision. Forget optimization. Decision is a kick of life administered in the cut of its threat-based present. It is directly an ontopower. In the context of full-spectrum war, "managing risk" means actively taking a risk. The best mechanism available for risk management is problematic future-sampling in a constitutively paradoxical life-space.

Traditional risk-averse approaches cannot work in a complex environment. One may conditionally reduce the emergence of risk by "preparing the battlefield" for future-sampling enactive decision (PE 168). But this is more a productive preemption of risk than an actual management of it. The produced conditions will prove just as complex and will incubate other threats. There is no alternative but to "put ourselves in position" (assume the posture) "to exploit the anomalies" that arise in a nonlinear system, as they arise (NCW 163). In comparison to traditional risk management, this real-time "exploitation" of change at the instant of its arising is "less engineered and more 'grown'" (PE 169).

## 9. Capacity-Pack the Past

In order to sow future-sampling on the ground of war to "grow" the ability to profit militarily from change, the field must be prepared. To prepare the battlefield is to prime it. To prime the nonlinear battlefield is to prime it for nonrecognition. As we have seen, this involves cultivating a bodily openness to multiple primes and an ability to play their corresponding commanding forms against each other to best effect, with the understanding that the "best" to be expected is short of optimal but at least makes time for survival, so that life (and war) may continue. The strategic issue is how "best" to open a body. How can a body be exposed to a plethora of unpredictably arising cues in an uncertain environment without it either becoming a Pavlovian slave to the most immediately beckoning cue, or having its response ability jammed by the clammer? The question is complicated by the fact that military bodies come in companies. How can the real-time actions of a number of individual bodies on the battlefield be correlated to achieve a best effect, given that each is embedded in the shared war environment from a unique angle and brings to that complex field idiosyncrasies of response owing to differences in experience and temperament, not to mention physique, carried from the pre-service past? In the absence of a preestablished scenario, how can their working at cross-purposes be avoided? How can improvised real-time response in a chaotic field not give rise to more chaos? The answer lies in integrating two fundamental aspects of full-spectrum war: "capabilities-based" operations (PE 225)[11] and "effects-based" operations.

The notion of capabilities-based operations might seem at first sight to go against the grain of effects-based operations by returning action to a causal foundation in the past. A capacity, however, is a bodily potential. It is contracted in the past, like a habit, but carries a future charge. Like a habit, it only enters the present as the calling forward of its pastness toward a future iteration. To speak of capacity or potential as opposed to habit connotes a greater charge of futurity. It is to speak of skill.

A skill is acquired and becomes habitual in the sense that the more practiced it is, the more automatic and unreflective its exercise. You have not mastered a skill until you can perform it without consciously reflecting upon how you do it as you do it. A skill, however, is more flexible than the average habit. Part of what is learned is how to adapt the performance that the skill holds in potential to differences in circumstance. You have truly mastered a skill when you can perform it *adaptively* without consciously reflecting upon the adaptation. The adaptations are made in real time as if they had been thought out, when they are directly acted out instead. A "thinking" occurs that is one with the execution of action. Skill is what thought would be were it only in action. It is thought enacted, self-performing: a habit of thought. Too much emphasis should not be given to the word "adaptive." The performance of the skill is adapting less to the context as given than to the future that might be enacted through perceiving chance. An adaptation to a nongiven future is an *improvisation.*

The distinction between skill and habit is in no way cut and dried. Habits also have a certain degree of flexibility, or they would be more often maladaptive than not. The difference is in the degree of variation held in enactive potential. A habit has a narrower bandwidth of variation within which to operate before it must cede to a conscious pause of reflection to correct its course. To in-train a skill is to augment a body's capacity for unreflected action. It is to increase its intelligent nonconsciousness quotient. A skill is more future-charged than a habit because its wider margin of maneuverability makes it more enactively tolerant of chance situational differences, which are then more likely to be greeted as positive opportunities to generate variations in performance rather than being discounted as incongruities to roll right past and smooth over. Habits are ontopowerful. Skills are more so—all the more so when they are coupled with the nonrecognition-based art of the perception of chance.

Carrying out capacities-based operations involves inculcating in the militarized body the widest possible range of skills running the full spectrum of force from hard to soft. On the asymmetrical field of war, a body is confronted by a clammer of cues, each sparking a potential action-environment. The aggregate of potential action-environments present themselves together in monadic disjunction, adding up a ragged landscape of non-overlapping futurities from which the next act will performatively sample. Each cued region of potential available for sampling presently envelops a future terminus of action. The terminus is an attractor: it exerts a future time-pressure for the unfolding of an action-line leading to it through the cue-cut present from a region of pastness comprising a reflex, habit, or skill that answers the call of the future with a push forward of its own from the past. It actuates a commanding form.

The key to effectively best operations is to ensure that the pull of the past that comes forward to meet the terminus's backward push to the future is a militarily in-trained skill and not a reflex or baseline habit. For every cue-sparked future there should be ready for enactive service an acquired skill carrying as high an intelligent nonconsciousness quotient as possible. The body must be well provisioned with skills, so that every change that the field of war throws up "cues" sparking the futurity of an in-trained skill apt to improvise survival. The act that comes to be performed and effectively samples the future will have triggered a skilled response whose seeds were carried onto the soil of war by the body's military training, where it "grows" into an actually executed commanding form.

Pre-mission briefing may selectively refresh certain skill sets, giving them more impetus to contribute to their corresponding commanding form. This pre-weighting will alter the competitive balance between commanding forms and in so doing modulate the sampling. In this fashion, unpredicted changes in the environment will operate as primes for acquired military skills. The cued act that comes to be performed will sample the future in a way modulated by training and mission intent. This does not pre-decide any body's action at any given moment. There is still no preestablished scenario. But since all of the fielded bodies will have undergone the same basic training and have had coordinated briefings, their skill responses will be similarly weighted and the various actions they perform are more likely to correlate positively. They are more likely to produce modulations that resonate to desirable surplus-value effect. Capacity-based operations are thus not opposed to effects-based operations. They are in fact a way of weighting the massing of effects so that they remain within certain bounds. "The overall design of command and control, the way each mission, function, and task will be managed, needs to be conceived in such a way as to bound the overall behavior of the forces" (NCW 162).

## 10. Command to Prime

The notion that command is a practice of modulating emergence in a complex environment so that what transpires remains within certain bounds of variation brings us full circle to the point of departure of this chapter. The vocabulary is now in place to understand how this view of command reinforces the military operationalization of perception, and how in relation to this, information as normally understood becomes ancillary even as information technology takes center stage.

The role of command becomes limited to "establishing conditions necessary to create, nurture, and bring to fruition disruptive innovation" (PE 226). Command sets the initial conditions for engagement. It is a basic principle of chaos theory that a chaotic or quasi-chaotic system (one "on the edge" of chaos) retains a sensitivity to initial conditions. The field conditions at the outset return in some degree to in-form each successive step in the chain of subsequent events. Command in full-spectrum war transforms training into a practice of perceptual priming. The capacities it in-trains heighten military bodies' sensitivity to initial conditions, drawing those conditions into selective relation with a landscape of presented futurities.

Each and every battlefield cue is a cut of the present holding the bare-active body in hyperactivated suspense for the smaller-than-smallest perceivable interval. Out of the cut unfolds the dynamic registering of a change in an adaptively enactive response: a "disruptive innovation." In asymmetrical warfare, orders cannot be fed sequentially to the troops on the ground in order to centrally guide their progress. If a command were able to receive enough information on changing field conditions to make a steady stream of central decisions, decision would in fact be disabled. It would drown in information overload. In a threat-based war environment, when it comes to information, enough is too much. The turnaround time for a well-reflected decision would be way too slow for the pace of the action. Centralizing decision would only displace the need for "intuitive" decision making, if that is an accurate characterization of the enactive thought in primed perception described above.[12] In displacing it, centralization would also impoverish it. Decision making would have only information content to go on, rather than situationally embedded action-cues. It would lack the immediacy of bare-active body implication in changing field conditions. It would be more guesswork than a thinking-in-action. Decision, in a word, would re-cognitivize. To avoid this, command must take stock of the inherent limitations of cognitive guidance. At the distance from embodied action at which it operates, command can only inch forward cognitively, when what is required is "orders of magnitude faster sensemaking" (PE 74). That is precisely why command must restrict itself to setting initial conditions for military actors who will subsequently go forth and operate with an autonomy that is effectively bounded in a way that is "appropriately permissive" (PE 171).

Command is the permissively nonlinear art of setting going a self-running: a self-adaptive process in which decision is effectively distributed to the enactive capacities of the lowest level "force entities" (NCW 66, 116; PE 203–205). Command can always cut back in at a global level to interrupt the process as a whole if it seems to be in danger of running out of bounds. It can meta-suspend the process's self-running, then reset conditions as it sees fit. This amounts to changing the default settings and pushing the restart button. Central command doesn't have the cognitive wherewithal to produce a continuous stream of just-in-time deliberative decisions, but it does have occasion to intervene punctually from time to time. Command is relegated to punctual meta-operation from a posture of exteriority to the very process it concerns. In military doctrine this is termed "command by negation" (NCW 75–76; Ullman and Wade 1996, 52).

Central command emplacements are now located far from the theater of war. They operate before the process begins, in the setting of the initial conditions, and again by punctually interrupting the process globally once it has gotten going. They command to prime, and command by negation. This exteriorization of central command spins off human cognition and deliberative decision making into a relation of adjacency to the unfolding of the war process. The center is peripheralized. Central command becomes exorbital to war as a self-running complex system whose engine is perception, where perception is thinking-in-action, or the immediate coming-together of thought and action: an unreflected "real-time awareness" that is a "real-time transaction" (NCW 48). Central command's own (cognitive) mode of operation has become foreign to the (enactive) mode of the actual conduct of war. The centrality of command spins out into a peripheral position of adjacency to a self-running war machine systemically dedicated to the doing of full-spectrum violence through enactive perception. Perception attack becomes the do-all of war.

The main task in commanding to prime is to compose "mission capability packages" or MCPs (PE 123–127, 171; NCW 6–9, 193–198).[13] Mission capability packages bring together all aspects of preengagement preparation into an integrated unit of readily available action-potential. Their composition is transversal, cutting across the customary divisions of the traditional military hierarchy (which due to the entropy of vested interests in such organizations remains very much in place, but now more as a condition of possibility for this transversality than an end in itself). An MCP "consists of a concept of operations, a command approach, organization, systems, and people with a prescribed level of expertise" (NCW 193). It combines conceptual, material, and personnel resources in a convenient action pack.

Every mission must be given many MCPs. They come in sets. A necessary part of each is a mission intent. The designated intent assigns, in more or less general terms, a terminus toward which the packed action-potential of an MCP will unfold if it comes to be triggered into operation. This orients the resulting action's recursive inclusion of an end point at its outset, creating an affinity between that MCP and certain termini potentially cued-in by changes of circumstance it may encounter on the battlefield. If all goes well, this will add weight to the attractive pull of chance-encountered termini which happen to echo the assigned terminus enveloped in the MCP, increasing the likelihood that certain kinds of commanding forms will actually take effect in preference to others.

Mission intent gives MCPs a weighted action-posture, or predisposition. The range of MCPs for each mission is guided by an overall mission intent arrived at by central command. This deliberative mission-will must not be thought of as a directive scenario or a pre-decision. It operates as a selective principle for determining how the coming battle will be primed with a range of autonomous monads of potential whose chancy triggering and variable unfolding will be left to the complexity of the field of war effectively to decide. Mission capability packages are a mechanism for enfolding the cognitive functioning of command and the human element of intentionality into the self-running of the perceptual war machine in the form of a dispositional tendency. They operatively translate cognitive

command and human intent into a modulatory mechanism for the tendential leveraging of surplus-value effect from the nonlinearity of field of
potential of war. They "synergize" the human element of conflict into the
complex-systemic machinery of war.

### 11. Make Information Pointy

"Often, the phrase 'pointy end of the spear' is used to distinguish a
critical mission from a supporting activity. This distinction is no longer
useful" (PE 173). Capability packaging makes missions dynamically self-
supporting. When a mission is off and running, each participating force
entity is tendentially oriented. It is not controlled step-by-step by central command. The challenge becomes one of coordination. Each unit's
slightest action will alter the field conditions in which the others operate.
Enemy actions will change the conditions for all of them. The complexity
of the already complex battlefield leaps to a higher order of magnitude.
This is reflected in the extent to which "friendly fire" has become the un-
heralded trademark of asymmetrical war. To handle the complexity without endangering itself or others, each force entity must have the means at
its disposal to adapt to the changing conditions at the same pace at which
the changes are occurring: in real time. Information delivered in real time
to the cutting edge of conflict becomes crucial. "Information is now literally the pointy end of the spear" (PE 174).

Information delivered as well-reflected content for analysis and delib-
eration is a blunt instrument. Blunted information may be good enough
for exorbital command. It has to be resharpened into a weapon to go into
action. To make it pointy, information must undergo a transformation,
to the point of changing its very nature. It must find a way to fit into the
smaller-than-smallest interval in which action is brewing. This a perceptual
interval. Information does not have the luxury of resting in content. It must
regain active perceptual form. It must mix back in with the bare-active welling of action-perception's incipiency. It must become generative, on a level
with priming. It must enter into the no-time of the decision that is one
with perception, where perception is already in action before reflection.
Making information pointy means making it fit back into the cut of forming experience.

To fit the cut, information must be overlaid upon the environmental cues catalyzing action-perception in the interval. These have already been made to do double duty. At the same time as they prime the field of action toward a constellation of competing future termini, they prime their corresponding unfoldings with skilled response abilities. This is not really an "overlay." On cue, the activated vectors, of battlefield futurity on the one hand and in-trained pastness on the other, absolutely coincide. They cue directly into each other. This is an operative *fusion* (Massumi 2011, 74–76; Massumi 2015a, 47, 62). The cue is the hit of a change in environmental conditions and a priming of a corresponding action-perception in the same strike. Their fusion has its own emergent form: it is expressed as the push-pull of the commanding form that comes into force to creatively resolve their differential in the dynamically unfolding unity of an oriented tendency or potential action. The commanding form is the vectors' active integration toward the specious present of action-perception. The fusion it expresses integrally imbues the battlefield with "higher," acquired, functions such as skill and collective intent. Separately, these would be cognitive functions. In fusion, they directly present themselves in perception as action in the making. They are present enactively, without having to be consciously thought-out. They are dynamically lived-in. Information must be "overlaid" upon the field of experience to this same fusional effect. It too must cue in. It must infuse the field. It must be "actionable" (PE 4, 192). "Sensing, deciding and acting" must be brought together into a single "complex functionality" (NCW 116–117), with information integral to the mix.

This can be achieved in a number of ways. One way is to embed an information feed in a sense-mode such as vision. A transparent smart visor, for example, can overlay targeting information or indications of friend and enemy movements directly on the visual field in real time. This can be done, for example, with cues presenting themselves as visual icons or cursor-like indexes. Another name for a cue that makes perceptibly present a tendential unfolding fusionally imbued with "higher" functions is an *affordance*.[14]

The unity of an experiential field is composed of a multiplicity of co-present affordances leading in potentially divergent directions. These often lead beyond the periphery of the present field. I reach a turn in the hallway and am afforded a potential nap going one way, and going another way a work session in the study. I experience these divergent potential futurities now, in the form of the corridor. The mutually exclusive termini of bed and desk make themselves felt where I stand. I directly sense them in my seeing of the corridor. The corridor affords them to my body. They come to me affectively, in bodily intimation. The sweetness of sleep wafts across my pores like a gentle breeze. The tenacity of the effort of writing micro-tenses my muscles. The differential pull of the competing termini endows the moment with a singular existential quality or affective "complexion" (Guattari 1995, 80–81).[15]

The constituent multiplicity of the sensing embedded in vision at that moment in no way detracts from the unity of the experience. The two affordances have enfolded the outside of the present field into its very constitution. The "complex functionality" of two mutually exclusive life-paths has become essentially ingredient to the field's experiential unity. The paths come to it in differential unison, as a simultaneous contrast between the affective qualities their attainment would afford, a complexion integrally woven into the very woof of the experience. The present sensing of the complexion will already have been a decision by the time the momentum of my walk has carried me through the coming step. What the enacted decision is will depend on how my body happened to have been primed as it entered the situation. As it happened, the cat who greeted me on the landing was yawning in contented appreciation of a catnap from which my arrival awakened him. Without so much as a thought, and without even making the connection to the yawn, my path is chosen.

Information embedded in vision through the device of a smart visor can function in much the same manner (with mission training in place of a cat). If the display is well designed, taking into technical consideration the way vision operates fusionally, the information embedded in visual experience will dissolve into its operation as affordances rather than featuring in it as focused content. This "enhances" vision by effectively "extending" it beyond its periphery and past its actual line of sight. In the present vocabulary, it would be more accurate to say that the technology "intensifies" visual experience by "enfolding" its outside integrally into it in the form of an affectively valenced existential contrast. This infuses the field of vision with a directly and unitarily perceived complexion of potential.

The field thus complexioned is space-like without actually being a space, since it mutually includes paths that can only actually diverge in space. It is also time-like without being contained in an actual point in time: it packs the specious present with futurities directly resonating with the immediate past in the emergent stir of life's next iteration. To say that embedding information technology "extends" perception can be misleading because the included "outside" of experience is outside actual space and time. It is cognitively and ontologically "prior" to their frame and measure of experience. The field of experience is an open field of a complexioned spatio-temporal fusion. It is not entirely without measure of a sort, for included in the complex is an element of value.

The affective qualities through which the termini make themselves felt will be weighted by the body's priming, and that weighting will modulate what transpires. The sensing that is the incipiency of an action that is already a decision will have also been a *lived valuation*: an enactive existential "judgment," flush with perception's dawning in action.[16] Saying that technology "enhances" experience can be misleading because it implies that there can be an embodied perception that is not already tendentially self-enhancing in an active valuation fusionally including complex enculturated functionalities. There is no raw perception. A body takes active integral measure of its life across all its levels, a step at a time. All this, packed into an interval smaller than the smallest cognitive yawn elicited by rational choice theory.

The field of potential experience may also be intensified by perceptually enfolding linguistic or numeric marks of "higher" functioning. Experimental studies of priming have long shown that reading can occur in the cut of perception in the making. In the psychological literature, this generative gap in consciousness is the moment of "attentional blink" in which the coming experience is physically and existentially "potentiated" but not yet actuated (see chapter 3). In the bare-active interval of potentiation, the emergent experience is wide open for modulation by cues fit to the cut. Words and numbers can function, in "direct perception," as primes.[17] Like all primes, they afford life-valued potential. Due to their

highly intelligent nonconsciousness quotient and the intensely enculturated pastness they bring into present futurity, linguistic and numerical
cues offer special advantages. Numerical cues can be used to increase
the accuracy of a coming action. A numerical indication of distance on a
smart visor can increase the accuracy of targeting. But this can work only
if the number is not experienced in such a way as to trigger a calculation
in the shooter's skull. It is already a calculation *in the machine* precisely
so it doesn't have to be one in the time-pressured war head. Instead, its
seeing must instantaneously, unreflectingly trigger a postural modulation of the shooter's body or an instantaneous recalibration of the weapon
setting. The number must be performatively transduced into posture and
gesture, in the instant. It must already have hit the body as "actionable"
information. This can only be if the entire Jamesian loop, by which a terminus determines an event's starting point as the retroactive "knower" of
the unfolding that will have occurred, has been compressed into an interval smaller than the smallest necessary for it actually to have taken place.
The ensuing action will have been cognitive in effect: as effectively *as if* an
actual calculation had been made in the brain.[18] This nonlinear feat of un-
reflectively effecting cognitively inflected action-value, in the immediate
form of a lived event, is made possible by the body's in-training. The event
is lived. The cognition isn't. It remains effectively virtual.

Numerical cues are of great value in priming for nonrecognition. An
effective targeting action must include in its formative interval an instantaneous orientation expressing real-time change in enemy position. Linguistic primes may cue in to change as well, also on the condition that in
the instant of their hit their semantic content transduces posturally and
gesturally into an action orientation, an existential leaning if not an accurate targeting. This is the case, for example, for signs of alarm. Signs of
alarm catalyze an urgent landscape of potential, triggered with minimal
semantic distinction. "Fire!" . . . Wait, in what sense? The kind that requires water or bullets? There is a semantic element involved in the warning, but it functions to cue pragmatically into a significance that exceeds
language. That pragmatic import is codependent upon co-present environmental cues. It is the full-spectrum field of cues that enables a misfire to
be avoided. Given the minimal nature of the semantic element involved,
it behooves a body to have more than the performative minimum in its

capabilities-based arsenal, so it can "judge" on the run to best effect, before it is too late.

Every cue triggers a "cross-modal" relay: an unfolding that mobilizes more than one sense modality and passes through phases in which the dominant mode of bodily involvement may change. There is always a primary phase of *proprioception*. Proprioception is the body's self-feeling of a posturing for movement, and in that posturing of a future carriage through the movement. This pre-posturing is the in-bracing of bare activity. It is nonconscious by nature. It absorbs the body into its own dynamic potential, no sooner to unfold that potential into action. Bare activity is essentially proprioceptive. It is lived-in potential, consciously unfelt, in the interval of its proprioceptive taking effect. It can only be lived out, actually felt in duration, as effectively transduced into something else. The something else into which it is transduced is the ensuing action-line, imbued with an enactive awareness of its own movement, one with its actual unfolding. This real-time *kinesthesia*, occurring at no reflective remove, backgrounds a continuing nonconscious proprioception. This recessive in-posturing of movement's carriage, continuing through the action it informs, may under certain circumstances come to the fore. When it does, it foregrounds itself as again transduced, this time into a feeling of effort (for example an effort of balancing required to correct a near stumble). Even a purely visual effort, such as focusing or discriminating, is an outcome of proprioceptive in-bracing, transduced into an action-line provisionally limited to the muscles of the eyes. Proprioception's pre-posturing toward action is the condition of possibility of any and all orientation. Without it, the eyes would be lost in a directionless welter of light, edge and shadow, and the hands would flail. Visual focus and manual grasping are transductions of the same primary proprioceptive experience into the action of different muscle sets. Both emerge from it and operate against the background of its continuing unperceived (or as side-perceived in the feeling of effort accompanying the action it orients).[19]

All manner of eventual variation is present in potential at the pre-postural strike of the cue. An action that has been triggered by a visual cue may emerge from the interval of bare activity into actual action and a sense of effort in a different mode, such as hearing. The cue may itself involve more than one sense modality. The notion of cross-modality is in the final analysis not adequate to this coming-together on cue. There is no "relay." The differing sense modalities strike in unison, to unified effect. They operate fusionally, in a way neither could in isolation. They figure contrastively, to absolutely integral effect. This is what Michel Chion, studying sound-vision interaction, terms "synchresis."

The word synchresis is a neologism combining "synchronism" and "synthesis": a synthesis in no-time passed. Audiovisual synchresis is a "spontaneous and irresistible weld produced between a particular auditory phenomenon and visual phenomenon" (Chion 1994, 63). The effect is a mode of experience irreducible to either of its contributing modalities taken separately, even if the product may present itself as if it were in one or another. For example, in an action film the image most often cuts before the bullet hits the skull, but we feel we have seen the impact, and may well even remember having seen it, when we actually only heard the splatter. On impact, the splatter triggers an instantaneous disturbance, a startle, which modulates the unfolding action-line. The modulation is negligible because the action-line itself is defined as negligible by the cinematic situation, designed as it is to immobilize. The action-line is sitting, and the modulation a shifting in the seat. What stands out is less the action-line or its modulation than the startle of impact filled with the splatter we will have remembered seeing. It is because the produced visuality stands out in startling relief against a backgrounded action-line that the experience presents itself as a perception as opposed to an action. Perception as it is lived, however, is never opposed to action. All perception is action-perception. When we feel ourselves to be perceiving "rather than" acting, it is because an emergent quality of experience, in this case a visuality, has been produced in such a way as to stand out from an action-line backgrounded by the situation. The opposition is not between action and perception, but rather between action-perception as it is proprioceptively lived-in and action-perception as it is kinesthetically lived-out.

What functions as a cue for the formation of Chion's synchretic cinematic experience is the *disjunction* between hearing and seeing. A seeing is primed into experience by the sound's coming at the cut between visual takes. The disjunction between modes of perception is filled by a cued *creation*. What has been created is an additive to vision: an experience presenting itself in visual mode, but actually occurring over and above what vision is capable of producing in its own right. What has been created is a surplus vision event. Although the emergent effect is irresistibly in surplus visual mode, the creative process to which it owes its emergence has passed between modes. It has come of their disjunction. The cue-cut has produced a weld or effective fusion between modes of perception. It has produced, in the instant, the novelty of heard sight.

Here, priming is not backgrounded, even if it is still imperceptible as such, coming as it does in the cut and conditioned as it is by a disjunction. But rather than qualitatively modulate a stand-out line of action while backgrounding itself, as it does in the modes of priming discussed up to this point, it foregrounds its own emergent product. It is the action-line that is backgrounded by the priming's qualitative product. The disjunctive visual cue, in synchronicity with a sound, induces the creation of a synchretic stand-out quality of experience.[20] It is this produced quality's taking on relief that determines what the experience really will have been. The startle, the instantaneous micro-shock of the cue's taking effect in the bare-active interval, presides over a full-spectrum creation of experience. The shock itself is immediately experienced, in an indistinction between the "here" of the coming shifting in the seat and the "there" of the heard-seen strike of the bullet against the body on screen: in a proprioceptively all-over here-there-and-now. In its commotional immediacy, the shock is all. It is all, ready: it already carries a differential. The here-there dimension of the here-and-now of the impact gives a germinal spacing to the forming experience. The *differential* between here and there is lived-in—without the accompanying sensation of the distance that differential normally betokens. This is bare-active spatial potential, proprioceptively felt, all-over, in all immediacy. But the potential is no sooner lived-in than it is lived-out. No sooner has the shock of the strike registered its all-absorbing commotion than there bleeds from the germinal cut an affective quality indissociable from the produced visuality: a horror experienced as one with the strike. The visual horror bleeds from the conditioning interval backward and forward, irrigating the immediate past and the immediate aftermath with an experiential fill spilling from the cut: emergent content. Irrigated by this synchretic bleed, the immediate past and the immediate present flow into each other. They too are fused. The synchretic event of fusion actually *produces the specious present*, in the very act of filling it with its own qualitative content. The interval has taken on duration. The instantaneous, insubstantial cut between two visual scenes has assumed an extended time aspect: from the absorptive, intensive in-no-time-flat of the here-and-now to the extended now-time of the specious present. The synchretic event has extruded its own moment. In the same stroke, it has filled the moment with its own perceptual creation. Priming does not only modulate coming experience. It *makes* the moment. The prime time of experience is fusionally emergent. Its genesis, purely qualitative: a visual effect imbued with affective quality (so thoroughly imbued that we could say the reverse: an affective quality expressing itself as a vision effect).[21]

The synchretic event extrudes not only an extended time, but spatiality as well. Coeval with the making of the moment is a development of the spatial potential already germinally implanted in the horror at the strike of shock. In the bleed of affective quality from the cut, the horror presently pools over "here" as the strike sets into having been seen over "there." The proto-spatial differential is in the process of being lived-out. The affective quality takes on a vague extensity of its own, filling the distance. It soaks the experience through and through, irrigating it with the singular ambiance of its affective tonality. It is vaguely environing. Its ambient quality is what defines the "thisness" of the experience: the quality of the moment now taking place. And the moment in the making is now literally *taking place*: a space of experience has been extruded. Space is felt in both its experiential dimensions: the co-presencing of juxtaposed locations (here and there), and the envelopment of this juxtaposition in a general environing (all around).

This creation of space and time out of the interval co-operates with the futurist time-pressure and potential experiential landscape produced by priming in its other mode, in which it in-forms a coming action-line for modulation, foregrounding the action-line while backgrounding itself. The qualitative moment-making and future-tending action modes of priming co-operate. They cocreate what Whitehead calls the "extensive continuum." The extensive continuum, or extensive plenum, is the "general scheme" (not to be confused with a sensorimotor schema) of potential space-time relationships, as it is integrally produced and differentially modulated from the singular "standpoint" (standing-out) of a particular experiential event.[22] The terra-forming functions of perception attack discussed in chapter 3 are large-scale extrusions, fusionally emergent from an iterative distribution of perceptual strikes, of the extensive plenum of war: the full spectrum. In no case are space and time a priori categories of experience, whether we are talking about the local movie theater or the global theater of war. Space and time are synchretic productions of the prime cut of life.

Synchresis is a directly lived production of experience. It is vitally creative. Chion speaks of an "added value" to perception: an excess experiential effect, or surplus-value of perception. In synchresis, perception creatively surplus-produces its own lived reality. The term designates perception as inherently an ontopower. It shows it capable not only of generating particular action-perceptions, but of bringing to emergence, in the interstices of the senses, in the bare-active interval, new and singular modalities of experience. Each such emergence carries an immediate affective valence. This affective tonality is a value "judgment" integral to the perceptual event, occurring as one of its immediate dimensions. It determines the lived quality of this experience, as it happens. It is through surplus-value production that experience *makes time* for itself and fills the made moment with the lived quality that is life's content.

Synchresis may occur between senses other than hearing and vision. It can occur even without the actual operation of one of the participating sense modalities. For example, when we are blindfolded a texture or edge can produce a feeling of the seeing of the thing unseen: a tactile visual effect, blindly produced. Or a sound of shattering may give us a tactile sensation of virtual sharpness: an auditory tactile effect. These synchreses, or to use the more current term, synesthetic experiences, virtually involve another sense whose operation actually appears only on the level of effect. Synesthesia, understood as a synchretic surplus-value of perception, must be considered more the rule than the exception in the life of the body, if we take into account the in-lived proprioception of bare activity, and its living-out in the background of unfolding kinesthetic experience (itself often backgrounded by vision).

The participation of the virtual in the production of synesthetic effect is also the rule. In the heard seeing example, both vision and audition were in actual operation. The coproduced effect was in visual mode: a seeing of the hearing. The seen strike, however, did not correspond in particular to any actual visual input. It was what Whitehead calls a "nonsensuous perception": an actual experiential effect, a really lived experience that has no actual isolatable cause.[23] There was no actual stimulus or input genetically connected to it in linear fashion. There were no light rays striking the retina corresponding to the sight we heard. There actually were sound waves striking the ear, and there actually were light rays corresponding to other elements of the scene. But the seeing of the strike was a pure creation. This is not to say that it was created ex nihilo. It was not out of nothing—it was out of lived relation (cut, commotion; shock, absorption; differential, fusion). It is a surplus-value of the interrelation of different dimensions of experience in actual-virtual participation. The implications of this for the theory of perception and the philosophy of experience are far-reaching. The ubiquity of synchresis radically undermines any classically empirical stimulus-response or input-output model of experience. For the moment, what is important is that every experience involves synchresis, at least between proprioceptive in-bracing and one other sense modality. All experience is synesthetic (Massumi 2002, 162–176, 186–194).

A synchretic event between two modalities of experience is less the rule than a limit-case. C. S. Peirce asserts that all modalities of experience are virtually active at all times. There is no feeling that is not integrally coproduced. "When any particular kind of feeling is present, an infinitesimal continuum of all feelings differing infinitesimally from that is present. . . . A finite interval of time generally contains an innumerable series of feelings" which come "welded together," "affecting" each other with "an energy that is infinite in the here-and-nowness of the immediate sensation, finite and relative in the recency of the past" (Peirce 1992, 324–325). The infinite energy of the here-and-nowness of the immediate sensation is the proprioceptive in-bracing of bare activity. For it is proprioception that nonconsciously supplies the web of potential transitions between feelings relaying at infinite speed, in the smaller-than-smallest interval, to form virtual series. Each relay corresponds to a virtual change of posture and variation in forward carriage. The bodily field of potential always includes the full spectrum of experience. It is action-packed with virtual series proposing themselves as potential commanding forms for the coming event.[24]

Integral to each self-proposing commanding form is an affective tonality, a singular quality of the experience, also proposing itself for the present. This makes for the intensity of the here-and-now as it self-extends into the specious present: its action-packing with futurity packs an overload of affective qualities. From the loaded interval infinitesimally fissuring into futurity, there issues a fusion. On cue, a commanding form is synchretically enacted with its present fill of affective tonality. Doubling the intensity, there emerges extensity. This is the synchretic extrusion of the specious present's taking place.

Paradoxically, the present comes at a lag. The cue-strike registers in the appearance of its product. In other words, it presents itself as already just having hit. The extensity of the specious present is at one and the same time the finite recency of the past: a just was-there. "Say 'now' and it *was* even while you say it," writes (wrote) William James (1996b, 254). Present and past are fusional and together emergent. Futurities are fractal and recessive. They are here-and-now in infinite seriating regress from the fusion. They self-envelop, swallowed in their own infinite fissuring. They cut away from the emergent duration. Two systems processually interlocked: an emergent (past) present duration, and a recession of futurities self-enveloped in their own serial proliferation. The cutting-in of the cue binds them to each other, across their difference, in the same event. Its cut forms the hyphen of the future-past (present).

The two systems interlock as dimensions of the same surplus-value production of experience. For the next prime will cue into action one from among the recessive series, as the commanding form governing the unfolding of the next duration. Another iteration of experience emerges. The two systems are processually coupled, to experiential added-value effect. The present system adds a surplus-value accumulation of lived quality. The future system constitutes a surplus-value *speculation* on the more to come of life. The cut of the cue is the operator of this differential, and the differential is the drive of the process. It constitutes a creative off-set, an ontopowerful imbalance between fusion and fissuring, that pulses the process self-creatively forward. In drive, the present system extrudes the was-there of an experienced spatiality. The future system, for its part, envelops a multiplicity of potential regions speculatively proposed here-and-now—in "real time"—to coming experience. All of this adds up to a dynamic topology of experience: a continuous spatiotemporal variation of the perceptually enacted form of life's unfolding.[25]

Translating the self-creative topology of experience into a topology of power is the mission of the military in adapting to the threat-environment of asymmetrical war.

The preceding discussion in earlier points necessitates an extension of Peirce's generative spectrum of experience. The full-spectrum stretches not only across the modalities of perception but across all the "faculties" of the living body. Add to Peirce's proliferating infinity a further infinity of higher enactive functions such as reading, calculation, skill, intent, and valuation, all of them functioning synchretically with what we experience as sense perception. All of them fusionally transduce into emergent perception while receding into proliferating potential. This raises the onto-powers of the living body to an even higher power by enlarging the creative off-set formative of experience. It quickens the pulse of the self-creating topology of experience, adding new gears to help leverage the imbalance into forward drive. The body's synchretic invention of new modalities of experience expands in capacity. As Spinoza might have remarked, we know not yet what a primed body can do.

The military effort to make information "pointy," to make it "actionable" or enactive through the embedding of advanced technology in the field of action, is a recognition of the plastic powers inherent in the creative life of the body. When the fulcrum of military force moves to perception, when perception attack becomes the ur-weapon of war, synchresis is on the front line. Efforts to operationalize synchresis militarily may be as simple as voice-feeds fusing into the field of visual action, or as experimental as creating virtual vision using pressure-point tactile stimulation of the skin. Whatever their level technically, processually their implications are great.

## 12. Self-Synchronize and Differ

The most far-reaching implication is that if the project of making information pointy succeeds the military machine will jump-start into "an accelerated evolution" (PE 86) by which "the very nature of the organization will have been transformed" (PE 6). The change in the nature of the organization consists precisely in its becoming coextensive with its own process of transformation. The military machine tends toward becoming a complex, self-adaptive evolutionary system whose organization *is* the enactment of its process.

The way this comes about is through "self-synchronization" (PE 27–31; NCW 175–180). It is only an apparent contradiction that self-synchronizing involves an "unfetter[ing] . . . from the requirement to be synchronous in time and space" (PE xiii). Self-sychronization is an operational concept. It is the "how" of achieving "value-adding interaction" (NCW 175) such that the overall productivity of the machine "exceeds the sum of the productivity of its parts" (NCW 90). The self-exceeding productivity expresses itself as "momentum" (PE 141), an unrelenting forward drive. There is no longer a steady state as a base state. There is no gravitational center to return to to rest and recoup. The machine is perpetually "on the fly" (PE 158). The very notion of a central base of operations reeks of the traditional "platform-centric" approach to war rendered long-since obsolete by the contemporary threat-environment (NCW 65). Platform-centric warfare's infrastructural emphasis assumes frictional force-against-force as the default operating mode. For the organization to self-synchronize, platforms must "evolve" into "nodes in a network" resembling "dynamically reconfigurable packs, swarms."[26] In network-centric warfare "the very notion of platform will evaporate." Infrastructural solidity melts into a "series of transformations" (PE 169) in forward drive, "shifting seamlessly" among alternatives (PE 143). Momentum, alternatives: the mode of operation is future bound.

It should be clear by this point that binding operationally to the future is not about advance planning. Planning must become one with execution (NCW 74–75). This is all about "real time." "Real time" in today's war time is an odd bird. Real time, as the here-and-now of perception attack, includes sampled futures. Riven with futurity, it is "asynchronous in time and space" (PE 75). Odd phraseology. Asynchronous . . . space? The phrase treats space as a time-variable. This is not, at this point, an unfamiliar move. The notion of terra-forming presented in chapter 3 explicitly treated space as a time-variable. This chapter's account of space as the extrusion of a perceptual event considered the emergence of space to be coextensive with that of the specious present as momentary durational experience. Time that is "asynchronous" has no self-consistent duration. It is out of joint with itself. The production of space still hinges on time, but the time it hinges on is the in-no-time-flat of the future-fissured here-and-now. This radicalizes the time-variability of space. The space of war becomes the direct expression of the self-receding here-and-now, so that the space produced is similarly out of joint. It doesn't add up to a self-consistent expanse. The space of war is not a contiguous extension. It is composed of local patches of emergent extensity that do not connect at the edges, each of which is genetically fractured by the fractal fissuring of its birth time.

This "asynchronous" battlespace is not less than but rather "far more than a contiguous physical space" (NCW 60). From its patching and fractality there synchretes "a whole new dimension" (NCW 61). The new dimension is a "complexity" arrived at by the multiplication and distribution of synchretic fusions. Operations are distributed among countless nodes in a network. Each node has the capacity to "sense, decide, act" autonomously (NCW 94, 116). In fact, operating synchretically in these three modes at once is what defines a node as a "battlespace entity." That is what a node does, and what a node does is what it is (PE 94). Nodes, as battlespace entities, are enactive. "Real-time awareness and real-time transaction" come together in each of their operations (NWC 48). Each operation fuses perception and decisive action into an autonomous, real-time, future-sampling decision. A distributed micro-present and a distributed fragment of extended space may potentially extrude from this fusion, but only locally, in the vicinity of the node. The fusion's synchretic effect doesn't add up to a whole-field present or a contiguous global space because it is made possible, in its autonomy, by multiplication and distribution.

Self-synchronization is an effects-based concept. It means producing "synchronous effects" (PE 103) from a fractal population of distributed fusion. The imbalance between the synchretic fusion and the fractal fissuring produces the far-from-equilibrium momentum driving the process. Each local fusion at one node entrains all of the other nodes, without unifying them. The only "space" where everything comes together is the forward momentum thus produced. What the multiplication and distribution of effects is "synchronous" with is that momentum itself.

Momentum is a vector concept. The concept of the vector integrates space-like and time-like characteristics, without equating with either. A vector is a moving intensity of oriented force. It is time-like under its movement aspect. As oriented, it is spacey. Self-synchronization does not refer to a structural property of an organization. The overall momentum of the process is the resultant of a multiplicity of micro-moves or mini-vectors. These micro-sallies self-execute without central planning. Although each is local and autonomous in execution, their effects are correlated. The nodes are effectively linked in-no-time-flat by a horizontal web of "interoperability" to form a "spectrum of connectedness" (PE 109). As their operations' effects propagate complexly and instantaneously across the spectrum, they mass into a coordinate movement. The elementary units are not parts of a structural whole. They are part-operations executed by interoperating sub-actors whose decisions do not add up to self-consistent extension of a whole, but rather multiply into a distributive unity of movement, like a swarm of storm-tossed ripples converging in a pilot wave.

Self-synchronization is a wavelike "emergent *behavior*" (PE 209). It is an operational concept, not a structural concept. It is predicated on a destructuring: a fluidification transforming organization into a self-massing "dynamic reconfigurable *force*" (NCW 120). A wave-force turns over on itself as it advances. A self-synchronized military force feeds self-adaptively on the momentum of its own "real-time modification" (NCW 159). The sub-acting nodes ripple away in "unrelenting operational tempo" (NWC 82), in response not to central planning directives but to the ineradicable "contingency" (NWC 159) that is the groundless ground of war. Out of contingency arises a "coevolution" (NCW 227), by the coordinate graces of the networked spectrum of connectedness. The generation of this "synergistic [synchretic] effect" (NCW 92) defines self-synchronization. Its upswell is the creative "magic" of network centric warfare (PE 208–209).

When the overall spatial aspect of war is analytically isolated from war time, it must be treated as an operational space rather than as a continuous spatial extension. "Battlespace" is a vector space from bottomless to top, or trough to crest. Battlespace is distinct from the battlefield (NCW 63). A battlefield is an expanse of space traditionally conceived, located on a preexisting coordinate grid. Battlespace, constructed as it is from a massing of effects channeling into vectors, has emergent coordination rather than preexisting coordinates. The extent of a battlefield is measured in constant, conventional units (square meters or kilometers). The magnitude of battlespace is a variable. Its measure is the "number and variety of targets of interest and their dispersion" (NCW 62). The measure of battlespace is the span of its distribution—its degree of fractality. Its fractality is a measure of the intensity of the force afield. The higher the degree of fractality, the larger is the distributive spectrum, and the greater the magnitude of the battlespace: the more intense is the action-perception potential for vectoring the field. Each increase in intensity means that more emergent threats have been detected and can be potentially countered through the system's self-synchronization around the irruption of the threats.

Targets "of interest": battlespace intensity varies according to the degree of the machinery's perceptual engagement. The more interest, the more attention paid to perceiving chance, the more emerging threats detected, the more threats nodally preempted. The fact that the variability is tied to perception does not contradict its nature as essentially a time-variable. As discussed in chapter 3, attention is only apparently the action of a subject, even when we are talking about an individual human body and not a population of battlespace entities which may or may not be human (a node can be a sensor, a self-guiding ordinance, an autonomous probe or vehicle, an antenna array, a software hub, a human, a group of humans, or a combination of the above). Attention, even in the unnetworked human, is a name for the operator of the fissure of time from which the specious present may emerge (see chapter 3). The subject is the "superject" of a shift in "attention to life": an emergent creation geared into formation by the attentional cut separating the next experiential moment, or momentous (interest bearing) experience, from the last.[27]

In conventionally measurable space, or metric space, scale is a matter of segmentation. A small-scale battlefield spans fewer conventional units. Since space is indefinitely divisible, the segmentation can go on forever. The difference between the infinite metric divisibility of the battlefield and the infinite fractality of battlespace is that metric segmentation is "reductivist" (NCW 70). Levels of complexity are excluded from view with each drop in scale. This is because as a metric concept, scale is linked to a quantitative divisibility. Battlespace, for its part, is not segmented (NCW 70) and the corresponding concept of scale carries an ineradicable qualitative aspect. A fractal is qualitatively self-similar at whatever scale. This is also the case with battlespace. Battlespace scale is a matter of "granularity" (NCW 80).

The concept of granularity is tied to resolution. Resolution has a perceptual connotation (how fine a capacity to discriminate). But it also has a power connotation. A "resolution of forces" is "the process of substituting two forces in different directions for a single force, the latter being the resultant" (Walker 1991, 760). This is another example of fusion (much like granular synthesis in sound processing, where finest resolution samples complexly co-occur, and rather than registering individually synchrete a novel note). The granularity of battlespace combines the two meanings of resolution, pertaining to scale and to a fusional power-effect. A battlespace entity is enactive in that it fuses sensing and acting into immediate decision. This is never simply a transmission of raw data. Battlespace entities do not deal in information. They deal in micro-perceptual synchretic events. These bubble in the here-and-now of the emergent space-time of war without either settling into a stable spatiotemporal structure or registering in a higher-level reflection as a cognized specious present. Say "now," and they have already been vectored.

Even the most lowly sensor figures in battlespace as an enactive resolver of forces. Take for example a movement detector for use in targeting. It will never transmit to the network a raw, instantaneous reading of a vector of movement. It will be part of an array. Battlespace entities always come in populations. Battlespace is populated "all the way down." At least one other sensor will take a reading from a different angle or at a different resolution. The two vector readings will be combined locally into a "composite track" (NCW 142), or resultant vector. What is transmitted is the resultant of the differential between readings: a resolution of vectorial forces. A surplus-value of tracking has already been extracted from the readings before they even appear in battlespace. As soon as the readings take on resolution, as soon as they appear in battlespace, a counter-vector is launched: a missile, for example, automatically guided by the result of the readings. The launch itself will not appear in battlespace until it hits (or misses) the target. The emergent outcome is the "resolution" of this attack vector with that of the composite track. It is relational and eventful: the product of an encounter.

The relational product is a resolution in both senses of the term. The resultant of the resolution of forces gives the event battlespace-resolution in the sense of discriminability. The encounter passes a threshold of perceptibility. It appears, minimally perceptible, in battlespace. More precisely, the effects of the encounter emerge and propagate across the fractal spectrum of interoperability connecting battlespace entities across the intervals separating them. The propagation modulates the "whole" of battlespace, like a ripple. The registration of the rippling modulation constitutes the here-and-now of battlespace. But this is a distributed here-and-now, lacking stable extension even as it is bubbling with emergent space-times. Calling it a "whole" is a stretch. It is fractal at bottom, and a fractal is by definition of fractional dimension. It is more precise to use dynamic vocabulary for this dynamic event, especially given that battlespace, constantly rocked by ripples from one node or another, or many at once, is in ceaseless, oscillatory reformation. It is more precise to say that the effect, upon passing a threshold, passes to the limit of the system (even though the limit is not specifically assignable in the contour of a whole). The here-and-now is an instantaneous wave-form modulation that affects, at the limit, all of the local nodes in the horizontal network in real time: in-no-time-flat.

In spite of the networked connectivity, the local space-time of a given event may fall into the cracks between the interoperating nodes. Any extension the event may have taken on may remain an emergent patch unintegrated with others of its kind, floating there in the operational here-and-now of battlespace. This is because even though all nodes will *potentially* register the event's synchretic effect, most will not be "interested" in enacting on it due to the parameters with which its particular initial conditions have been set. Uninterested, they will not extrude a follow-on event. The unenacted ripple will remain dormant in them, until they register another vector with which to resolve the first, in its own interested, enactive fashion. Until then, the ripple-effect, although registered, will not have hit that node effectively as a cue. It is suspended in a not-yet of effective perception. It remains, unresolved because uncomposited: minimally felt but unconsummated, unfused into a follow-on perception-action. It is in pointedly nonconscious perceptual limbo, much the way a word is on the tip of the tongue, potentialized for active duty yet hanging in linguistic suspense. (This is not to be confused with the readiness for reflection of the preconscious cognitive dormancy of blunted information.)

A term in philosophy for a minimally felt experiential constituent that does not appear in its own right but in-forms what does is a "micro-perception" (Deleuze and Guattari 1987, 162, 213, 283; Deleuze 1993, 86–87). The differentials that enter into a fusion, such as the constituent vectors resolved in a composite track, or the ingredients of a synchresis, are micro-perceptions which appear only in their integral follow-on effect. Battlespace as a whole is noncontiguously connected because its connectivity is never fully consummated. Its spectrum of connection is never fully actualized. It is riddled with unresolved micro-perceptions that are like sinkholes of potentiation cutting out from actual continuity. The spectrum of connection is effectively mottled (PE 92, figure 10). The flash of an action-perception is like a white ripple-crest appearing against the backgroundlessness of a black sea of potentiation. At each flash of enactive perception, or constellation of flashes, the rest of battlespace blinks with potential. The blink is not a total absence of perception. It is the almost-presence of myriad micro-perceptions.

Battlespace as a fractal "whole" dynamically reconfigures itself around each nodal event's effects, in a patchwork of action-flash and potentiation. Its "shape" is the changing pattern of actuation and potentiation rippling across its spectrum of connectedness, in-forming it with potential. Its "size" is the number, variety, and dispersion of the patterned enactions. But once again, battlespace doesn't really have shape or size in any usual sense. What it has is intensity. Its intensity increases when a critical massing of effects resolves myriad ripples into a macro-wave integrating populations of emergent battlespace-times. Now, the enactive potential of battlespace more integrally forms a vector. The component vectorial forces have been concentrated. The resultant of this concentration is a factor of power. This factor of power, taking effect as it does in the in-formed here-and-now of battlespace potentiation, is a militarized force of time: a force to "own" time militarily (chapter 3).

Power is "the ability to make something happen. The amount of power is expressed as a vector" (PE 166). The more capacity to act, the more integral the vector, the higher the intensity of power. Battlespace is an effects-based "dynamically scalable environment" (PE 186) of power. If it has an overall measure, it is not a size but a power factor. Power is not only its measure, but its very fabric. Power is the dynamic stuff constitutive of battlespace. Except there is no stuff, the heavy-metal platforms of traditional war having "evaporated" (PE 169). Of course there is still infrastructure and there may be heavy equipment on the battlefield. But it must be remembered that battlespace is not the battlefield. Battlespace is the integrally self-differentiating power factor that oscillates through the battlefield. Battlespace is the operational space of a surplus-value generation of power, as an emergent property of the real-time blinking into action-perception of continuous conflict.

Returning to the question of "connectedness," what connectedness means in battlespace is the propagation, across the fractal gaps between autonomous battle entities, of resultant vectors that are potentially re-resolvable in a more integrative vector susceptible to further propagation, or in a node-specific potentiation latently awaiting resolution. "Connectedness" is the distributed ingredience of one entity's local emergence in another entity's autonomy of sensing, acting, deciding. The term "datum" can be applied to these processual inclusions. But the word is then being used in a meaning that is neither cybernetic information, nor the raw sensory input posited by the classically empirical view of perception (which is associationist rather than fusionist-emergent). It is being used in a sense more akin to cueing or priming of action-perception.[28]

The operation of a node or battlespace entity is always a generative "data fusion" figuring as part of a qualitative "value-adding process" (NCW 141). The value added is the adaptive reconfiguration of the network of war directly expressed as a power factor. The reconfiguration is cued-in by a synchretic fusion event registering in one way or another throughout battlespace. Battespace is always under modulation. It is always emergent and occurrent. Each reconfiguring iteration of its process is a refactoring of its constitutive power.

It is no accident that the terms used here to describe the operation of a nonhuman sensor array are identical to those used earlier to describe human perception: differential imbalance, fusional resolution in a surplus-value production, enactment, modulation, cueing (priming). The military theory texts make no distinction between human sensing and cybernetic sensor activity. As battlespace entities, the human senses are spoken of as a subset of a larger category: "organic sensors" (NCW 172). This follows naturally from the overall mission of the military as interpreted in this chapter: to contract all of war into the micro-interval of perception, in order to re-factor its power potential. War contracts all the more into the cut, even as the power intensity of its machinery increases with growing connectedness, and the scale of its potential battlespace integrations tends to planetary dimensions.

What lies at the heart of the self-synchronization process that drives this mission is the production of a "situational awareness" that can be "shared" (PE 99) in such a way as to feed a real-time "sense-making" that "goes beyond what is happening and what may happen to what can be done about it" (PE 102) given the essentially uncertain ground of war (PE 200). Read: node-level fusion for "situational awareness"; interoperable propagation of in-forming fusion effects across fractal gaps for "shared"; synchretically future-bound for "goes beyond what is happening or what may happen"; and real-time enaction of integral power vectors for "what can be done about it." The translation is fair enough. Except that the military texts adopt the cybernetic commonplace of "distributed intelligence" to characterize the self-adaptive process. From the philosophical perspective developed here, this misses on three counts. First, it reduces the process to cognition, glossing over the broader-spectrum experiential event, whose "self-synchronized" productivity extends even to its own emergent space-time. Second, it fails to acknowledge force and power as constitutive factors in experience. And third, it assumes an identity between the human and nonhuman battlespace entitites (as opposed to an operative solidarity, across their difference).

Philosophically, human and nonhuman entities are in a relation of isomorphy, not identity or even convergence. An isomorphy is a processual parallelism, not a substantial sameness or identity of nature. A processual parallelism is an operative analogy: "an identity in operative relations" across an ontological difference in the status of the entities between which the analogy is made. For example, a cybernetic sensor can detect movement, and so can a human body as organic sensor. The operation of detection is same enough even though the operators differ in every other way: material composition, genetic composition, number and kind of parts, and so forth. So far this is a fairly standard definition of operative analogy. It is revised by Gilbert Simondon to adapt it to the philosophy of creative emergence. The difference between paralleled entities is not only an ontological one. It is ontogenetic: ontologically productive. The parallel operations are effectively linked, so that the entities on both sides come out of an iteration changed in unison, but each on its own side, in its own way. An operative analogy is not a description. It is an ontopower in action, an enacted logic of becoming. Double becoming. Operative analogy is an effects-based process of "co-individuation" or collective individuation: a coevolution. This coevolution is really an "aparallel" evolution, because the becoming of each, on its own side in its own way, can in fact broaden the ontological difference between them, even as they enter into value-adding synchretic resonance across their inexpungible difference. The relation of the human to the nonhuman in the process of war must be approached in this way: as coevolutionarily mutually in-forming. The machinery of asymmetrical war is a process of ongoing collective individuation producing surplus-value of being through self-synchronizing operations of perception-attack. Participating battlespace entities are in aparallel evolution, in interoperative relation to each other. Battlespace is an ever-emergent property of their aparallel evolution.[29]

### 13. Take It to the Edge

"In a remarkable number of cases, the adversary has not fully committed to a single course of action" (PE 148). The enemy has blinked. Its lines of action are in potentiating suspense. Its perception-action is in the bare-active interval where multiple alternate action-lines are co-present in pressing futurity. The mission of the full-spectrum war machine is to compress its own operation into that interval to the greatest extent possible: to contract its battlespace into a smaller-than-smallest adversarial interval of perception. Hit them where they potentiate. What comes out of the enemy bare-active interval will then be different than it otherwise would have. You have productively preempted. Hit them again, in the next blink. Shift seamlessly from one perception attack to the next across the spectrum of connection of your battlespace following the propagating ripple-effects of the serial hits. Constellate your own blinking so that your intervals never overlap with the enemy's. To do this, set each node's initial conditions so that it awakens on cue from micro-perception and cuts into action at the slightest fusional sign of an enemy vector of "interest." You have made "information" doubly pointy, fit to the cut of your enemy's interval, to productively preempt, and cueing into your own, to self-adapt in real time. Your operations now self-synchronize in syncopation with the enemy interval. The "shape" (distributive intensity) of your battlespace rhythmically reconfigures as its nodes cut into the enemy's interval and cue into their own in a complex, adaptive pattern. You have transacted the enemy's instant of bare-active vulnerability into your own emergent power factor. You have made your operational space a dynamically self-scaling, rhythmically reconfiguring, real-time topology of power.

This is the meaning of taking power to the edge. The double-edged sword of ontogenetically pointy "information" is everywhere. Every enaction takes effect in a cut of the instant. The military machine is all on edge, pointedly pivoting on the fractal here-and-now, for cut and cue. Organizationally, this marks the "demise of the middle" (PE 177).

In an "edge organization," there is a predominance of direct, real time peer-to-peer relations: node to node, battle entity to battle entity, enaction to enaction, effect to effect (PE 176). "Everyone is at the edge because they are empowered" (PE 176). This "flattens" the organization, cutting out the middle levels of organization that separate central command from lowest-level actor. There is no longer a linear chain of command. There is a complex web of enaction instead. Operations are no longer shackled to a hierarchy. Where hierarchical centers of command persist, the self-synchronization of battlespace has made the hierarchy the functional equivalent of horizontality. The separation of functions guaranteed by a centralized hierarchy ripples resolvingly away. Planning and execution "merge" (NCW 75). The distinction between strategy and tactics "collapses" (NCW 70). Most significantly of all, command and control collapse into enaction. "Command and control and execution processes . . . merge into a single, integrated process" (NCW 157).

This really amounts to an "uncoupling of command from control" (PE 217) in such a way that control becomes immanent to the iterative emergence of the time-based topology of power, and command becomes just another control node. "Control," writes Deleuze, "undulates." It moves in serpentine fashion in a "continuous beam." Wavelike, it is "short-term in rapid turnover [it blinks], but at the same time continuous and unbounded [it is on a spectrum of connection]," so as to "effect a universal modulation" (Deleuze 1995, 180–182; trans. modified). Translated back into Revolution in Military Affairs speak:

> Control needs to be thought about and approached differently. Control is not something that can be imposed on a complex adaptive system, particularly when there are many independent actors. Control, that is, ensuring that behavior stays within or moving to within acceptable bounds, can only be achieved indirectly. The most promising approach involves establishing, to the extent possible, a set of initial conditions that will result in the desired behavior. In other words, control is not achieved by imposing a parallel process [of hierarchical decision making], but rather emerges from influencing [modulating] the behaviors of independent agents [also called autonomous battlefield entities]. Instead of being in control, the enterprise creates the conditions that are likely to give rise to the behaviors that are desired (PE 209). . . . Control is not a function of command but an emergent property that is a function of the initial conditions, the environment [force of circumstance], and the adversaries. (PE 217; emphasis in the original)

Control is not advance central planning, but "planned opportunism": adventitious coevolution. In military affairs, it immanently governs an aparallel evolution with the asymmetrical enemy in an environment of threat.

The uncoupling of command from control spins it off into the exorbital position described earlier. Command comes before the fact, in setting the initial conditions for planned opportunism to take place within a desired "bandwidth" of variation in battlespace intensity. It does this by in-training human bodies, priming human nodes with Mission Capability Packages, priming nonhuman nodes with the cybernetic equivalent of MCPs (programmed algorithmic starting points and parameters), and in-folding into these initial conditionings the recursively causal terminus of mission intent. The process is then fielded. The modulatory effects of the preconditioning undulate into battlespace and propagate across its coevolution. Command also comes after the fact, if the modulations propagate in such a manner as to overspill the desired bandwidth or turn maladaptive. Command then cuts in as command-by-negation to reset initial conditions.

Before the fact as after the fact, command activity per se is external to the process. By this is meant that command only effectively has macro-perceptions—and it is only command that has macro-perceptions. Command still functions as a central node in the sense that it is designed to register sufficiently large-scale battlespace modulations, and once they register, can discern enough of their genesis and mode of propagation for the purpose of tweaking or resetting the parameters of the process's conditionings. At this resolution, the micro-grain of battlespace is lost. The constituent micro-perceptions are left in the dark. Only already large-scale effects fuse for command. If there is a whole to battlespace control, it is here: apart from it, in exorbital command, in the was-there of the process. If there is a specious present of war time as a whole, it has taken on duration in differential imbalance with this was-there of the process. If there is a global cognitive overview, it is a synchretic effect of this exorbital specious present. If there is military cognition and deliberative judgment, this is its reflection. Globality, actually, is the local of command. Centrality, processually, is a peripheral spin-off. It can only reenter battlespace by abdicating its macro vantage point, submitting its actions to a rebecoming micro-perceptual, in the self-synchronizing thick of things.

Command feeds off of a spun-off surplus-value of perception whose emergent time and space is far more conventional than that of the war machine left to its own process. Command is always in perceptual off-set from the real-time experience of war. It is because of this processual aloofness that command is so prone to err. The more aloof, the worse its reflection. Exhibit A: Donald Rumsfeld. Even though he made a command mission of setting in place the initial institutional conditions for the new machinery of war, he erred mightily in maximizing his aloofness at every opportunity and in arrogantly neglecting the implications of his processual off-set from the very war machine he commanded into becoming. His command suffered, to put it mildly, from a tweaking deficiency. Exhibit B: George W. Bush. Given the constitutional off-set between the deceptively solid present ground of the commanding global view on the one hand and the infinite granularity and dynamic scaling of the real-time war process on the other, not to mention the constitutional disposition to error this offset entails, a dose of modesty may be recommended to those in high command. Barack Obama: Exhibit C. Obama's policies in Iraq and Afghanistan were certainly modest. But they were modest in a way that substituted civilian, all-too-cognitive, reflective civilian hindsight (decisions prioritizing domestic political considerations, and haunted by fears of repeating the past) for forward-driving battlespace awareness at junctures where the threat-environment was ripe, from the neoconservative perspective, for drastic action (Libya in 2011, Syria from 2011 to the present, Ukraine in 2014). Although the terminus of self-synchronization toward which power to the edge vectorizes is clear, the path of its realization is riddled with pitfalls, curtailing countertendencies, and compromises with countervailing formations. This is all for the best. It buys time for counter-ontopowers to stir.

# 5    Embroilments and History

Demise of the middle, death of hierarchy, evaporating platforms, self-synchronization, power to the edge: who would know, looking at the burgeoning U.S. military and Homeland Security budget, the many-leveled, byzantinely bloated defense establishment, and the regular descent into less-than-synchronized backbiting and bickering among the various forces and their civilian counterparts and keepers? The suspicion is hard to shake off that this intricate vision of war is no more than a lofty ideal. True, the main author of the essay that first introduced the concept of network-centric war, Vice Admiral Arthur Cebrowski, was recruited by Secretary of Defense Rumsfeld in the immediate aftermath of 9/11 to head the newly founded Office of Force Transformation which was entrusted with implementing the Revolution in Military Affairs championed by Rumsfeld, Vice President Dick Cheney, and their allies in the revolving door between public service and private enterprise in the extraordinarily high-growth area of defense and security consulting and contracting. John J. Garstka, also a retired air force officer and coauthor with Cebrowski of the original network-centric war article as well as coauthor of the book *Network Centric Warfare*, served as Cebrowski's second in command at the Office of Force Transformation. Revolution in Military Affairs concepts of shock and awe, minimal troop levels, rapid dominance, intensified networking, and full-spectrum force informed the U.S. strategy for the invasions of Afghanistan and Iraq. However, there are many who are of the opinion that these strategies were not well implemented in either case. Harlan K. Ullman, main author of *Shock and Awe*, is among them. He was highly critical of what he saw as a simplistic implementation of the concept in the initial attack against Iraq and a halfhearted and insufficiently full-spectrum follow-through after the fall of Baghdad (Von Drehl 2003; Ullman 2006). The kind of shock-and-awe campaign Ullman advocated in the lead-up to the war emphasized using force-against-force in a highly selective manner and specifically for purposes of perception attack, an approach he termed "muscular containment" (no ground invasion in this case, air force shock strikes only, against key targets strategically chosen to create an awe-paralyzing threat-environment—a more accurate description overall of Obama's strategy than Bush's; Ullman 2002).

In the minds of more traditional currents, the Revolution in Military Affairs itself was to blame for the miring in Iraq, although neither the troop "surge" of 2006 nor the post-Rumsfeld strategy of shifting the balance more toward the soft end of the spectrum of force through reinvigorated "human terrain" operations (involving among other things "embedding" sociologists and anthropologists with the troops) contradicts the RMA doctrine in and of itself.[1] When the Office of Force Transformation was closed in late 2006, with Rumsfeld's departure as secretary of defense palpably in the offing, there were not a few who saw it as the death-knell of the Revolution in Military Affairs, which in many quarters had become a pejorative term. Others, however, saw the closing instead as an indication that the RMA had done its work and was now mainstream. Its functions, after all, had not been abolished but divided and transferred to two core offices of the Department of Defense (policy, and acquisition and technology). The high-tech DARPA research programs inspired by it have continued, and funding within the army for quicker implementation of their results has been a priority (Boyce 2008; Weinberger 2008; DARPA 2014). A key adviser to General David Petraeus, commander of allied forces in Iraq under Rumsfeld's successor Robert Gates, advocated a suspiciously RMA-ish "low footprint / high tech" formula for the anticipated wind-down in Iraq following the putative success of the troop "surge."[2] This formula continued to serve as the model for the Obama administration and its actual winding down of the wars in Iraq and Afghanistan.

In a word, the situation is sorely embroiled and not a little murky. What is the situation "really"?

It all depends, as President Bill Clinton famously said, on what "is" is. That is, on what is taken to be "real." If potential is taken to be real, the problem is different from sorting out the "hard facts" of the course of history as notably evidenced in personal words and deeds, interpersonal exchanges, and manifest acts of government. The concern must be not only for the "is" but also for the "almost-was" of the futures sampled along the course. Not the bare facts and nothing but the facts, but also the bare activity. Not just the actuated, but also its potentiation. Not just the notable points of emphasis, but also the ellipsis points of pregnant pause. "History," writes Whitehead, "includes the present *and the future* together with the past." The futurity is never fully containable in reflective consciousness, even in the instant, and thus can never be reconstituted historiographically on the model of "hard" fact. "Pure history . . . is a figment of the imagination" (Whitehead 1967a, 3–4; emphasis added).

The focus of this book is precisely on that confounding aspect of the real that can be counted upon to render history "impure." That reliably embroiling factor is potential. No one ever speaks or acts as if all would then be said and done. Words and deeds are always for what more may come. What comes, of course, is contingent on circumstance. But the trigger-hold circumstance has on potential is what makes it a force of history. Circumstance cues in history's in-the-making, cursoring it from instant to instant, running it forward. The infinite circumstantial richness of each field of experience fractures the instant even as it crests as a historically placeable moment, repacking it with futurity as it happens. Circumstance is a happenstance. It is cocreative of the events that may come to figure in history. It is co-determining, with potential and tendency, of the run of registrable history. The question is what manner of thinking is adequate to historical happenstance at that crossroads of circumstance, potential, and tendency. One thing that is certain is that it is a manner of thinking in no way assimilable to any established classically empirical discipline. Potential is in the instant enactively, forever bringing the run of history to ground in the interval of immediate experience. As telescoped into this infra-level, it eludes the grasp of conventional historiography. No sooner has it telescoped into the infra of the instant than it accordions back out into the course of history in the macro-making, exceeding individual experience. *In the same movement by which potential eludes historiography, it exceeds psychology.* There is no "pure" thought of potential, in the sense of it fitting a specific discipline or it accommodating itself to any specialist method, because its movement creatively crosses boundaries. There can be no "pure" thought of potential, in the sense of prehending it in itself, because though it is more than the instant, it is nothing outside of it. It is the ever more *of* the instant.[3]

The only kind of thought willing or able to grapple with the ins and outs of it is philosophic. Even philosophic thought will not suffice if it is practiced as a discipline in its own right. Philosophy has to dirty its abstract hands in the history and psychology it finds potentially challenged (to mention only the most pertinent disciplines for the present project). It must proceed impurely, in friendly handshake with non-philosophy.[4] The handshake is a sleight of hand, extracting from the disciplines their missed potential. A taking of what eluded grasp is not a loss—unless the aggrieved party fails to take it back as a gift. The philosophic gift of disciplinary potential is not necessarily innocent. To traditional disciplinary practitioners, it may yet be poison. This is philosophy as a radical empiricism: the kind you can't trust to respect your disciplinary holdings (and especially not your holdings-back). Philosophy of this sort is pesty and embroiling. All the better for the potential of thought.

Potential does register, in a way. It expresses itself in the way it comes out of itself, repeatedly, into the constitution of what will come to be seen retrospectively as the fact of the matter. Potential comes *across* the facts. It runs *through* the course of history. It is *transversal* to history. It oscillates across the hard-fact field of history in the same way battlespace ripples and waves across the heavy-metal battlefield. Potential expresses itself in *tendency*. Understood in terms of potential, tendency is an internal factor, or constitutive dimension, of the rhythmic emergence of fact. In the instant, tendency is immanent to the constitution of each individual fact; it is in-forming. Overspilling the instant, it rolls across each and rhythms all; it is field-filling. Tendency is a surplus-value of history. It is realized punctually in the enaction of each action-perception, but in such a way as to roll over in rhythmic excess of any one. It is the processual quality of history's dynamically self-recomposing field of factual emergence. It is not the fact of the matter, it is the matter of fact: the dynamic stuff of the run of history.[5]

The concept of the terminus, mobilized in chapter 4, is a useful tool in thinking tendency philosophically. The terminus, as the name implies, involves a certain notion of finality. If you extrapolate the end point that an emerging experiential vector would reach if it could roll itself out to the limit of its capacities, this ultimate expression would be the terminus. The terminus, however, is restive. It doesn't wait around for the rollout to reach it. It reaches forward to meet the approaching vector of experience, upon which it exerts a force of attraction that pulls the experience toward itself with an intensity equal to the trigger-force of circumstance cueing it forward by activating habitual and skilled inheritances from the past. All this happens in the instant, in the smaller-than-smallest perceivable interval. The terminus is at once instantaneous in its action and recursive in its causality. This means that the terminus dynamically recomposes at every experiential iteration throughout the field, in a rhythm with the field's oscillations. It is integrally ingredient to each event, at the same time as it differentially multiplies throughout the field. The terminus is not *an* ideal, in the sense of a utopia or otherworldly model of perfection. It is as much all, as one. But it is ideal, in a sense: in the sense that its one-and-allness has no thickness of being, being the sort of "stuff" that only does, and does only in self-differing. Whatever "is" is, the terminus isn't exactly. Potential is in dynamic offset to any and all particular experience, like an abstract double or imperceptible shadow haloing each action-perception and their shared field with a penumbral excess of the processual more to come. It is extra-being: surplus-value of being.[6]

The terminus is ideal in the sense that it is not contained in space or time, even though it is nothing outside their emergent reiteration. As an attractor governing a tendency, it must be conceived as exerting an abstract force of cocreation.[7] Exerting a force, it must be accounted as real. Although not in time, the terminus is nothing if not time-like, since it is an internal factor of the experiential event's extrusion of the time of its making. The terminus is not a past, in the sense of a was-there in particular. Its restiveness and tendential iteration make sure of that. Neither is it a future of the kind that can be divorced from the past. Its recursivity sees to that. Nor is it the durational fusion of these in the specious present. Its recurring to emergence at every instant forbids its occurring durationally itself. The terminus in-forms every instant and out-fields every tense. The time of the terminus is the complex time-likeness of iterative emergence: for the first time for all of time and yet (again).[8] Its ideality is what makes it a privileged operator of a *logic* of enactive experience. It also makes it such that this operative logic of experience necessarily includes a metaphysical dimension.

"Terminus" is a word that repeatedly features in William James's writings on radical empiricism, although it is not highlighted as a feature of his official terminology.[9] James sees radical empiricism as the philosophic mode of thought best suited to helping fulfill the project of pragmatism. This subjects the metaphysical notion of the terminus to the same criterion James's pragmatism lays down for any concept worth thinking. A concept is truly a concept, he often reiterates, only if it makes a difference, only if it has effects that would not otherwise have been generated (James 1996a, 72). Radical empiricism partners with pragmatism in an effects-based operation. It is free to entertain metaphysical notions, even at the extremity of abstraction, as long as they effectively do work.

The work of the concept of the terminus, in tandem with tendency, is as an enabler of the thinking of complexity. It is a tool for grasping an event, or action-perception, without analytically isolating it from its becoming. Terminus and tendency together make a vector: an oriented force or momentum. This situates the event in the arc of its action-line. At the same time, it expresses the event's differing from itself as situated. The vector is creative, the force a force for change, and the momentum that of a variation. As discussed earlier, this formative movement is a fusion event integrating a generative differential infra- to the cut of the instant. Terminus and tendency trouble any hasty identification or reductive categorization of what something is or was. It obliges a thinking of what actively conditions a given passage from recessive differential into extruded fusion. Because the conditioning is active, the "ground" of an emergence is not a preconstituted schema, of space, time, the body, or anything else, but an as-yet undetermined "something doing" (James 1996a, 161). What is doing is emerging into a determinate variation on something like itself. Terminus and tendency remind us that there is always generatively more in an event than actually transpires. There is always more to come in an action-perception than what was "there": there is variation. Every emergence expresses a variation while carrying afield the potential for more. An emergence reconditions the field from which it emerges, in the rippled real time of its arising. This modulates other emergings, with which it is then complexly correlated in ways that will not be wholly apparent. Aspects of the full spectrum of complexity recede into the fractal fissure of the instant in a rhythm with the real-time wave of emergings, pulled in by the ontogenetic undertow, to eddy in the reservoir of tendency. A something doing is always a pulse in a coevolutionary rhythm, "full of oneness and manyness, but in respects that don't appear" on the whole (James 1996a, 93–94). The reservoir of tendency is an ontogenetic remainder left-under from each field-filling wave of emergence, still available as a surplus of in-formative force for the next arising coindividuation.[10] The remainder stands abstractly for the potential that each something doing may always have done otherwise, had the force of circumstance, in its relation to the other processual factors coproductive of the event, happened to have played out differently. Terminus and tendency point to the matter of fact that a something doing includes its "would have beens." This is where the terminus must separate for a conceptual moment from tendency to take on a logical consistency of its own before rolling back around.[11]

The terminus is a way of conceptualizing the remainder of potential that is left-under each iteration, remaining active as an ontogenetic surplus-value of being for the coproduction of the next tendential wave of becoming. The terminus is the extra-being of tendency. In connection with a particular action-perception, it may be conceived as a function of unspent momentum: the difference between the capacities that the event effectively fulfilled, and the utmost that the something that was doing might have reached had it passed to the limit of its constitutive tendencies. To return to a mundane example from chapter 4, this is like the difference between wearing a bicycle helmet and wearing a seat belt to drive a car. A bicycle helmet would afford some protection in the event of a car accident, but less than a seat belt. The tendency toward transportational safety is fulfilled by the helmet to a lower degree. The capacity to wear a seat belt is not something foreign to a traveling human body. The acquired tendency to safeguard travel did not reach the higher degree of fulfillment that was within its capacities, due to force of circumstance. The cue that might have triggered wearing the seat belt did not register as important enough to deviate the action-line. Importance is a directly felt relevance to the situation (Whitehead 1968, 9). That particular prime did not figure as relevant: it did not strike in felt relation with the other constituents of the situation. It did not hold together with them. It did not enter co-operatively into their shared dynamic.

When an action-line does not reach a higher degree of self-accomplishment, it is because of a looseness in the holding-together of the constitutive elements of the dynamic situation: a lack of operational "solidarity" among them, as Simondon would say.[12] On the other hand, when an action-line does reach what in retrospective will appear a reasonable degree of accomplishment, there is always a surplus of ways the governing tendency might have been taken even further. Beyond the seat belt lies the air bag. The traveler might have had one installed. Beyond the air bag, there is reinforced armoring of the vehicle. Or, if Google has its way, the self-driving automobile. There are many ways to make a vehicle increasingly secure. Pushing safety further and further, they come in absolutely infinite variety. But the further the tendency is pushed, the more irrelevant its forms of fulfillment become. The primes that might have cued a move toward one of them or a set of them are less and less in solidarity with the everydayness of the situation. This is due once again to force of circumstance: there is neither the time nor the money nor the immediate wherewithal to accomplish these modulations. It is also due to the acquired countertendency of standard operating procedure. Convention builds certain habitual bounds into the initial conditions of the event. It is not generally considered important or reasonable to take the tendency to safety to such extremes.

The terminus is the absolutely infinite variety of potential endings to the tendency, as governing a movement to the limit extending far beyond the outer bounds of habit and convention. In itself, the terminus is far too complex to be given an image. It is too multifarious and too overfull to fit into perception, or even into conception in its general sense. Thinking it out would involve an exhaustive inventorying, which would itself be governed by a tendency to run on infinitely, in the course of which it would progressively lose relevance for most situations. The terminus is purely abstract, even for thought process. It is multifariously ulterior to thinking as to doing. It nevertheless still effectively figures in the experiential event. It is ingredient to the event as a ratio: the differential between a passage in thought or deed toward one or more of the potentials lurking at the tendential ulterior limit, and the movement that can be seen upon retrospective reflection to have actually been capacitated. The infinity of potential end points enveloped in the terminus should not be taken to imply that the terminus is a fundamentally quantitative concept. The degree to which the processual quality (safety) primed into the event effectively informed and ambienced its unfolding.

The degree to which an action-perception determines the fulfillment of the governing tendency of its action-line is the intensity of its capacitation. The intensity is actively expressed in the event as the "bandwidth" of the modulatory ripples and waves triggered by the situation's constituent cues. Intensity is a measure of an action-perception's ontogenetic power factor in a coevolutionary field. Each experiential event has its own unique power factor. Each event is utterly singular in its power, because its power factor is utterly bound up with the circumstances unique to its occurrence. At the same time, every event is an iteration. There have been and will continue to be other movements governed by the same tendency (safety is not only for bicyclists) and tending toward the "same" terminus. Except both will be different, because of the differences in circumstance. The terminus itself is iteratively re-produced as a variation on itself by each singular event, as multiply as they come. Strictly speaking, it is neither one nor many, but singular-multiple (involving the singular-multiplicity of part-subjects as discussed in the afterword). It is neither a whole nor a collection of parts, but an abstract variety (a nonsensuous prime cueing in a complex of "themes," as Ruyer would say, which express themselves in the ongoing of action as commanding forms, as discussed in chapter 4). It is an effective abstract variety, insofar as it acts as a force of becoming co-ingredient to a power of being.

In terms of chaos theory, this means that the terminus qualifies as a "strange" attractor. A strange attractor is one which co-implicates a multiplicity of end points in restive relation. Any tendency toward a strange attractor will feel the pull of all of them, more or less distinctly, to greater or lesser intensity. The intensities interfere with each other, causing vacillation. The action-perception is in suspense. It is bare-actively attuned to the potentials. Depending on the circumstances, the interference will be presently resolved, either by excluding potential endings, or by transforming the interference into a positive feedback so that the tendentially proposed action-lines fall into resonance and creatively fuse into a novel emergence. Accidents of circumstance will figure in the resolution. But then what is an accident of circumstance if not an actually occurring prime that falls into the cracks between tendencies proposed by the nonsensuous priming of the singular-multiple terminus? Is an occurrence that is too multiply potentiated to predictably trigger a capacitation an accident? An "accident" is in matter of fact an expression of the interference between dynamically interrelated end points co-enveloped in the ulteriority of the terminus. In process, there is as a matter of fact no such thing as a pure accident, any more than there is such a thing as linear causality. One goes out with the other in the effects-based ontogenetic operation that is this emergent world of complexity. The "accident" is a punctual expression of the constitutively problematic nature of the world. In the problematic world of emergent complexity, plied as it is by tendency, rippled as it is by interference and resonance, each event a mini-motor of a coevolution, there is never pure chaos. On the other hand, there is never not "quasi-chaos" (James 1996a, 63): a margin of indetermination permissive of novelty.[13]

The co-operation of terminus, tendency, and force of circumstance as understood in this way is what Deleuze terms the "problem" (1990, 120–123). For Whitehead, it is the "proposition" (1978, 11, 185–186). The resolution "accidentally" introduced by tendential interference is what Whitehead calls "decision," appealing to the etymological meaning of the word, which is "cutting off."[14] The cutting-in of cue resolves the emerging action-perception to unfold from its formative vacillation. The unique resolution of the problem thus effected cuts *off* the event from the field conditions from which it arose. The something doing folds integrally into its own time-making, place-taking fulfillment. As presently fulfilled, it was-there, and future-more. It has bequeathed a ripple of reconditioning for the self-renewal of the field in further emergence. It has passed and pulsed. The process of the world has rolled over. The terminus rolls back around, left-under again for a next pulse of becoming.

The pragmatic difference these metaphysical somersaults make is that they authorize an understanding of events in terms of novelty, that is, qualitative emergence and modulation. Sorting out the unique mode of ingredience in a given event of terminus, tendency, and force of circumstance enables a rigorous thinking of qualitative emergence as embedded in a coevolutionary field. The intensity of the coevolutionary emergence enables the event to be understood as a qualitative power of existence, a power for coming thus to be: an ontopower. All of this makes a difference that is as political as it is philosophical.

First, the instant of qualitative emergence appears as an instance of decision that does not presuppose a subject of the decision. The entire issue of what constitutes decision is reopened.

Second, the fulfillment of the emergent event correlates to a thematic region of the world's worlding that cannot be reduced to a set of objects passively occupying space for a metric time, and playing no actively determining role in the decision. The thematic region, composed of a time-looping complex of abstract varieties, is more capacious than any mere context.

Third, the coevolutionary field requires thinking the singularity of an event as immediately implicating a multiplicity, undermining any presumed separation between the individual and the collective, now processually wed in coindividuation. This demands an ecological approach to political history, and to psychology in its sociopolitical dimensions, as well as other disciplines.

Fourth, the variety in the ecological field is understood in terms of terminal potential rather than origins or inherited empirical need or necessity. The futurity of the terminus opens a processual window of creative modulation for change. More than that, it integrally includes, as active factors of production immanent to every event, potential passages to the limit tending to surpass the bounds of convention. This disables relying on normative criteria of evaluation.

Lastly, the potential for a processual tendency to spread and even to return after a historical hiatus is left open by the remaindering in real time of the surplus-value of being. This forbids reductive explanatory schema, for example, in terms of ordered civilizational stages, as if history were following a linear trajectory, all quasi-chaotic evidence to the contrary. It also forbids reducing the spread of tendency to intersubjective "influence," or conversely laying the failure of a tendency to keep its momentum going to personal or institutional shortcomings that can be retrospectively second-guessed by the superior personal reflections of the commentator.

Shortfall is built into the thinking and the doing because the event *becomes* finite, as a function of a limit that can never be reached.[15] A something doing emerges into its self-fulfilled finitude under terminal conditions of infinite variation.[16] When all is said and done, it always isn't. Something's still doing. With each new circumstance, the process integrally rejigs. The thought equivalent of the force of circumstance is the detail. With each new detail, the thinking must also integrally rejig. By opening itself to the force of detail, the thinking of the process remains in operative analogy with it. It leaves itself formatively open to the tiniest force of detail, while at the same time straining tendentially to the metaphysical limit of what it can think doing can become. This is radical empiricism as James conceived of it. Radical empiricism is an enactive logic in circumstantial coevolution with its "object" (or "subject") of inquiry. It is itself an operative logic, in a double becoming with its field. It does not place itself in a posture of superiority, but rather in aparallel evolution. It is allagmatic (chapter 4, note 29). It relishes getting its abstract hands dirty. It is self-embroiling. It consents to conceptual risk, knowing in advance that it will fall short no matter how far it is able to go, so that it might as well go it to the limit. It is a modest sort of extremism.

Going it to the limit involves putting both the accomplishments and shortfalls of a tendency in their overall processual place. In order to do this, the infinity of potential in the field must be taken seriously while at the same time the finitude of its expressions is accounted for. The infinity of potential features in the form of the extrapolation of an extremum. This is the *extremist* element: thinking the terminus. It involves giving an impossible image of thought to a tendency's highest intensity, its reaching for the limit of what it can do, which of course it can never do. This thought of and striving toward the effectively impossible as a creative factor in becoming must be as pragmatic as it is metaphysical. Its utility is in enabling an evaluation of an action-perception's degree of eventful self-accomplishment, its effective capacitation: in other words its onto-power. This pragmatic evaluation is what gives the thought of the potential infinity that is the impossible terminus its relevance to history. This is the modest part, because the evaluation is essentially contestable, by other approaches to thought as well as by the subsequent course of history itself. Since its relevance is always in question, the political thinking of potential must be openly adaptive. It must integrate self-corrective tendencies into its mode of operation (by always resurrendering itself to the force of detail). Everything connected to history is always contestable in any case. In this case, it is a self-formative point of pride.[17]

With respect to the tendency in the contemporary practice of war that has gone by the name of the Revolution in Military Affairs, the terminus appears in the concept of "self-synchronization." This terminal processual concept is produced by the current within the RMA tendency that might be considered the most extremist organizationally (if not necessarily the most extreme by conventional left-right political yardsticks) in order to think the vectorial orientation of which it is a part, and to produce self-evaluative criteria for its accomplishments and shortfalls. A thinking of contemporary war wishing to enter creatively adaptive operative analogy with its field must accept this terminus into its own correlated but aparallel orientation in thought.

Self-synchronization is the utmost of "interoperativity." It is an impossible image of the tightest operational solidarity thinkable between the processual elements felt necessary to move the tendency forward, as enumerated, for example, in the subheadings of chapter 4. The concept of self-synchronization is the most abstract self-expression of where RMA heads. Taken up here philosophically, it is given even a more extreme expression by smoothing over elements in the military discourse that still give the nod to what are in matter of fact countervailing tendencies such as democratic humanism and reflectively informed deliberative politics in general. In its aparallel philosophical expression, self-synchronization must be taken to a purest of conceptual extremes by filtering out cross-tendencies.

This actually increases the concept's pragmatic thought-value. The potential for this purification is given by the military process itself. It a product of a certain philosophic thought entering into operative analogy with its "cutting edge" expression. The pragmatic thought-value it affords is in giving radical-empirical reason for asserting that the terminus of self-synchronization effectively in-forms the military field and is coproductive of its tendencies. This allows each action-perception and serial iteration of action-perceptions (action-line) to be situated in the overall military field as an effective power factor of this military tendency: a "power-to-the-edge" factor. Events may then be evaluated as intensities of tendential self-fulfillment, or variable degrees of "concretization" of this full-spectrum military process.

When an action-line falls short, as they all essentially do (and as the invasion of Iraq did spectacularly), the reasons for the shortfall will be sought in what Whitehead liked to call the "welter" of detail. In other words, the singular way in which forces of circumstances will be seen to have played out. These "accidents" of history can be interpreted as indicative of interference between competing currents within the same tendency, or between one military tendency and others, or more broadly between processes of militarization and other processes plying the coevolutionary field. These coindividuating processes may be social, economic, political, or even psychological. When a competing tendency has been able to cause the military movement to take power to the edge to short-circuit, it is because that tendency has been able to capacitate the "accidents" of history more effectively toward its own end. Its terminus succeeded in more powerfully "capturing chance" and attracting the ensuing proliferation of effects more toward itself. The success of one tendency over another can result in its adjoining to itself what will, by this act, have proved to have been the weaker process. This extends the capture of chance into processual capture. The thinking of the terminus must be supplemented by an intensive analysis of the competitive and co-adaptive in-mixing of tendencies, across their shared full-spectrum field that is the world environment. The result is a multi-vectored political ecology of universal processual embroilment. It is the extreme metaphysical device of "purifying" the terminus that conceptually enables the pragmatic evaluation of the dynamic "impurity" of this mixed coevolutionary field, quasi-chaotic by its embroiled nature.[18]

A process at work in history can only be understood with any faithfulness to its creative quasi-chaos, oriented complexity, and co-adaptability if approached in this open-systemic, metaphysically enabled way. It cannot be understood prioritarily in terms of subjects or objects, a structure of parts composing a whole, individual needs or desires, collective agglomerations or mediations of these, identities at any level, or even state and nongovernmental institutional interactions. It cannot be reduced to any

category taken classically empirically to preexist. The formative tendencies of the ecological field run across them all. They oscillate emergently
through them, just as battlespace oscillates through the bodies and hard-
ware and rock of the battlefield. They redouble them with surplus-value
of being. They are in processual excess of anything moderately empirical.
Only an excessive theorization, unafraid of conceptual extremism, has any
chance to faithfully aparallel them.

# PART THREE

# The Power to Affect

# 6 Fear

## (The Spectrum Said)

That momentary paralysis of the spirit, of the tongue and limbs, that profound agitation descending to the core of one's being, that dispossession of self we call *intimidation*. . . . It is a *nascent* social *state* which occurs whenever we pass from one society to another.

—Gabriel Tarde, *The Laws of Imitation*

The future will be better tomorrow.

—attributed to George W. Bush

In March 2002, with much pomp, the Bush administration's new Homeland Security Office introduced its color-coded terror alert system: green, "low"; blue, "guarded"; yellow, "high"; orange, "elevated"; red, "severe." The nation has danced ever since between yellow and orange.[1] Life has restlessly settled, to all appearances permanently, on the red-ward end of the spectrum, the blue-greens of tranquility a thing of the past. "Safe" doesn't even merit a hue. Safe, it would seem, has fallen off the spectrum of perception. Insecurity, the spectrum says, is the new normal.

The alert system was introduced to calibrate the public's anxiety. In the aftermath of 9/11, the public's fearfulness had tended to swing out of control in response to dramatic, but maddeningly vague, government warnings of an impending follow-up attack. The alert system was designed to modulate that fear. It could raise it a pitch, then lower it before it became too intense, or even worse, before habituation dampened response. Timing was everything. Less fear itself than fear fatigue became an issue of public concern. Affective modulation of the populace was now an official, central function of an increasingly time-sensitive government.

The self-defensive reflex-response to perceptual cues that the system was designed to train into the population wirelessly jacked central government functioning directly into each individual's nervous system. The whole population became a networked jumpiness, a distributed neuronal network registering en masse quantum shifts in the nation's global state of discomfiture in rhythm with leaps between color levels. Across the geographical and social differentials dividing them, the population fell into affective attunement. That the shifts registered en masse did not necessarily mean that people began to act in similar form, as in social imitation of each other, or of a model proposed for each and all. "Imitation renders form; attunement renders feeling" (Stern 1985, 142). Jacked into the same modulation of feeling, bodies reacted in unison without necessarily acting alike. Their responses could, and did, take many forms. What they shared was the central nervousness. How it translated somatically varied body by body.

There was simply nothing to identify with or imitate. The alerts presented no form, ideological or ideational and, remaining vague as to the source, nature, and location of the threat, bore precious little content. They were signals without signification. All they distinctly offered was an "activation contour": a variation in intensity of feeling over time (Stern 1985, 57–59). They addressed not subjects' cognition, but rather bodies' irritability. Perceptual cues were being used to activate direct bodily responsiveness rather than reproduce a form or transmit definite content.

Each body's reaction would be determined largely by its already-acquired patterns of response. The color alerts addressed bodies at the level of their dispositions toward action. The system was not in any direct way a subjective positioning device. It was a body-aimed dispositional trigger mechanism. Bodies would be triggered into actions over whose exact nature the governmental emission of the perceptual cue had little direct control. Each individual would inevitably express an attunement to the affective modulation in his or her own unique way. It was in a second moment, through the diversity of the resultant actions thus triggered, that each would position him- or herself subjectively in relation to others. Any moment of reflection that might come would come after, in discussion or retrospective review. The system addressed the population immediately, at a presubjective level: at the level of bodily predisposition or tendency—action in its nascent state. A color shift would trip each body's tendencies into an unfolding through which its predispositions would regain determinate form in particular actions attuned to a changed situation. Each body's individuality performed itself, reflexively (that is to say, non-reflectively) in an immediate nervous response. The mode under which the system operated was cued directness of self-expression, in bodily action. It was less a communication than an assisted germination of potentials for action whose outcome could not be accurately determined in advance—but whose variable determination could be determined to occur, on hue.

The system was designed to make visible the government's much advertised commitment to fighting the "war" on terror it had so dramatically declared in the days following 9/11. The collapse of the World Trade Center towers had glued the populace to the TV screen with an intensity not seen since the assassination of President Kennedy in the medium's early days, and in its recent history comparable only to the Gulf War show. In a time of crisis, television was once again providing a perceptual focal point for the spontaneous mass coordination of affect. Any ground television had lost to the web as an information source and as the pivot point for family entertainment was recouped in its resurgent role as the privileged channel for collective affect modulation, in real time, at socially critical turning points. Television become the *event* medium—for a final moment of social-political salience before being engulfed by the rising tide of social media.[2] The terror alert system sought to piggyback on television as event-medium, capturing the spontaneity with which it regained that role. To capture spontaneity is to convert it into something it is not: a habitual function. The alert system was part of the habituation of the viewing population to affect modulation as a governmental-media function.

This taming of television's affective role accomplished a number of further conversions. For one, it yoked governmentality to television in a way that gave the exercise of power a properly perceptual mode of operation. Government gained signal access to the nervous systems and somatic expressions of the populace in a way that allowed it to bypass the discursive mediations upon which government traditionally depended, and to regularly produce effects with a directness never before seen. Without proof, without persuasion, at the limit even without argument, government image production could trigger (re)action. But what public government function gained in immediacy of effect it lost in uniformity of result. If skillfully played, the system could reliably determine people to action, but the nature of the trigger, or inducer, as an activation contour lacking definite content or imitable form meant that it could not accurately determine *what* actions would be signaled forth. This was an admission of political reality: the social environment within which government now operated was of such complexity that it made a mirage of any idea that there could be a one-to-one correlation between official speech or image production and the form and content of response. The social and cultural diversity of the population, and the disengagement from government on the part of many of its segments, would ensure that any initiative relying on a linear cause-effect relation between proof, persuasion, and argument on the one hand, and on the other, the form of a resultant action—if in fact there was to be any—was bound to fail, or to succeed only in isolated cases. The contradiction-friendly pluralism of American politicians' public address is evidence that this has long been recognized in practice (the fact, for example, that George W. Bush would address car workers in his down-home Texas-transplant drawl as a man of the people looking out for the struggling families of Middle America, then make a telling quip at a fund-raising dinner that his "base" is the "haves and have-mores"; Nagourney 2000). Addressing bodies from the dispositional angle of their affectivity, instead of addressing subjects from the positional angle of their ideations, shunts government function away from the mediations of adherence or belief and toward direct *activation*. What else is a state of alert?

Orienting for the indeterminacy of pure activation assumes that the nature of the actual responses elicited will be finally determined by offscreen cofactors that are beyond politicians' ken, and not for lack of effort but because they are highly contingent and therefore highly changeable. The establishment of the alert system as a linchpin in the government's anti-terror campaign was an implicit recognition that the production of political effects, for them to be direct and widespread, must unfold in a manner that is nonlinear and cocausal; that is to say, complex. The perceptual mode of power set in place by the yoking of governmentality to television in this affective way coupled its functioning with the contingency native to complex systems, where input does not necessarily equal output, because all manner of detourings, dampenings, amplifications, or interference patterns may occur in the playing-out of the signal. With affect, perceptually addressed, chance becomes politically operational. A political uncertainty principle is *pragmatically* established. It practically acknowledges that the systemic environment within which power mechanisms function is meta-stable, meaning provisionally stable but excitable, in a state of balance but ready to jog (Simondon 2005, 26, 205–206, 326–327).

The necessity for a pragmatics of uncertainty to which the color system alerts us is related to a change in the nature of the object of power. The formlessness and contentlessness of its exercise in no way means that power no longer has an object. It means that the object of power is correspondingly formless and contentless: post-9/11, governmentality has molded itself to *threat*. A threat is unknowable. If it were known in its specifics, it wouldn't be a threat. It would be a situation—as when they say on television police shows, "we have a situation"—and a situation can be handled. A threat is only a threat if it retains an indeterminacy. If it has a form, it is not a substantial form, but a time-form: a futurity. The threat as such is nothing *yet*—just a looming. It is a form of futurity, yet has the capacity to fill the present without presenting itself. Its future looming casts a present shadow, and that shadow is *fear*. Threat is the future cause of a change in the present. A future cause is not actually a cause; it is a virtual cause, or quasi-cause. Threat is a futurity with a virtual power to affect the present quasi-causally. When a governmental mechanism makes threat its business, it is taking this virtuality as its object and adopting quasi-causality as its mode of operation. That quasi-causal operation goes by the name of security. It expresses itself in signs of alert.

Since its object is virtual, the only actual leverage the security operation can have is on threat's back-cast presence, its pre-effect of fear. Threat, understood as a quasi-cause, would qualify philosophically as a species of final cause. One of the reasons that its causality is quasi- is that there is a paradoxical reciprocity between it and its effect. There is a kind of simultaneity between the quasi-cause and its effect, even though they belong to different times. Threat is the cause of fear in the sense that it triggers and conditions fear's occurrence, but without the fear it effects the threat would have no handle on actual existence, remaining purely virtual. The causality is bidirectional, operating immediately on both poles, in a kind of time-slip through which a futurity is made directly present in an effective expression that brings it into the present without it ceasing to be a futurity. Although they are in different tenses, present and future, and in different ontological modes, actual and virtual, fear and threat are of a piece: they are indissociable dimensions of the same event. The event, in its holding both tenses together in its own immediacy, is *transtemporal*. Since its transtemporality holds a passage between the virtual and the actual, it is a *process*—a real transformation that is effected in an interval smaller than the smallest perceivable, in an instantaneous looping between presence and futurity. Since it is in that smaller-than-smallest of intervals, it is perhaps best characterized as *infra-temporal* rather than transtemporal.

As William James famously argued, fear strikes the body and compels it to action before it registers consciously. When it registers, it is as a realization growing from the bodily action already under way: we don't run because we feel afraid, we feel afraid because we run.[3] He means "consciously afraid." We have already begun to experience fear nonconsciously, wrapped in action, before it unfurls from it and is felt as itself, in its distinction from the action with which it arose. Activation is a better word than action, because fear can be, and often is, paralyzing. When it is, in the place of action there is agitation, a poising for action, the taut incipiency of action that may fail to take definitive form. Where a specific action does unfold, its onset still will have been in an indistinction with affect, in that vague feeling-acting-coming-on, in a durationless moment of suspense in the time-slip of threat. It will have been a shock to the system whose immediacy disconnects the body from the ongoing flow of its activities while already poising it for a restart.

Fear at this level of pure activation in the time-slip of threat is the *intensity* of the experience, and not yet a content of it: bare activity. Threat strikes the nervous system with a directness forbidding any separation between the responsiveness of the body and its environment. The nervous system is wired directly to the onset of the threat. *The reality of the situation is that activation.* If an action triggers, the activation follows, prolonging the situation along a line of flight. The fear follows down the line, gathering into itself the momentum of the run, using that accumulation to fuel each successive footfall, moving the activation through a series of steps. The fear snowballs, as the reaction runs its course. The fear is a dynamic ingathering of action assuring the continuity of its serial unfolding and moving the reality of the situation, which is its activation, down the line of fright.[4] *The experience is in the fear*, in its ingathering of action, rather than the fear being the content of an experience. At the starting line, the affect of fear and the action of the body are in a state of indistinction. As the action unfolds, they begin to diverge. The action is linear, step-by-step, and dissipative, it exhausts itself. It runs its course along the line of flight. The affective intensity, on the other hand, is cumulative. It snowballs as the action unfolds, and when the running stops, it keeps on rolling. Its rolling on after the running unwraps it from the action. It comes out into itself. It is only now, past action's stop-point, that it registers as a *feeling* of fear as distinct from its acting out. What registers distinctly with that feeling is the reality of the situation—which was and remains fundamentally affective in nature. The reality of the situation is its affective *quality*—its being an unfolding of fear, as opposed to of anger, boredom, or love.

To say that at this level the experience is in the fear, rather than the fear being the content of an experience, is to say that its momentum-gathering, action-driving, reality-registering operation is *not phenomenal*. It is the in-which of experience; in other words, experience's *immanence*. But on the stop-beat, the experience comes out, into itself, registering its quality. Its unfolding then continues, along other lines. For it is only with the luxury of the pause that the body can begin to distinguish the details of the situation, previously lost to shock. It can look around, seeking to identify clearly the cause of the alarm, and take in the surroundings in case further action is necessary. It begins to *perceive*—to divide the situation into component parts, each with a location relative to the others and each with a recognizable constancy of form. Objects in spatial configuration begin to appear, distinguishing themselves from the fear in which they were enveloped. This enables *reflection*. What just happened is placed under retrospective review and mapped as an objective environment. The location of the threat is sought by following the line of flight in reverse. The cause of the fright is scanned for among the objects in the environment. Directions of further flight or objects that can serve for self-defense are inventoried. These perceptions and reflections are gathered up in *recollection*, where their intensity will ultimately fade. It is at this point, in this second ingathering toward lowered intensity, in the stop-beat of action, that the fear, and its situation, and the reality of that situation, become a content of experience.

The unfolding reality of *that fearful feeling* has become the *feeling of that fear* enfolded in perception.[5] The perception has been wrapped in reflection, and the reflection in turn has been taken up in memory. In recollection, the affective unfolding has folded back in, at a different level, in a different mode, after passing a threshold marked by the exhaustion of the action with which the feeling grew. The threshold is a conversion point, on a number of counts. It is where the nonphenomenal in-which of experience turns phenomenal, passing into the content of experience, its immanence translated into an interiority. At the stop-beat, the affective quality of the event comes out in its purity from action, but as it does, it becomes quantifiable. It had been, in its indistinction with action, the totality of the situation. The situation has now branched, the affect separating from the exhausted action by virtue of its continuing. The situation further divides into a *collection* of perceived objects, then again into reflections distinct from the perception, and recollections of some or all of those components. The fear that came out in its affective purity at the stop-beat is retrospectively but one of a number of ingredients of the experience. It is a countable component of an experience. That experience, which began as the dynamic unity of feeling-in-action, is now a collection of particular elements. The whole has become divisible, and what the experience was globally now counts in it as one of its parts. As a content of experience, this fear becomes comparable to other fear incidents in other recollected situations. It can be now be counted as a greater or lesser fright. Where once it was intensity, it now has magnitude. It still qualifies the situation, but its quality is now quantifiable, in two ways: it counts as a one among a number, and it can be assigned a relative magnitude. In intensity, it could only be *lived through* the body. As bodily lived it was unrefusable, a direct and immediate activation. It was *compelling*, and its compelling was one with the propelling of an action. Now it has taken its place as one content of the experience among others. It can be approached inactively as from the outside. It can be set alongside the other components and compared to them. As a quality, it still retains a certain ungraspability. Thus the objects to whose perception it led, whose appearance, as it happened, was a differentiation of the fear, now seem more solid and dependable than it. Retrospectively, they take on a larger share of the recognized reality of the event. The emotion is sidelined as its merely subjective content. Yet another branching has occurred, between the subjective and the objective. This bifurcation structures recollection.

If the event is recounted, the narrative will place the objective unfolding of the occurrence on a parallel track with its subjective registering, as if this duality were operative from the onset of the event, rather than being an artifact of its self-differentiating unfolding. The personal history of the narrating body will have to negotiate this duality, presenting a public face allied with the content defined as objective, in contradistinction to the subjective content, defined as private. The private content may fail to be recounted, or may be edited for reasons of tact or to avoid embarrassment. The emotional content may then waver and even start to break away from its anchoring to the objective narrative. The two-track narrative of the event may lose its parallelism. Unanchored, the vivacity of the emotional content diminishes, to the point where the emotion can be second-guessed: "I wasn't really scared—just startled." The emotion pales, as if it could be separated even as it happened from the immediacy of bodily response, and as if the subject of the experience could choose to have it or to pass it up. To treat the emotion as separable in this way from the activation-event from which it affectively sprang is to place it on the level of representation. It is to treat it, fundamentally and from the start, as a subjective content: basically, an idea. Reduced to the mere idea of itself, it becomes reasonable to suppose that a private subject, in representing it to itself, could hold it and the aleatory outside of its arising as well as the body in live-wire connection with that outside, at a rational, manageable distance. It makes it seem comfortably controllable.

A startle without a scare, however, is like a grin without a cat. The separation between direct activation and controlled ideation, or affect in its bodily dimension and emotion as rationalizable subjective content, is a reflective wonderland that does not work this side of the mirror. James is quick to make the discomfiting point: "Where an ideal emotion seems to precede [or occur independently of] the bodily symptoms, it is often nothing but a representation of the symptoms themselves. One who has already fainted at the sight of blood may witness the preparations for a surgical operation with uncontrollable heart-sinking and anxiety. He anticipates certain feelings, and the anticipation precipitates their arrival" (James 1983, 177). What he calls a representation here is clearly a *re*-presentation: the heart-sinking *is* the anticipation of the emotion, in the same way that he argues that in a case like running in fear "our feeling of bodily changes as they occur *is* the emotion" in its initial phase of emergence (James 1983, 170). Anticipation is similarly a triggering of changes in the body. That affective reactivation of the body then develops unrefusably into a reemergence of the fear. What we sloppily think of as the idea of an emotion, or the emotion as an idea, is in fact the anticipatory repetition of an affective event, precipitated by the encounter between the body's irritability and a sign. In the surgical example, the blood functions as a sign of fear. Like a red alert, it directly activates the body. But the context obviates the need to run. You are in a condition to react to the blood precisely because you're not the one under anesthesia on the operating table. This is also a reason why actually running away would be somewhat off the point. The particular nature of the context inhibits the acting out of the movement. The activation of the body, however, was *already* that movement in incipient form. The failure of the movement actually to express itself does not prevent the development of the emotion proper, which should rightly phase in, on pause, after the action's actualization. Here, the body gives pause in advance, due to contextual constraints. In this context, the emergence of the emotion *preempts* action. Actual action has been short-circuited. It is *in*-acted: it remains enveloped in its own activated potential. The development of the emotion is now bound entirely to potential action. It can regenerate itself without the detour through actual movement: it can be *enacted* through in-action.

Part of the affective training that the Bush color alert system assures is the ingraining in the bodies of the populace of anticipatory affective response to signs of fear even in contexts where one is clearly in no present danger. This significantly extends the purview of threat. An alert about a suspected bombing plan against the Golden Gate Bridge (one of the early alert episodes) can have direct repercussions in Atlanta. As a plus, the enaction of the affective event in in-action has obvious political control benefits.

The purview of threat is extended in another way as well. When an emotion becomes enactable in anticipation of itself, independent of action, it becomes *its own threat*. It becomes its own virtual cause. "I am told of a case of morbid terror, of which the subject confessed that what possessed her seemed, more than anything, to be *the fear of fear itself*" (James 1983, 177). When fear becomes the quasi-cause of itself, it can bypass even more readily any limitation to contexts where a fearful action is actually called upon and, in so doing, bypass more regularly the necessity to cycle through an unfolding of phases. The phases telescope into each other, in a short circuit of the affective process. The affective event rolls ever more tightly around the time-slip of threat, as fear becomes its own pre-effect. "We see plainly how the emotion both begins and ends with what we call its effects" (James 1983, 177). Fear, the emotion, has revirtualized. Its emergence as an end-effect has threateningly looped back to the beginning as its cause. This marks another turning point. Now, fear can potentially self-cause even in the absence of an external sign to trigger it. This makes it all the more uncontainable, so much so that it "possesses" the subject. It wraps its time-slip so compellingly around experience that it becomes experience's affective surround. Without ceasing to be an emotion, it has become the affective surround of existence; its in-which. Self-caused and all-around: at once the ground and background of the experience it now tends to take over. Call an emotion that has revirtualized in this way to become self-caused ground and enveloping background of overtaken existence, an *affective tone* or *mood* (as equally distinct from action, vitality affect, pure affect, and emotion proper). *Affective atmosphere* is another way of naming it, emphasizing the aspect of its power of envelopment.[6]

Fear's intoning revirtualization does not mean that it will never again feature narratively as a contained emotion. Efforts to contain it will in fact have to be redoubled in order to mitigate the subject's possession by it. But it is a vicious circle. The more successful the efforts, the more the subject's existence is wed to the process. Having fear as a subjective content against the background of fear revirtual becomes *a way of life*. However many times fear is contained it will always also exceed the containment, because its capacity to self-regenerate will continue to loom and that looming will define the surrounding mood. Any particular fear clearly featured as an emotional life content will stand out against that comparatively vague or generic affective background from which it emerged. It will be clearly redundant: wherever it actually occurs as emotion it will already have been as affective tone. Everywhere, fear double-features: as vaguely and clearly featured; as generic and particular; as ground of existence for itself as a way of life. Fear, in its quasi-causal relation to itself, has become redundantly self-sufficient—an autonomous force of existence. It has become *ontogenetic*: an ontopower.[7]

This autonomization of fear is a next natural step from its preemption of action in the sign-response short circuit. Its development is conditioned by the independence that preemption enables from actual contexts of fear. When fear itself is frightening, its capacity to self-cause means that it can even trigger in the absence of any of its external signs. Politically, fear's autonomization risks undoing the control gained in that phase: fear can now *run away with itself*. It has the capacity to be self-propelling. This ups the ante of unpredictability. Where fear unleashed can lead is any alert-emitter's guess. While the signs of danger may no longer be necessary for the triggering of the affective event of fear, their repetition and multiplication seeds the conditions for their own overcoming. They prepare the (back)ground.

It is only superficially that self-propelling fear can forgo sign action. According to Peirce, "every thought beyond immediate perception is a sign" (Peirce 1998, 402). When fear is of fear itself the retriggering of its affective process hinges on a thought-sign. This triggering still entails bodily activation. "There is some reason to think that, corresponding to every feeling within us, some motion takes place in our bodies. This property of the thought-sign, since it has *no rational dependence upon the meaning of the sign*, may be compared to what I have called the *material quality* of the sign; but it differs from the latter inasmuch as *it is not essentially necessary that it should be felt* in order that there should be any thought-sign" (Peirce 1998, 402).

Consider that the only way to regain control over one's possession by fear once it has become self-propelling is to not feel it. "Put a stopper on the gush," as James indelicately puts it. In a word, suppress it. We are all taught how as children. "When we teach our children to repress their emotions, it is not that they may *feel* more." The emotion doesn't build up volcanically because fear as self-propellingly in need of being controlled is not a sulphurous content but a revirtual cause. It has no substance to build up (only efficacity to intensify). So it is not that they may feel more, "quite the reverse. It is that they may *think* more" (James 1983, 179). To suppress emotion is to produce more thought-signs, in an even tighter short circuit. Now it is not only actual action but the feeling itself that is bypassed. The bodily activation continues necessarily to occur. But there is no "more" of it to build up either. It is not quantitative. By Peirce's reckoning, it is a material *quality* of the body (a mode of its irritability). It may pass *unfelt*. The thought-sign is now intensively coupled with an incalculably qualitative unfeeling upon which it has "no rational dependence." Fear is coming to revolve more and more tightly around the logical vanishing point of an unexperience where matter and quality are one. This vanishing point lies at the very limit of the phenomenal. Fear's passage to this limit carries its virtualization close to as far as it can go. Fear's quasi-causality can cycle in the shortest possible circuit, with the fewest actual requisites or intervening phases, between the qualitative-material unconscious and the thought-sign. This intensifies its efficacity, reinforcing the autonomy of its ontogenetic powers.

What Peirce means when he says that there is no rational dependence on the meaning of the sign is that "there is nothing in the content of the thought which explains why it should arise only on occasion of . . . determining thoughts" (Peirce 1992, 45). In other words, there is no need for the thought-sign of fear to have any rational connection to contexts in which thoughts logically relating to it might occur. "If there is such a relation of reason, if the thought is essentially limited in its application to these objects [objects with which it is logically connected by context], then the thought comprehends a thought other than itself" (45). Without a relation of reason determining it, the thought may still occur, but when it does, it comprehends only itself. Fear has *self-abstracted*. It has become exclusively self-comprehending. It has become the autonomous thought of itself. It can now boldly go wherever thought can reach. And thought can reach wherever *attention* goes. Unfelt bodily motion (what Peirce calls "sensation") and attention are, he says, "the sole constituents" of thought. "Attention is the power by which thought at one time is connected with and made to relate to thought at another time. . . . It is the *pure demonstrative application* of a thought-sign" (46; emphasis in the original). In the case of a thought determined by and comprehending only itself, the thought to which attention demonstratively links it at one time as to another is— itself. In thought, fear becomes intensively self-relating, independent to the extreme of actual context, or even other thoughts. It demonstratively signs itself. It has become a self-effecting operative logic.

This implies that *techniques of attention* applied against the background of the affective tone of fear revirtual may purely and demonstratively re-generate thought-signs of it, along with the unfeeling of its corresponding bodily activation. Fear has attained a summit of virtualization, almost fully autonomized (contingent only on the vagaries of attention) and abstracted from its actions, contexts, external signs, logical content or meaning, and, last but not least, its own feeling.

We have now entered the wonderland world where the startle can come without the scare: body activation without the feeling James insists that it *is*. We have passed to the other side of the affective mirror where fear "reflects" only its own Cheshire catlike occurrence, at the phenomenal vanishing point, where it is without.

Fear can now operate as the nonphenomenal background of existence, or outside in-which of experience, in its role as the affective tone or generic context for a way of life. It can also still be contained, featuring as a particular life's phenomenal content. In addition, it can function purely self-demonstratively, as a self-sufficient thought process unencumbered by the bodily activation still necessarily accompanying it. Which of these modes, or which combination of them, will be in operation at any given point will depend on the regime of external signs in play, the nature of the contexts through which they multiply, the acquired skills of suppression impressed upon the bodies populating those contexts, and the techniques of attention in operation (for example, as associated with the media, in particular as they disseminate themselves more widely and finely through the social field assisted by miniaturization and digitization).

In this journey through fear, we have cycled, more than once, from virtual cause to virtual cause, the degree of virtuality increasing at each loop. In a first loop, we saw a self-differentiating unfolding into a variety of modes: from activation to feeling-in-action; from feeling-in-action to pure expression of affect; from pure expression of affect to branchings into perception, reflection, and recollection; then on to affective containment. The process then continued, looping back into itself, through and in excess of its own containment. It attached itself to signs, then to thought-signs. At each cycle, its quasi-causal powers expanded. Its modes of expansion emerged sequentially, as phases of a continuing process. But beyond the threshold of affective suspense in the first loop, the emergence of the modes was additive. The branching was onto levels of operation that were in co-operation, potentially working with or in some cases on each other. Although the phases emerge sequentially, they operate con-jointly to form a complex, multilayered formation. The overall process is at once additive and distributive.

If the different phasings unfolded from the initial activation, their full variety must have already been in it, in their incipiency—in *potential*. The intensity of that activation was the immanence of their potential. Rather than layered in a structure, they were immediately, virtually, co-occurring. In the feeling-in-action of the first run, they were all coursing together, in a state of actual indistinction from each other. They were actively fused, in dynamic superposition. This means that in any reactivation of the event by a virtual cause, the variety of modes become re-fused. They roll back into one another in shared potential. They *dephase* or dedifferentiate, then phase back out or re-unfold.[8] Another occasion of experience self-differentiates into an unfolding variety. Experience regenerates itself. The strike of an-other threat will initiate a reemergence. But, given fear's emergent self-reflective capacity to be its own beginning and end, or to be the threat of itself, so too may any sign of the threat's potential effect (as in the sight of blood). A thought-sign may also initiate a recurrence, even if it is not logically the thought-sign of a threat or a fear (given the thought-sign's independence from its rational determinants). Once fear has become the ground of existence, every change can regenerate its experience under one or a combination of its species. Every shift in attention against the back-ground mood of fear may carry the ontogenetic charge of an alert trigger-ing a regeneration of experience and its variation (what Benjamin termed "shock").

George Bush's color alert system was designed to exploit and foster the varieties of fear while expanding upon their ontogenetic powers, or ontopower. It assumed the full spectrum of fear, up to and including its becoming-autonomous as a regenerative ground of existence, in action and in-action, in feeling and without it with thought. This refocusing of government sign-action on complex affective modulation is a tactic of incalculable power. It allies the politics of communication with powers capable of "possessing" the individual at the level at which its experi-ence reemerges (dispossessing it of its own genesis). In other words, it operates co-optively at what Simondon calls the "pre-individual" level. By pre-individual he does not mean "within the individual" but rather "at the limit between the subject and the world, at the limit between the individual and collective" (Simondon 2005, 254). That limit is the body bare-active, the body activatable—the bodily irritability that is the generic "material quality" of human life.

For "action and emotion to be in resonance with each other" in the affectively self-regenerating ways just described "there must be a superior individual that encompasses them: this individuation is that of the collective" (Simondon 2005, 253). When an individual life overflows its containment in private narrative and representation—as each life tends affectively to do—the living runs straight to the limit of the collective. There, it irritably rejoins the potential from which it arose, toward a next iteration of its many-phased ontogenesis. "The subject can coincide with itself only in the individuation of the collective" (Simondon 2005, 253). This is because that limit is where the phases fold into each other toward a next deployment. It is there, in that immanence, that a life coincides with its affective potential. For better or for worse.

The alert system is a tool for modulating collective individuation. Through the media, it addresses itself to the population from the angle of its potential to reindividuate differentially. The system recenters government sign-action on Gabriel Tarde's nascent social state of intimidation in order to induce its collective individuation to pass from one form of society to another. All for the better, Bush says. The future, he promises, will be better tomorrow. America will be a stronger and safer place.

But tomorrow's future is here today, as virtual cause. And America is neither stronger nor safer than it was yesterday. If anything, it is more precarious than ever because the form under which the promise of tomorrow is here today is ever-present threat. This hinges its actualization on nonlinear and quasi-causal operations that no one can fully control but which on the contrary are capable of possessing each and every one, at the level of their bodily potential to be individually what will have collectively become. The outcome is anything but certain. All that is certain is that fear itself will continue becoming—the way of life. The grounding and surrounding fear that the system helps develop tends toward an autonomy that makes it an ontogenetic force to be reckoned with. That reckoning must include the self-propelling mode of fear-based collective individu-ation we call fascism. Although there is nothing in the content of any thought that explains why it *should* arise, the passage to a society of that kind is a potential that cannot be excluded. The Bush administration's fear in-action was a tactic as enormously reckless as it was politically powerful.

Confusingly, it is likely that it can only be fought on the same affective, ontopowerful ground upon which it itself operates.

# 7  The Future Birth of the Affective Fact

*Future Superlative*

"The next pandemic," screams a 2005 headline in Quebec's reputedly most sober newspaper, "does not exist yet." Beneath, in a supersize, full-color portrait, deceptively innocent-looking, peers a chicken. "The threat, however, could not be more real" (Soucy 2005).

*Observation*: We live in times when what has not happened qualifies as front-page news.

Human-adapted avian flu is just one of many nonexistent entities that has come from the future to fill our present with menace. We live in times when what is yet to occur not only climbs to the top of the news but periodically takes blaring precedence over what has actually happened. Yesterday was once the mainstay of the journalist's stock in trade. Today it may pale in the glare of tomorrow's news. "I think we agree," prophesied a future president on the cusp of a millennium whose arrival was overshadowed by a nonexistent bug of another color, "the past is over" (Bush 2000).

*Question*: How could the nonexistence of what has not happened be *more* real than what is now observably over and done with?

Threat is from the future. It is what might come next. Its eventual location and ultimate extent are undefined. Its nature is open-ended. It is not just that it is not: it is not in a way that is never over. We can never be done with it. Even if a clear and present danger materializes in the present, it is still not over. There is always the nagging potential of the next after being even worse, and of a still worse next again after that. The uncertainty of the potential next is never consumed in any given event. There is always a remainder of uncertainty, an unconsummated surplus of danger. The present is shadowed by a remaindered surplus of indeterminate potential for a next event running forward back to the future, self-renewing.

Self-renewing menace potential is the future reality of threat. It could not be more real. Its run of futurity contains so much more, potentially, than anything that has already actually happened. Threat is not real in spite of its nonexistence. It is superlatively real, because of it.

*Observation:* The future of threat is forever.

### Futures Past

*Rewind:* It is the summer of 2004. George W. Bush is campaigning for a second term as president. He is on the defensive about the War in Iraq, as pressure mounts for him to admit that the reasons his administration set forth to justify the invasion, in particular the allegation that Saddam Hussein possessed an arsenal of weapons of mass destruction, had no basis in fact. For the first time he admits what had been known all along to those who cared to examine the evidence. He goes on to argue that the lack of factual basis for the invasion does not mean that he made the wrong decision.

> Although we have not found stockpiles of weapons, I believe we were right to go into Iraq. America is safer today because we did. We removed a declared enemy of America, who had the capacity of producing weapons of mass destruction, and could have passed that capability to terrorists bent on acquiring them." (Schmitt and Stevenson 2004)

The invasion was right because *in the past there was a future threat.* You cannot erase a "fact" like that. Just because the menace potential never became a clear and present danger doesn't mean that it wasn't there, all the more real for being nonexistent. The superlative futurity of un-actualized threat feeds forward from the past, in a chicken run to the future past every intervening present. The threat *will have* been real for all eternity.

It will have been real because it was *felt* to be real. Whether the danger was existent or not, the menace was felt in the form of fear. What is not actually real can be felt into being. Threat does have an actual mode of existence: fear, as foreshadowing. Threat has an impending reality in the present. This actual reality is affective.

Fear is the anticipatory reality in the present of a threatening future. It is the felt reality of the nonexistent, loomingly present as the *affective fact* of the matter.

Once a nonexistent reality, always a nonexistent reality. A past anticipation is still an anticipation, and will remain having been an anticipation for all of time. A threat that does not materialize is not false. It has all the affective reality of a past future, truly felt. The future of the threat is not falsified. It is deferred. The case remains forever open. The futurity doesn't stay in the past where its feeling emerged. It feeds forward through time. It runs an endless loop forward from its point of emergence in the past present, whose future it remains. Threat passes through linear time, but does not belong to it. It belongs to the nonlinear circuit of the always will have been.

*Proposition*: If we feel a threat, there was a threat. Threat is affectively self-causing.

*Corollary*: If we feel a threat, such that there was a threat, then there always will have been a threat. Threat is once and for all, in the nonlinear time of its own causing.

## Double Conditional

The felt reality of threat legitimates preemptive action, once and for all. Any action taken to preempt a threat from emerging into a clear and present danger is legitimated by the affective fact of fear, actual facts aside.[1] Preemptive action will always have been right. This circularity is not a failure of logic. It is a different logic, operating on the same affective register as threat's self-causing.

The logic of affectively legitimated fact is in the conditional: Bush did what he did because Saddam could have done what he didn't do. Bush's argument doesn't really do justice to the logic of preemption. Saddam didn't actually even have the "capacity," and that poses no problem for preemptive logic which is based on a *double conditional*. "The Pentagon neocons argued that the CIA overemphasized what Saddam *could do* instead of stressing *what he would do if he could*" (Dorrien 2004, 186).

Bush was being modest in a CIA kind of way. From the prevailing neoconservative perspective, he was understating why he was right. He was right even though Saddam did not have the capacity, because Saddam "would have if he could have." The case remains open. At any moment in the future, he could have acquired the means, and as soon as he could, he would. Would-have, could-have: double conditional.

Present threat is logically recessive, in a step-by-step regress from the certainty of actual fact. The actual fact would have been: Saddam Hussein has weapons of mass destruction (WMD). The first step back from that is: he had the capacity to have WMD. The next step is: he didn't have the capacity, but he still would have if he could have. The recessive assertion that he "would have" is based on an assumption about character and intent that cannot be empirically grounded with any certainty. But it is proffered with certainty. It carries a certainty, underivable from actual fact, which it owes to the affective fact of the matter. The felt reality of the threat is so superlatively real that it translates into a felt certainty about the world, even in the absence of other grounding for it in the observable world. The assertion has the felt certainty of a "gut feeling." Gut feeling was proudly and publicly embraced by Bush as his peak decision-making process in the lead-up to the war in Iraq and beyond (Woodward 2002, 16, 136–137, 145, 168).

Preemption's logical regress from actual fact makes for a disjointedness between its legitimating discourse and the objective content of the present context which its affirmations ostensibly reference. Its receding from actual fact produces a logical disjunction between the threat and the observable present. A logical gap opens in the present through which the reality of threat slips to rejoin its deferral to the future. Through the logical hatch of the double conditional, threat makes a runaround through the present back toward its self-causing futurity.

The affect-driven logic of the would-have/could-have is what discursively ensures that the actual facts will always remain an open case, for all preemptive intents and purposes. It is what saves threat from having to materialize as a clear and present danger—or even an emergent danger—in order to command action. The object of preemptive power, according to the explicit doctrine, is "not yet fully emergent threat." The doctrine doesn't say emergent danger—let alone clear and present danger.[2] And again (and again), when threat strikes it is once and for all.

*Problem*: How can preemptive politics maintain its political legitimacy given that it grounds itself in the actual ungroundedness of affective fact? Would not pointing out the actual facts be enough to make it crumble?

*Observation*: Bush won reelection.

## Right Again

*Fast forward*: One year later, summer 2005. For the first time in the polls, more than two years after the invasion, a majority of Americans oppose the War in Iraq. The legitimation of preemptive action—or that particular action at any rate—is faltering. The downturn had begun long after the lack of actual facts behind the decision to invade had become common knowledge. It began with the counter-affective strike that came with the release and widespread circulation of shocking images of torture at Abu Ghraib.[3] It was only then that the lack of actual-factual basis for the invasion began to resonate with a voting public rendered less receptive, for the moment, to the logic of preemption by the affective counter-coup of torture graphically revealed. Bush makes a valiant attempt to kick-start the logic of preemption again. He delivers a major radio address to the nation explaining his refusal to withdraw. He deploys an argument that he will continue to use for at least the next two years.[4]

"Some may agree," he says, "with my decision to remove Saddam Hussein from power, but all of us can agree that the world's terrorists have now made Iraq a central front in the war on terror" (Bush 2005a). The presence of terrorist links between Al Qaeda and Saddam Hussein had been the second major argument, behind WMD, originally used to justify the invasion. The Bush administration had already been obliged to withdraw the assertion long before this speech. The fact that Al Qaeda had not been in Iraq at the time of the invasion now becomes the reason it was right to invade. The fact that they are there now just goes to prove that if they could have been there then, they would have.

The could-have/would-have logic works both ways. If the threat does not materialize, it still always would have if it could have. If on the other hand the threat does materialize, then it just goes to show that the future potential for what happened had really been there in the past. In this case, the preemptive action is retroactively legitimated by future actual facts.

Bush does not point out that the reason Al Qaeda was in Iraq is *because of* the invasion that was mounted to keep it out of Iraq—that the preemptive action actually *brought about* the result it was meant to fight.[5]

*Observation:* Preemptive action can produce the object toward which its power is applied, and it can do so without contradicting its own logic, and without necessarily undermining its legitimation.

*Proposition:* Because it operates on an affective register and inhabits a nonlinear time operating recursively between the present and the future, preemptive logic is not subject to the same rules of noncontradiction as normative logic, which privileges a linear causality from the past to the present and is reluctant to attribute an effective reality to futurity.

## Flour Attack

*Pause:* Around the same time, a state of emergency is called at the Montreal airport. There has been a "toxic substance alert." White powder has been seen leaking from a suitcase. The actual facts of the case are still two weeks in the future after the necessary lab work will have been done. Action, however, cannot wait. It *could be* anthrax. That potential threat must be acted upon. The airport is closed. Highways to the airport are closed. Men in white decontamination suits descend. SWAT teams and police pour in. Terrified passengers are sequestered in the terminal. News helicopters hover overhead. Live coverage takes over the local airwaves. All of the actions that *would be* taken if the powder were anthrax are taken preemptively. The dramatic rapid response of the public security apparatus causes a major disruption of commerce and circulation. The site is quickly decontaminated, and life returns to normal.

*Observations:* Preemptive power washes back from the battlefield onto the domestic front (even in countries not militarily involved). On the domestic front, its would-have/could-have logic takes a specific form associated with public security procedures involving the signaling of alert. The alert, set off at the slightest *sign* of potential threat, triggers immediate action. The actions set in motion in response to the threat are of the same kind and bring on many of the same effects as would have accompanied an actual danger. The preemptive measures cause the disruption to the economy and everyday life that terrorist attacks are designed to produce beyond their immediate impact.

*Proposition*: Defensive preemptive action in its own way is as capable as offensive preemptive action of producing what it fights. Together with the increasing speed and vigor of defensive action, this blurs the boundaries between defense and offense, between domestic security and military action.

Two weeks later, the powder is identified. It is flour. News articles following up on the story after the discovery of no toxic substance continue to refer to the incident as a "toxic substance alert."[6] No one refers to the incident as a "flour alert." The incident is left carrying an affective dusting of white-powdered terror. Flour has been implicated. It is tainted with the fear of anthrax, guilty by association for displaying the threatening qualities of whiteness and powderiness.

In preemptively logical terms, the incident *was* a toxic substance alert— not because the substance was toxic, but because the *alert* was for a potential toxic substance.

*Observations*: An alarm may determine the generic identity of a potential threat, without specifically determining the actual identity of the objects involved. This declares what will later prove actually to have been innocent objects (or in other circumstances, persons) as officially threatening for the duration of the alert, based on their displaying material properties answering to the generic description. Afterward, they remain tainted by their affective involvement in the incident, for they really always will have been associated with the fear produced by the alert, and fear feeds threat forward.

*Proposition*: The affective reality of threat is contagious.

*Proposition*: Threat is capable of overlaying its own conditional determination upon an objective situation through the mechanism of alarm. The two determinations, threatening and objective, coexist. However, the threat-determined would-be and could-be takes public precedence due to its operating in the more compelling future-oriented and affective register. This gives it superior political presence and potential.[7]

The incident comes to a close with follow-up articles about improvements in government safety procedure as a result of the toxic substance alert. The false alert is presented in the news media as having palpably increased the security of airplane passengers (*La Presse* 2005a).

*Proposition:* The security that preemption is explicitly meant to produce is predicated on its tacitly producing what it is meant to avoid: preemptive security is predicated on a production of insecurity to which it itself contributes. Preemption thus positively contributes to producing the conditions for its own exercise. It does this by capturing for its own operation the self-causative power native to the threat-potential that it takes as its object.

## Specifically Imprecise

*Rewind:* New York City, October 2005. Mayor Michael Bloomberg puts the city on alert, citing a chillingly specific threat to bomb the metropolitan subway and bus system simultaneously at "as many as nineteen" different locations. "This is the first time we have had a threat with this level of specificity," he says at a televised news conference (Bajaj 2005). The FBI announces that arrests related to the plot have already been made in Iraq, based on "reliable" information. "Classified operations have already partially disrupted this threat." Although offensive preemptive action has already been taken, there is still felt to be a menacing remainder of threat. Preemptive action is retaken, this time defensively. Transit passengers on the home front are briefed on security procedures and asked to contribute to the city's surveillance by keeping an eye out for suspicious persons and objects. A suspicious bottle, which could have been filled with hazardous material, is sighted at Penn Station. It is isolated and destroyed (if it could have, it would have . . . ).

The next day, the Homeland Security Department weighs in to say that "the intelligence community has been able to determine that there are very serious doubts about the credibility of this specific threat." The threat had been "very, very specific. It had specific time, specific object and modality," the city police commissioner assured. "So, you know, we had to do what we did. . . . I believe in the short term we'll have a much better sense of whether or not this has, you know, real substance to it" (Weissenstein 2005).

A threat can have specificity, and lead to decisive preemptive actions with a corresponding level of specificity, without having "real substance" or objective "credibility." The preemptive actions taken in response to the threat are still logically and politically correct if they were commensurate with the urgency of the threat, if not with the urgency of the actual situation. They will still have been justified even if the information proves objectively imprecise and there was no actual danger.[8]

*Proposition*: An alert is not a referential statement under obligation to correspond with precision to an objective state of affairs. The measure of its correctness is the immediacy and specificity of the preemptive actions it automatically triggers. The value of the alert is measured by its *performance*. Rather than referential truth-value, it has performative *threat-value*. More than any correspondence between its semantic content and an objective referent, it is the performed commensurability of the threat and the triggered actions that qualifies the alert as correct. Its correctness, felt as a question of collective security, is directly political. The threat-alert, as *sign of* danger, is subject to different criteria of reliability and effectiveness than referential language *about* danger.

*Proposition*: Threat has no actual referent.

*Corollary*: Preemption is a mode of power that takes threat, which has no actual referent, as its object. When the politics of preemption captures threat's potential for its own operation, it forgoes having an actual object of power.

## "The 9/11 Generation"

*Fast forward on rewind*: It is now the lead-up to the 2008 U.S. presidential elections. Ex-mayor Rudolph Giuliani of New York is revving up his campaign by looping back to 9/11, toward future preemptive action. He writes an article in *Foreign Affairs* taking a hardline neoconservative position in continuity with Defense Secretary Donald Rumsfeld's first-term Bush administration policies. The article argues that the 9/11 attacks inaugurated a new world-historical era. The fall of the Twin Towers was an originating moment of what he calls, following Rumsfeld, the "Long War" against terrorism, in much the same way that the building of the

Berlin Wall inaugurated the Cold War, according to Giuliani. "We are all members of the 9–11 generation," he declares (Giuliani 2007).

The 9/11 attacks were an actual event that put thousands of lives in immediate danger. People were agape in shock at the enormity of it. The immediate shock gave way to lingering fear, relaying the danger into a remainder of surplus threat. The attacks were an excess-threat generating actual event which has perhaps done more than any other threat-o-genic source to legitimate preemptive politics. It was continually cited by the Bush administration to reinvoke potential threat for use in legitimating policy. Candidates of both parties in the race to succeed Bush also invoked it regularly in order to establish their own national security credentials.[9] And yet . . .

Question: Can the threat-potential fueling preemptive politics have an identifiable origin?

There were precursors to 9/11. The "war on terror" was declared by President Richard Nixon in the early 1970s. Between that time and September 2001, there have been any number of attacks characterized as terrorist, including the earlier, less successful, 1993 bombing of the World Trade Center. Since 9/11 there have been further attacks. If the historical and geographical parameters are enlarged, attacks that could be qualified as "terrorist" stretch indefinitely.

Observation: 9/11 belongs to an iterative series of allied events whose boundaries are indefinite.

An event where threat materializes as a clear and present danger extrudes a surplus-remainder of threat-potential which can contaminate new objects, persons, and contexts through the joint mechanisms of the double conditional and the objective imprecision of the specificity of threat. Threat's self-causing proliferates. Threat-alerts, performatively signed threat-events, are quick to form their own iterative series. These series tend to proliferate robustly, thanks to the suppleness and compellingness of the affective logic generating them. As an indication, according to the Homeland Security Department, in the United States alone in 2003 there were 118 airport evacuations. In 2004, there were 276. None was linked to a terrorist attempt, let alone an actual bombing.[10]

As the series proliferate, the distinction between the series of actual attacks and the series of threat-events blurs. At the same time, the range

of generic identities under which the threat and its corresponding performance may fall also expands. The terrorist series includes torpedo-
ing buildings with airplanes, air missile attacks, subway bombs, suicide
car attacks, roadside bombings, liquid explosives disguised as toiletries,
tennis-shoe bombs, "dirty" bombs (never actually observed), anthrax in
the mail, other unnamed bioterrorist weapons, booby-trapped mailboxes,
Coke cans rigged to explode, bottles in public places . . . The list is long,
and ever-extending. The mass affective production of felt threat-potential
engulfs the (f)actuality of the comparatively small number of incidents
where danger materialized. They blend together in a shared atmosphere
of fear.

In that atmosphere, the terrorist threat series blends into series featuring other generic identities. There is the generic viral series including
threats, real and nonexistent, as heterogeneous as human-adapted avian
flu, SARS, West Nile virus, and the Millennium Bug, just to mention a
few from the first years of this century. There is no apparent limit to
the generic diversification of threat, which can cross normative logical
boundaries with impunity, like that between biological and computer
viruses. Or food and pathogens: "Comparing junk food to a possible
avian flu epidemic, provincial Health Minister Philippe Couillard said
yesterday that the province is preparing a crackdown to get sugar-laden
soft drinks and junk food out of schools" (Dougherty 2007). The series
combine and intertwine, and together tend to the infinite, preemptive
action in tow.

The atmosphere of fear includes this tendential infinity of threat series
on the same performative basis as actually occurring terrorist attack. The
generic identity of threat overall stretches to the limit to accommodate
the endless proliferation of specific variations. The object of threat tends
toward an ultimate limit at which it becomes purely indeterminate, while
retaining a certain quality—menace—and the capacity to make that quality felt. The portrait of a chicken can embody this quality and make it felt
as reliably as a terrorist's mug shot.

At the limit, threat is a *felt quality*, independent of any particular instance of itself, in much the way the color red is a quality independent
of any particular tint of red, as well as of any actually occurring patch of
any particular tint of red. It becomes an abstract quality. When threat self-

causes, its abstract quality is affectively presented, in startle, shock, and fear.[11] As presented affectively, its quality suffuses the atmosphere. Threat is ultimately *ambient*. Its logic purely *qualitative*.

*Proposition*: Threat's ultimately ambient nature makes preemptive power an *environmental* power (see chapter 2). Rather than empirically manipulate an object (of which it actually has none), it *modulates* felt qualities infusing a life-environment.

*Question*: If 9/11 is not an origin, what is it? How does it figure in the tendentially infinite series to which it belongs? Is it possible to periodize preemptive power?

Rather than assigning it as an origin, we may think of 9/11 as marking a threshold. It can be considered a turning point at which the threat-environment took on an ambient thickness, achieved a consistency, which gave the preemptive power mechanisms dedicated to its modulation an advantage over other regimes of power.

*Proposition*: To understand the political power of threat and the preemptive politics availing itself of threat-potential, it is necessary to situate preemptive power in a field of interaction with other regimes of power, and to analyze their modes of coexistence as well as their evolutionary divergences and convergences.[12] In a word, it is necessary to adopt an *ecological* approach to threat's environmental power.

*Corollary*: Each regime of power in the ecology of powers will have its own logic implicating unique modes of causality and having a singular time signature. The causal and temporal processes involved will endow the objects of each regime of power with an ontological status different from those of any other regime. Correlative to its ontology, each regime will have a dedicated epistemology guiding the constitution of its political "facts" and guaranteeing their legitimation. The political analysis of regimes of power must extend to these metaphysical dimensions particularly in the case of *operative logics*.


STOP

*Question*: What is an operative logic?

Call an operative logic one that combines an ontology with an epistemology in such a way as to endow itself with powers of self-causation. An operative logic is a productive *process* that inhabits a shared environment, or field of exteriority, with other processes and logics. It figures in that field as a formative movement: a *tendency* toward the iterative production of its own variety of constituted fact. The forms of determination it brings into being as fact have an in-born tendency toward proliferation, by virtue of the self-causative powers of their formative process. An operative logic is a process of becoming formative of its own species of being.

Question: What does an operative logic want?

Itself. Its own continuance. It is autopoietic. An operative logic's self-causative powers drive it automatically to extend itself. Its autopoietic mode of operation is one with a drive to universalize itself. Depending on the logic, that drive will take fundamentally heterogeneous forms (from the ecumenical to the imperialist, from the pastoral to the warlike).

Proposition: An operative logic is a *will-to-power*.

This will-to-power is impersonal because it necessarily operates in a field of exteriority in perpetual interaction with other operative logics, with which it is always in a dynamic state of reciprocal presupposition. It is a field phenomenon. The interaction actualizes in a diversity of regimes of power cohabiting the same field in reciprocal exteriority and potential interlinkage. An operative logic's actualization may be to varying degrees, in more than one regime. An operative logic not fully actualized in any regime of power interacts with the others virtually (anticipatorily, as a present force of futurity; or, as "negatively prehended").[13]

Question: In the case of threat as an operative logic, how can an effective analysis of it be carried out, given that the kind of fact it constitutes is affective and largely independent of actual fact, not to mention that its object is superlatively, futurely nonexistent?

There is a common category of entities, known to all, that specializes in making what is not actually present really present nonetheless, in and as its own effect: *signs*. The sign is the vehicle for making presently felt the *potential force* of the objectively absent.

Proposition: To understand preemptive power as an operative logic it is necessary to be able to express its productive process of becoming as a *semiosis*. Since preemption's production of being in becoming pivots on affect as felt quality, the pertinent theory of signs would have to be grounded first and foremost in a metaphysics of *feeling*.

## Smoke of Future Fires

Imagine a dreamer who suddenly hears a loud and prolonged fire alarm.

> At the instant it begins he is startled. He instinctively tries to get away; his
> hands go to his ears. It is not so much that it is unpleasing, but it forces
> itself so upon him. The instinctive resistance is a necessary part of it. . . .
> This sense of acting and being acted upon, which is the sense of the real-
> ity of things—both of outward things and ourselves—may be called the
> sense of Reaction. It does not reside in any one Feeling; it comes upon
> the breaking of one feeling by another feeling. (Peirce 1998, 4–5)

A fire alarm is the kind of sign C. S. Peirce calls *indications* or indexes.
Indexes "act on the nerves of the person and force his attention." They are
nervously compelling because they "show something about things, on account of their being physically connected to them" (Peirce 1998, 5) in the
way smoke is connected to fire. Yet they "*assert nothing.*" Rather, they are
in the mood of the "imperative, or exclamatory, as 'See there!' or 'Look
out!' " (Peirce 1998, 16). The instant they "show," we are startled: they are
immediately performative.

A performative always strikes as a self-executing command. The indexical sign effecting the command may assert nothing, but it still conveys
a form. "The form conveyed is always a determination of the dynamical
object. . . . The dynamical object . . . means something forced upon the
mind in perception, but including more than perception reveals. It is an
object of actual *Experience*" (Peirce 1998, 478).

Now what happens when there is no fire and the alarm sounds nonetheless? The sign of alarm has asserted more nothing. It is still just as imperative, still as automatically executing of a command. It still startles us
awake to a sense of a reality of things, outwardly and selfward at once.
It still forces attention, breaking into the feeling before with a transition
to a next. Something still happens. A sign-event has transpired. This is
an actual *Experience*, including, all the more more-than-perception reveals.

It is not just that the putative object of experience, the fire, is nonexistent. It is that it is absent from perception essentially, not just circum-
stantially. There is no fire. The alarm was in error. How can a falsity have a
superlatively real hold on experience?

How could it not? For Peirce, the "dynamical object" is not the fire. The dynamical object is the "really efficient but not immediately present Object" (Peirce 1998, 482). Here, it is the quasi-cause that innervates the body. It is the threat of fire, from the angle of its insigning of the body. It is the awakening to alertness of the nervous body signed astartle. That event takes place wholly between the sign and the "instinctively" activated body whose feeling is "broken" by the sign's imperative to transition to a new feeling. At that instant, nothing but this transitional break exists. Its feeling, the sudden bustle, fills the still dreamily reawakening world of experience.

The "form conveyed that determines the dynamical object" is nothing other than the dynamic form of the body, its bare activity at this instant of reawakening to its world on alert, imperatively altering. It is nothing else than the activation event launching the body into a transition to a next experience in which its waking world will have undergone a change. Everything takes place between the activated body and the sign of its *becoming*. Fire or no fire, transition to and through alert is made.

What happens when the fire is not falsely nonexistent, but nonexistent in a future tense? What happens if the smoke is that of fires yet to come? What happens if the sign-event is triggered by a future cause?

That is the semiotic question of threat.

Semiosis is sign-induced becoming. It is the question of how a sign as such *dynamically* determines a body to become, in actual experience. It is the question of how an *abstract force* can be *materially* determining. The question is the same for a nonexistent present fire signed in error, and for the futurity of a fire yet to come. There is one difference, however. For the future-causal fire, there can be no error. It will always have been preemptively right.

That one difference makes all the difference. The question becomes, what are the experiential political implications of the a priori rightness of smokes of future fires? What are the existential effects of the body having to assume, at the level of its activated flesh, one with its becoming, the rightness of alert never having to be in error? Of the body in a perpetual innervated reawakening to a world where signs of danger forever loom? Of a world where once a threat, always a threat? A world of infinitely seriating menace-potential made actual experience, with a surplus of becoming, all in the instant?

Imagine a waker hearing a sudden and loud alarm and therewith falling forward back into a world where the present is a foreshadow cast retrospectively by the future. Where the present's becoming is the back-cast dream of a future's will have been.

## A Bustle of It All

Peirce insists that the sign's forcing itself upon the body, and the "resistance" the body instinctively feels "in reaction," cannot be "distinguished as agent and patient" (Peirce 1997, 179). The bodily activation event occurs at a threshold of reawakening where there is as yet no distinction between activity and passivity. This means that the body cannot distinguish its own "instincts" from the reawakening force conveyed by the sign's formative performance.

The zone of indistinction between the body reactivating and the action of the sign extends to the shared environment that encompasses and ensures their correlation. Is not the waking distinction between the body and its environment one of activity in a surrounding passivity, or of activity coming from the surrounding to passively impress itself on the body? Prior to the distinction between agent and patient, in the bustle of the reawakening, there is no boundary yet between the body and its environment, or between the two of them and the correlated sign, or between all of the above and other bodies. Or: between the dream and the event. Peirce's definition of the dynamical object as cited above was truncated. It continues: "The form conveyed is always a determination of the dynamical object of the *commind*" (Peirce 1998, 478; emphasis in the original). The commind "consists of all that is, and must be, well understood between utterer and interpreter, at the outset, in order that the sign in question should fulfill its function" (478). It is all that braces a body among others into the oneness of an event in which they will become together, in the utmost immediacy of an imperative to collective individuation (see chapter 6). The distinctions between one body and another, between the body and its environment, between these and the sign, will reemerge from the bustle, after a transition, in the settle into a next determinate feeling. The form conveyed is a felt dynamic form of unbounded activation germinal of determinate feeling.[14]

Pure affect. Collectively felt. In a redawning universe. This is what the sign "shows."

To understand the political ontology of threat requires returning thought to this affective twilight zone of indexical experience. In that bustling zone of indistinction, the world becomingly includes so much more than perception reveals. For that reason, thought's approach cannot be phenomenological. It must be unabashedly metaphysical. It must extend to that which conditions what is appearing *next*, itself never appearing: what Whitehead terms the reality *of* appearance.

The reality of appearance is the ontogenetic effectiveness of the nonexistent. It is the surplus of reality of what has not happened, paradoxically as an event, and in the event happens to be productive of a startling transition toward more determinate being—that is at the same time the production of a surplus of being (a collective becoming).

Look out!

"The occasion has gathered the creativity of the Universe into its own completeness, abstracted from the real objective content which is the source of its own derivation" (Whitehead 1967a, 212).

This "results from the fusion of the ideal with the actual" (211) in a mutual immanence of contemporary occasions "allied to the immanence of the future in the present" (217).

See there!

"The light that was never was, on sea or land" (211).

*Last question*: Does it shine beyond preemption?

# Afterword: After the Long Past

## A Retrospective Introduction to the History of the Present

Mark the singularity of events. . . . Grasp their return. . . . Define even their lacuna point, the moment they did not take place.
—Michel Foucault, "Nietzsche, Genealogy, History"

Philosophers of the event tend to have a bone to pick with history. As do philosophers of process and becoming. A. N. Whitehead minces no words when it comes to "the mass of fables termed history."[1] He laments the "unfortunate effect" upon our thinking exercised by "the long-range forecast and back-cast of critical thought." After all, neither the past nor the future exists. Our "habit of dwelling upon the long future and the long past" is a "literary" effort of "purely abstract imagination, devoid of any direct observation of particular fact." Dwelling on long-duration continuities, "time-spans of centuries, or of decades, or of years, or of days," is a way of not attending to what we can effectively experience: "conceptual persuasions in the present." Long-range fable-making "enfeebles the emphasis of first-hand intuition."

Wait: centuries, decades, years . . . *days*? Just how short-range are our "conceptual persuasions"? "In considering our direct observation of past, or of future, we should confine ourselves to time-spans of the order of magnitude of a second, or even fractions of a second." And did he say "emphasis *of*? Not "on"? In the fraction of the second that is the order of magnitude of what Foucault calls "effective history," firsthand intuition creates its own emphasis. It is not the forecasting or back-casting of the critical observer who places an emphasis on. There is no overlook allowing an emphasis to be laid on from outside or above. Rather, Whitehead says, the observer, is on the "utmost verge" of events' taking shape in their own "process of self-completion." On the verge of history, past and future are "immanent" to the present and, in that interval, to each other. The critique of history has nowhere to be but in the reciprocal immanence that is the verging toward the *self*-completion of events in the making. The fraction of a second-scale is where we must mark the singularity of events, and grasp their return. This is no easy task: because the verge of history is also events' lacuna point, the moment they have not taken place.

This is why Nietzsche argues that what history is most intensely about is the "untimely." This is why Foucault asserts the need for an effective history that is a "history of the present" (Foucault 1979, 31). "Effective history . . . shortens its vision to the things nearest it—the body, the nervous system . . . energies" (Foucault 1977b, 155). Only an immanent critique can effectively "observe" what is energetically not taking place, coeval with a moment's effective self-completion: in the interval of history's in-the-making.

This book has been an exercise in the history of the present. It has been a question of all that was just mentioned: of the singularity of events, their return, their energetically verging; of immanence and intuition; of the innervated body; of the power of short-range "conceptual persuasions" to energize, in the interval, a moment's self-completion, replete with what could have been, but did not take place. It has been a question of all of these things, in the field of events of what has been called the "Long War": the "war on terror."

The thesis of this book is that the Long War is actually the telescoping of war powers into the untimely interval, making them all the more effectively self-completing: history in the making, menacingly foreshortened. A corollary of this thesis is that the entire field of power deforms around this intensive contraction, like the fabric of space-time in the vicinity of a black hole. The name of this deformation of the field of power is "preemption."

It is neither possible nor desirable to entirely avoid the fabulation habit. Fables have their uses. They enable us to get an extensive hold on time.[2] But perhaps we can double down on our historiographical forecasting and back-casting and fabulate as well, on a fellow-traveling track, following a different tack, flush with the conceptual persuasion of the present, the elusive interval of history's untimely in-the-making.

## Operative Logic

Conceptual persuasion in this connection cannot mean a persuasive use of concepts that we personally deploy, mediating between our subjective intentions and the world "out there." It can only mean a persuasive force exerted directly *by* the conceptual, in the interval. This attributes an effectively historical reality to the conceptual. It asserts that there is an abstract force of history immanent to its in-the-making. The analyses of this book orbit around this concept of a strangely effective force immanently inflecting events, abstractly energizing their verging onto self-completion. The deceptively mundane name given to such forces in this book is "operative logics."

Preemption, it is argued, is the most powerful operative logic of the present. It is the untimely force of attraction around which the field of power is bending.

At first approach, the notion of a directly effective abstract force seems hard to bend one's head around. In reality, it is not so hard to see how a concept exerts a power of its own. Concepts, according to Gilles Deleuze and Félix Guattari, are only superficially enchainments of signifying building blocks adding up to a meaningful statement. Pragmatically, they are a simultaneous positing of *phases* adding up to a *problematic node* (Deleuze and Guattari 1994, 18, 25).

Take for example the phrase "of the people, by the people, for the people." This concept is the traditional problem of American democracy, in the positive sense of being the node to which it has repeatedly felt compelled to return, and in orbit around which it has produced historical variations on itself. The phrase was uttered by U.S. president Abraham Lincoln in his Gettysburg Address midway through the Civil War, the country torn apart. It was accompanied in the speech by wording from the Declaration of Independence in a way that implied that its three-part formula encapsulated the historical force of the country's foundation, carrying forward the inaugural act of the country's constitution "four score and seven years" before. The formula is in fact often mistaken for a phrase from the Constitution. The formula performs itself as a foundational force—under circumstances in which the unifying origin has been rendered null and void, lost to dismemberment. The phrase is uttered in this breach in the continuity of the country's history. As a concept, it agitates abstractly in the interval, for a return to unity.

All concepts, in their own infinitely diverse ways, perform themselves in this untimely manner. They instantiate themselves as a foundational force: in the interval, in the very breach left by the suspension of origins and the blink of the implosion of all they set in place. They beckon a return to a continuous unfolding, in the conflictual midst of its manifest impossibility. Paraphrasing Whitehead's famous formula, there is no continuity of becoming, but there is a becoming of continuity (Whitehead 1978, 35). A concept is a problematic node for the becoming of continuity. It is a catalyst for a manifestly impossible unfolding of a dynamic unity from the interval of suspension. The nodal problem of the phrase "of the people, by the people, for the people" is: how do "we" (the people, whoever that is) make ourselves whole again and continue dynamically along "our" path together, given how abjectly the history of the present has shredded any possibility of "our" and "we," and that the path is strewn with corpses?

The unity does not come all at once. It doesn't come all at once because it isn't already contained in the meaning of the conceptual formula. What could this unity of the "of," "by," and "for" possibly be, given the circumstances? What could it possibly mean? Especially considering that the formula itself is threefold. How does a unity grow from a multiplicity? And isn't there a slight incompatibility between government "by" the people and "for" the people? Is Lincoln really suggesting that the "by" and "for" coincide? That would imply a direct democracy without organs of representation. Wouldn't that contradict the very Constitution of the nation whose inaugural performative act the formula strives to repeat? And wouldn't the meaning of the genitive "of" have very different connotations depending on how the "by" or "for" actually panned out?

The point is not that the formula contradicts itself. The point is that the conceptual problem is not a problem of meaning. The conceptual problem is the incompatibility between the component parts of the formula that render it richly meaningless. In the utterance of the phrase, the "of," "by," and "for" are in irresolvable tension. Their contradictions can, of course, be interpreted away. The tensions can be overcome in a higher conceptual synthesis, using the word "conceptual" this time in its standard meaning of an abstract general idea (as opposed to a singular abstract force). But this would render it an episode in the history of philosophy—the more easily ignored as mere learned navel-gazing the more perfect the synthesis—when what it aspires to be is an unrefusable, formative force *of* history. The contradiction is not there to be overcome. The tension is there to be worked with, or worked through. A tension, unlike a contradiction, can be worked out. It can resolve itself, but only in the form of a provisional pragmatic solution. This working out can happen only if the formula extends into a process.

Start with the "for." Representative organs of government stand apart, and often against, the unity of the people. So be it. But not if it ends there. Continue: make a transition to the "by." Submit government representation to vetting "by" the people. The transition goes both ways at the same time, no sooner "by"-ing the people than returning the "for" to office. It is a question, of course, of elections. The success of the operation will hinge on how the elections are experienced "by" the people, in terms for example of fairness or inclusiveness. Every redeployment of the electoral apparatus will modulate the "by" and the "for" relative to each other, placing them more or less, or differently, in resonance or interference. The resonance or interference will determine how "of" the people the government is felt to be. The shifting tenor of the "of" measures the success of the unification project. The conceptual problem has now branched out into a set of practical problems. How can the "by" be extended to the secessionist South? Will it include freed slaves, not just formally but in fact? And later: will it include women? How does money enter into the equation? Each successive modulation is at the same time a case of solution to the conceptual problem and a generator of an ongoing series of practical problems, each of which is a seed of struggle and conflict that may at some point once again call the "of," "by," and "for" back into question, posing a refoundational question to the nation—and compelling the generation of another case of solution. The "meaning" of the conceptual problem is this serial generation of spin-off problems. The conceptual formula is "problematic" precisely in this sense: as an abstract matrix for the practical production of problems on an ongoing basis. This is the actual "continuity" that will become: an unfolding riven with tension, driven by the tension's working out, cut into by conflict every step of the way.

In the course of the unfolding of cases of solutions, formations not explicitly connoted in the formula will enter the fray, adding gears to the apparatus of the conceptual problem's working out. What of the judiciary? Should it be elected also? Is it really ensuring the "balance of powers" between the "by" and the "for"? And between the tributary formations of the "for"s electoral body and its executive functions? Namely, the bureaucracy. And the military. Not to mention nongovernmental organizations. Is the bureaucracy doing its job? Is the military overreaching? Do nongovernmental organizations have the access and influence to do their job? The working out of the conceptual problem annexes tributary formations to the provisional settlement providing a case of solution to the problem. Each such settlement involves a whole field of heterogeneous elements, from the angle of their potential coming-together around its matrixial tension. Every modulation of the formative tension expressed by the formula is a whole-field modulation. Its effects trickle to every corner of the field, poking and perturbing, agitating for adjustments. A poke in one place reverberates throughout. A concept is, in its effects, a full-spectrum force.

Some key points can be harvested from this example: the conceptual formula is an *operative* logic because it governs a pragmatic working out. It is an operative *logic* in a special sense, insofar as it lacks inherent meaning. Its working out gives it meaning, specific to each case of solution. The differential tension composing the formula is thus not a contradiction in meaning. It is a paradox demanding in response not an interpretation but a production. The logic is that of *productive paradox*.

The part-concepts composing the formula insist on their own disjunctness: in the formula, they are in a relation of nonrelation. But in the working out of the paradox, they effectively combine, becoming mutually presupposing phases of a process. This defuses their contradiction on the level of meaning by spacing them out of their problematic simultaneity, giving each its own time as part of an actual *circuit*, as when the "for" of American government submits itself to the election cycle. Transitions smooth over the apparent contradictions between the participating formations without overcoming their disjunctness. The disjunctness remains, in the form of struggle and conflict. The formations in the circuit functionally co-operate, but there is something left over, over and above the smoothness of their functioning. Struggle and conflict are the remain-

213 OF INTRODUCTION 213

der of the irresolvable tension between the part-concepts composing the operative logic. They are the form in which the formula continues to agitate its pragmatic field. The agitation represents an eventual phasing-out of the operative solidarity of the working-out that had settled in. This is a dephasing, already anticipatorily accompanying the phasing-in of the settlement it calls into question. Across this phase-shift, the surplus of tensional energy must be recaptured by the process, reinserted into the circuit: rephased. When this happens, a *surplus-value* has been produced. If the case of solution that had settled in is capable of recapturing the surplus-value and rephasing, it will be able to adapt to changes in its full-spectrum field of operation, and will continue across subsequent phase-shifts. In the example of the "of, by, and for the people" formula and its cases of solution, the surplus-value takes a directly qualitative form. It is the surplus-value of felt unity produced in and through the fractiousness of the field, experienced as community, national pride, or even a contestatory commitment to the logic.

The operative logic can be understood as doubly productive. First, of an ongoing series of cases of pragmatic solutions producing complex orderings that touch, to one degree or another, in resonance and interference, the entire field of life. Then in addition to that, of a something-extra, a something over and beyond the pragmatics of mere functioning that registers the hard-won success of the ongoing production of circuits and cycles of self-settling cases of solution in a supplemental creation of value (an added value). This surplus-value can be contrived to accumulate. The process generates, from its own operations' settling in, two outgrowths. Two organs. One is a reproductive apparatus ensuring the cyclic repetition of the circuit and its reorderings (in this case, the electoral apparatus). The other is what Deleuze and Guattari call an "apparatus of capture":[3] a set of mechanisms ensuring the accumulation of the surplus-value produced, making it available to be fed back into the processual circuit at strategic points (in this case, national days, veterans' associations, patriotic parades, discourses and media-image mechanisms harvesting and fostering the sense of community, national pride, and commitment to the process).

The heterogeneous formations that take charge of mounting and administering the apparatuses dedicated to translating the part-concept of the formula into the concrete hinge of a functional phase or actual circuit are never univocal, however hard they may try. Neither are the heterogeneous formations throughout the field that are annexed, in whatever capacity. Actual formations are always at a crossroads of tendencies. That is exactly what the operative logic ultimately consists in: tendencies. What gives consistency to the process is the tendential direction in which the formations possessed of it move together, across their tensions. Here, it is "unity." This is another abstraction, different again from both the abstract force of the problematic node that is the constitutive concept of the operative logic, and the merely general abstraction of the general idea of interpretation. It is a singular abstraction that exerts an attractive force. It is a prospectively felt abstraction. It is no less empty of meaningful content than the conceptual formula, but it stands tantalizingly outside it, whereas the conceptual formula agitates immanently to its own unfolding. This outside abstraction is the point toward which every pragmatic variation on every process governed by the operative logic tends—without ever being able to reach. It is the ulterior limit of the process. The limit is purely virtual. Its full realization is impossible. An operative logic is impossible twice over: once in the tensional differential between its part-concepts, and once in the destination of the processual movement that tension energizes. In between lies a full-spectrum field of operation that has been *made possible* by the play between the two impossibilities. Together, in their calling to each other at a doubly abstract distance, they have *potentialized* a movement that begins in the indeterminacy of a paradox. But this is an indeterminacy that, paraphrasing C. S. Peirce, is *determined to be determined*, through the serial production of cases of solution. Each case of solution *creates* its own possibility from the potentializing of the impossible, and deposits it in the world for future reference and repeat realization.

The operative logic serially works itself out through the cases of solution, each of which, while never fully reaching the tendential destination that is the ulterior limit of the process, nevertheless gives it an actual expression. Each actual expression is closer to or further from the impossible limit-case of full realization. Each fulfills it, to a degree. That degree is the measure of the *intensity* of the operative logic's actualization in that case. Each heterogeneous formation involved in the unfolding of the case of solution lies at a crossroads of tendencies, because each degree of each actualization of these formations' logics can take *itself* for a destination, for future repetition. The field fractures into a proliferating production of tendential variations, differently limited. Some of the variations may constitute countertendencies: problematizations that feel the abstract force of the productive paradox of the conceptual formula in a way that gives different weightings to the part-concepts and the phases between that compose it, and to the corresponding operations into which they have been circuitously translated by a particular case of solution. For example, a coming into emphasis of the "by" might activate a tendency toward direct democracy that runs counter to the representational model presupposed by the formula. Or, certain workings out of the "for" might affirm diversity, and counter-tend all that was implied in the destination of unity giving direction up to that point.

All of this is important for the status of what seem to be binary dualisms, as between unity and fragmentation (or to take a well-known scholarly example, between "smooth" and "striated" in Deleuze and Guattari). They are not binaries. They are divergent processual destinations. Binaries are general abstractions. They have to do with contradiction and opposition on the level of meaning. The limits toward which a tendency tends are *poles* bounding a dynamic field of process. They never come alone, and no sooner come in pairs than proliferate into a many. The multiplicity of the tendencies they orient and of the apparatuses tending the tendencies are expressions of the productive paradox of the operative logic. The paradox of the operative logic in-forms each and every tendential expression. It is everywhere immanent to the processual field, constitutive of its very problematic nature. It is the field's constitutive immanent limit. This limit answers, at an abstract distance, across the spacing out and stringing along in time of cases of solution, to the field's ulterior limits, or the ideal end points bounding the field's furthest reaches. Its answer takes the form of an inflection of the field's problematic working-out, tendentially bent as by an ulterior motive. The constitutive immanence of the problematic node—of the conceptual formula that is the engine of the process—means that it is in every iteration of a case of solution, throughout the field, in every spacing-out and at every timing, everywhere, always and again tendentially inflected by its own ulterior reaching. This is why the ulterior limit is not an "outside" limit in any usual sense of the term: it abstractly folds into the operative logic's working-out. This is also why the conceptual formula is *nonlocal*. It in-forms each singular event in the series with its productive tensions and resolving inflections. It returns as the matrix for each iteration. Its reality is felt even where the events it governs do not take place, as when they are deflected by a countertendency that has succeeded in short-circuiting or supplanting the working-out that is under way.

The keyest of the key points: "engine of the process"; "governs." These phrases attribute a real efficacy to the operative logic's abstract problematic node. They imply that the conceptual formula possesses some form of causal force toward its own inflected unfoldings. The causal force of the formula is of a special kind. It cannot fully determine an effect. It is not an efficient cause. What it sets in motion needs apparatuses to move through, and these supply the efficient causality. But the formula is still really potentializing. It in-forms process with the potential that comes to be expressed in the emergent cases of solution. It really, if abstractly, energizes the process at its every twist and turn. It more than compensates for its insufficiency of efficient causality through its incorporation of a certain final causality. Its working-out senses the attractive poles, the ends, toward which the process ever and repeatedly tends. These tendential destinations continually feed back from their boundary zone at the process's ulterior limits. They fold back into the potentializing matrix and inflect its coming expressions. They co-operate in the energizing of the process. Together, the immanent and ulterior limits of the process give it a power of animation and orientation that is fully real, without being fully efficient causally. The abstract force of an operative logic is *quasi-causal*. Quasi-causality is not historical in any normal sense. The nonlocality of the formula and the potentiation it effects move through every point in the field's spacing, and move in (in-move; immanently agitate; in-form) every moment the process circuits through. An operative logic transits points in space and moments of time. It is not only nonlocal. It is *transhistorical* by dint of its nonlocality. It is as "untimely" as it is nonlocal.

Before moving on, it is important to think about how the conceptual formula is composed in its own right. Much more has been said so far in this chapter about how it is expressed in the working-out of the cases of solution to its productive paradox. The formula was said to be composed of part-concepts and phases abstractly moving through them (from the "by" to the "for," and vice versa). The part-concepts and a selection of their phasings pragmatically work out as the circuits and cycles of the actual functioning of a historical process. In this historical translation, the conceptual phases are spaced-out, in a manner specific to each apparatus involved. The spacing-out enables a time sequencing of the transitions composing the actual circuits and cycles. The part-concepts of the formula are now functionally separated out from each other. They have been transduced into working parts of an operational machinery. An apparatus has been mounted. Paradoxically, the formula itself has no working parts— lacking as it does both meaning and function outside its cases of solution. In the formula, the phasings between the part-concepts run, abstractly, in all directions, as at the same time. This promiscuity of mutual phasing is not practicable. In each case of solution, the promiscuousness of the phasings has to be reduced. This does not mean that the functioning has to become one-way. In fact, retaining a certain mutuality is absolutely essential. This most often translates as a bidirectionality of feedback. For example, the "for" fed operationally forward to the "by," and the "by" fed back to the "for," and their cross-linkage modulated the "of." This selective, functionally limited, operational solidarity between working parts does not characterize the conceptual formula itself—which as a result can in no way resemble its cases of solution. The formula contains, in potential, all of the possible circuits its abstract force may quasi-cause. It includes even potential circuits that do not eventuate (that are not possibilized, for whatever reason of historical contingency, even though they are potentiated to one degree or another). The formula includes all of the transitions. All of the resonances. All of the interferences. All of the ways in which they mutually inflect, and spin off variations on the tendency that the formula's quasi-causality determines-to-be-determined. The problematic node that is the formula is abstract as a consequence of this overfullness of potential cases of solution, which must be counted as real—even if they do not take place. You can get an image of what the conceptual formula is as such if you try to imagine all the circuits moving through all the transitions, multidirectionally linking all the part-concepts in an infinite number of ways. Then you try to imagine all of that at infinite speed, so that the variations blur into a Doppler effect. The problematic node is that Doppler effect: the impossible mutual inclusion of all the variations potentially agitating the field, in each other. The part-concepts are in a relation of nonrelation not because they do not come together, but on the contrary because they are each so singularly impregnated with potential prolongations each toward the others that they stand out in all their paradoxically potential glory as a "remarkable" point.[4] They are disjunct by virtue of the singular angle of their Dopplered mutual inclusion of their fellow part-concepts—which is reciprocally, but asymmetrically, their own envelopment in the field of their virtually coming-together. The greatest paradox of all is that the relation of nonrelation at the heart of process is an uncontainable surplus of coming-together.

Such is a part-concept. But, as always, it all depends on what "is" is. Because a part-concept isn't. The conceptual formula they compose also doesn't exist—even though it acts. Even though it potentiates, and in the working out of each potentiation, energizes and orients. Even though it has an odd, and oddly powerful, causal force. Its force is that it is too powerfully abstract to be—but still causal enough to express itself (and to make history in the process).

## Ontopower

We seem to have wandered far afield from the topic of the book. It has been a necessary detour, in order to understand the status of the events referenced and the coming to historical significance of the transhistorical processes that move through them. It is the aim of this book to diagnose this complexity.

The book approaches the transhistorical processes discussed as operative logics. This is to say, in light of the foregoing discussion, that they are treated as tendencies. They govern a field of tendential expression inhabited by apparatuses for the spacing-out and taking time of the variations virtually mutually included in the problematic node at the heart of the process. The field of tendential expresssion is unbounded in the usual sense. It has no actual boundaries. It is virtually bounded by the immanent limit of the operative logic itself (the bundle of potential expressions it mutually includes) and the ulterior limit of the working-out of its cases of solution (the tendential end points by which the potential expressions' unfolding is oriented). Each case of solution involves a multiplicity of heterogeneous formations. It is only in the midst of that actual heterogeneity that the tendency, and its abstract force of becoming, can be grasped. Try grasping it directly, and it slips away as ghostily as a Doppler effect. The tendency can only be caught in the act, in the mix.

The work of the book's theorization is to distill the abstract force of the tendency from the actual mixity of its field of expression: to give expression to the problematic node, as it expresses itself in and through that which it potentiates. That is why the project of the book is not a historical enterprise. History deals with the actual conditions of mixity, and the meaning and function of the apparatuses in co-operation and conflict in that field of tendential expression. The project of the book is philosophical rather than historical. Philosophy has a bone to pick with history not because it is fabulously wrong, not because it has no value as a fabulated interpretation of forecast and back-cast co-operation and conflict. It has a bone to pick with history only to the extent that history mistakes the interpretations it produces for concepts—that is, when history considers that the empirical analysis of the problematic field alone is sufficient to understand what animates and moves it.

In order to grasp what animates and moves history, it is necessary to move to a more abstract level. For the force of history is more abstract than what it resolves into in its concrete expressions. It is a radically abstract force, and it is for that reason that philosophy has a historical calling: to trans-it. Philosophy's historical object is the transhistorical movement in-forming history. That "object" (which is not one) has the special status of a quasi-causal abstraction. Only a metaphysics is adequate to understanding that which "is" only abstractly, under-through and out the far side of historical formations. The historical task of philosophy cannot be achieved solely through empirical analysis of actually existing formations. It must dedicate itself to the superempirical flushing out of what in-forms the very possibility of empirical analysis. It must be *radically empirical*. Radical empiricism is defined by the postulate that relationality is a mode of reality in its own right, and that relation can be directly perceived (if only as in-forming the immediacy of its effects). What is the mutual inclusion of the component non-parts of an actually unbounded field of variation in each other, if not relation in the purest, most potent sense (as the real virtuality of an uncontainable surplus of coming-together)?

This relates to the status of the events referenced in the book. Each expression of a tendency actualizes that tendency in an actual variation that carries it to a higher or lower power, in the sense of moving closer or further away from the fullest realization of its ideal end point. This means that each empirically observable, actual working-out of the tendential problem is a *power expression* of the operative logic. A philosophical analysis of the historical field is tasked with evaluating the power expression. To do so, it must think as best it can the immanent and ulterior limits of the field of expression: the polarities bounding its furthest reaches and the differential engine everywhere at its heart. In other words, the task is to evaluate tendencies.

As earlier mentioned, each actual formation is at the crossroads of tendencies. But there are events in which a certain tendency is brought to a highest-degree expression. It is in these exemplary or exceptional events that the force and orientation of the most clearly expressed tendency express themselves most powerfully. It is to these events that a radically empirical study must look. It must distill the taking-to-the-highest-power of a dominant tendency from the welter of competing tendencies. It does so in order to better understand the *potential* expressed—and released—by that eventful iteration. The release is key. What remainder is leftover, to fold in back under, to move the process even further toward its virtual destination? How is this surplus-value of process captured, in order to be fed back into the process, potentially to move it to an even higher power of expression? For isn't that what tendencies want? To express themselves? To carry themselves forward, toward an intensest expression? Does not each power expression of the tendency self-validate it as a *will to power*? Paradoxically, do not the mechanisms that the working-out of the process provides the operative logic's tendency to reproduce itself actually curtail it? For they capture it in a particular form, within certain actual parameters of operation and set boundaries to meaning and functioning. Must not the operative logic, as a will to power, attack and exceed its own organs of reproduction? The object of history is often construed to be the mechanisms by which "society" (or "culture" or a political system or an institution) reproduces itself. Must not the philosophy of history, to the extent that it dedicates itself to the distillation of the abstract forces in-forming the field of history, attack and exceed such self-containments?

As Nietzsche, and after him, Deleuze and Guattari, have said, history is one thing; *becoming* is another. The project of this book is try to provide some elements for an understanding of the history of the present's be-coming, as seen through certain exemplary events, mainly belonging to George W. Bush's presidency in the United States, that brought its con-stitutive tendency to an intensive peak of expression. Seen from the angle of the becoming it catalyzes as a quasi-causal effect of the working-out of an operative logic, a power expression is an *ontopower*. An ontopower is a name for a power of becoming whose force is maximally abstract: whose power resides in a "conceptual persuasion" as glossed in this chapter in terms of operative logic. An ontopower is a power of emergence: a power for the serial production of variations belonging to the same power curve, or tendency.

This book is a study of ontopower. The power curve most at issue in its meanderings through the present field of emergence is governed by the operative logic of *preemption*. Although the exemplary events through which this operative logic is evaluated in the book are, for the most part, historically moored to the Bush administration, the power curve they ex-press exceeds it. Preemption is understood here as a transhistorical be-coming that is unbounded by the geographical limits of the United States and the time frame of its thirty-sixth post–Civil War president. The limits of its power curve are otherwise occupied.

The history of the present is not confined to the actual dates of its ex-emplary events. It is nowhere else than in those singular events. But is also in their return. And even in their not taking place. It is as nonlocal as it is transhistorical.

The question of the object of history has been broached. But what of the subject of history? In a word, it too is multiple. It goes without saying that the "people" the government is "for" cannot, in any of the iterations of the formula, entirely coincide with the "people" the government is effectively "by" (until such time as the impossibility of direct democracy gives rise to an apparatic invention repotentializing the political field to render such a thing possible). Each part-concept of the conceptual formula actualizes, as the operative logic works itself out, as a substantially different subject of history. If we say the word "people" we seem to be dealing with a single collective subject. But as soon as we ask the "of" or "by" or "for" question in the context of an operative logic, it is clear that the single collective subject singularly differs in relation to itself, which is to say at each stop in the circuit. "The" people is thus singular-multiple, in a processual way that is irreducible to any general idea subsuming a collectivity under a single, overarching unity of meaning. The singularity of the "people" does not abide overaching. It is operatively multiplied at each phase-shift, immanently to its own process. The part-concepts composing the formula express as processual *part-subjects*. No one owns the whole process, and to phase in, each needs the others, in relay. The process gear-shifts its operative focus from one part-subject to another. Functional overlaps may be produced, but they do not counteract the irreducible subjective multiplicity. They just add a new state of actual mixity.

Tendencies have only part-subjects, and only on the consequent level of their conceptual formula's working-out. There is no "the" subject of any tendency, concept, or historical event. It is of the nature of tendencies to drive *themselves* through their workings-out. Ultimately, through their own quasi-causal efficiency folding back on itself in and through its actual expressions, they subject themselves to their own variations. They fundamentally self-cause. They are self-causing *subjectivities without a subject*, whose abstract but forcefully real elements actually express as part-subjects. Any general idea of subjective unity sits myopically atop a moving multiplicity of part-subjects. Such a general idea is too meaningfully self-absorbed to register the commotion right under its nose. "The" subject is one of the most artificed and tenacious "fables" of our "literary habit" of dwelling on the long future and the long past (whether "long" is measured in the minutes or hours of an intentional sequence of actions, the years of a personal history, the centuries of a nation building, or the epochs of a civilization). For this reason, the concept of "agency," with its "the" subject-of-an-action connotations, is assiduously avoided in this book. It is replaced with more quasi-causal, field-friendly notions of "triggering," "catalyzing," and "priming."

## The Circuit

Chapter 1. The premise of this chapter is that the liberal democratic operative logic of the "of, by, for" the people has been backgrounded, if not entirely superseded, by an upstart operative logic that took on a prominent degree of consistency in the wake of the events of 9/11. The operative logic of preemption involves entirely different part-concepts.

Part-concept 1: The world is uncertain and full of dangers. It is nothing less than an all-encompassing threat-environment. Part-concept 2: In an encompassing threat-environment, you can't afford to wait for threats to fully emerge, because when they do it is always in an unexpected form. You have to catch them in their potential emergence. Part-concept 3: The best way to catch them in their potential is to flush them out of their potential—to make them emerge and take determinate shape. You have to produce the threats you are intent on guarding against.

The operative logic of preemption is that of security. The operative logic of the liberal-democratic state of the people has been abstractly head-butted to the sidelines by the neoliberalism of the operative logic of the security state. The problem posed by this now increasingly dominant processual matrix concerns perception and time, more than justice and fairness. Its cases of solution are sallies and attacks, more so than institutional arrangements. Perception, because the imperative to catch threats before they emerge raises a particularly thorny problem: How do you perceive what has not yet emerged? How do you perceive potential? This problem of perception is immediately a time-problem, in the most pragmatic of ways: by what mechanisms can the not-yet be operationalized?

The apparatuses dedicated to that operationalization are primarily, of course, apparatuses of war. Much of the book will deal with the way the operative logic of preemption plays out in the theory and practice of war. But this logic is in no way limited to the battlefield. The threat-environment is all-encompassing. It blows back to encompass the "home front." It in-forms any number of actual formations, in particular of policing and surveillance (see Note: Bush on Steroids? below). An operative logic, actually having no set boundaries, and being as it is a will to power, has a potent shape-shifting capacity. It can not only produce variations on the apparatuses through which it expresses itself in its native field (in this case, the amorphous battlefield of asymmetrical warfare that is the "war on terror"). It can also exploit its nonlocality (actually assisted by apparatuses of diffusion such as the media) and field-hop. It can insert its logic into new fields, where it expresses itself through an entirely different set of formations. In a sense, this is an expansion of the same tendential field of expression, complexioned into different, but co-resonating and mutually interfering, regions of process. The process animated by an operative logic is always pushing back whatever actual boundaries have been set down—in co-operation, struggle, or conflict—to contain it. The tendency of its tendency is to go feral, seeding new species of itself. An operative logic is unbounded (but not unlimited—its limits, as discussed above, are nothing less than its real but abstract *enabling* constraints). The history of our present is enablingly delimited (de-limited) by the open-ranging wildness of preemption.

Chapter 1 concentrates on the differences between the logics of prevention, dissuasion, and preemption. The emphasis is on how preemption takes the self-causative powers of operative logic to a level of intensity seen in few other processes in history. Readers familiar with Deleuze and Deleuze and Guattari will recognize many aspects of the "diagram" (Deleuze 1988, 34–44) and the "abstract machine"[5] in the way the logic of preemption is developed and ramifies throughout the book.

The question inevitably arises: What's so "new" about preemption? Hasn't preemptive attack always been practiced? Isn't it part of the classical doctrine of war? Yes and no. This question is beside the point because no claims are being made here about the absolute newness of any of the things at issue. The apparatuses that become possessed of an operative logic have a long history into the intervals of which the history of the present energetically inserts itself. Their component parts have their own histories. The part-concepts have been felt before, in the part-subjects of their expression. But yes, despite all that, there is something new: a new consistency, and a new intensity. The new consistency is the tightness of the mutual inclusion of the part-concepts composing the problematic node, under the pressure of new inflections. Preemption, in the classical doctrine of war, was justified against a "clear and present danger"—very different from a not-yet emergent threat. The part-concept "catch threat that has not yet emerged" inflects "imminent danger" toward "immanent threat." This changes everything, even when the actual apparatuses, and the general ideas they embrace, may stay suspiciously the same. The other two part-concepts (threat-environment and produce-what-you-fear) bend around this inflection. It is the *problem* that changes. The preemptive problem of how to perceive change, and how to do so in potential—which is to say, in an interval smaller than the smallest historically perceivable—is disturbingly fresh. This novel problematization gives an intensive tinge of newness even to events that have been repeated many times before (such as U.S. invasions of foreign countries). Events repeat. Through their repetition, problems renew. Due to the renewal, the repetition is never effected according to a logic of resemblance. Operative logics are logics of differentiation (of continual variation, becoming across discontinuous intervals).

The surplus-value produced by the operative logic of preemption is a surplus-value of threat. It has been a political added-value in countless ways since 9/11. The more tendencies change, the more they stay the same— when their will to power attains a high enough degree of self-driving intensity, and their actual expressions stay adequately spry through the serial renewal of their ongoing variation.

> *Note: Bush on Steroids*? Dick Cheney, vice president under George W. Bush and a lead neoconservative war promoter, saw it coming. Shortly after Barack Obama's 2008 election and before his investiture, Cheney cautioned the public not to hope for too great a change. "Once they get here," he said of Obama's coming administration with uncharacteristic understatement, "and they're faced with the same problems we deal with every day, then they will appreciate some of the things we've put in place" (Barr 2008). He was referring in particular to the Bush administration's radical expansion of the president's discretionary powers, in a continuing context in which the boundaries of "war" have become indeterminate, stretching indefinitely into the future of threat, and from end to end of the full spectrum of power, from the most muffled of the soft (surveillance) to the most ballistic of the hard (military attack).[6] Three years later, when the extent of Obama's counterterrorist "drone war" was sinking in, Cheney was in "I told you so" mode

and, more to form, belligerently demanded that Obama formally apologize to Bush for his criticisms during the election campaign of Bush's foreign policy and record on civil liberties (Warrick 2011). This was before reports broke of Obama's personal administration of an extrajudicial "kill list" for targeted assassinations, including, in an unprecedented move, of American citizens (Becker and Shane 2012; Greenwald 2012). Obama, in the admiring words of John Nagl, a U.S. Marine Corps counterterrorism and counterinsurgency expert who helped develop Bush administration strategy, has presided over the creation of an "almost industrial strength counterterrorism killing machine" (Grey and Edge 2011) supported by a cancerously expanding network of at least 750 U.S. military bases in dozens of foreign countries (Turse 2011, 2012; Johnson 2004, 151–186; 54 countries is a common estimate). Aaron David Miller, a career diplomat who served under six U.S. secretaries of state, echoed Cheney's 2008 election campaign warning during Obama's run for a second term in 2012. Obama, he quipped, had become "Bush on steroids." It was a compliment. Miller was celebrating the "extraordinary fact" that "what has emerged in the second decade after 9/11 is a remarkable consensus among Democrats and Republicans on a core approach to the nation's foreign policy" (Miller 2012).

This is not even mentioning Obama's massive expansion of the warrantless surveillance begun under Bush. Edward Snowden's release of government documents not only revealed that there was an unexpected quantity of surveillance under way, but also drove home that it had changed qualitatively. The mass trawling techniques used by the U.S. National Security Agency operate on a preemptive basis, oriented toward data mining for signs of threats that have not yet fully emerged, as the formula for preemption has it. Neither is it taking into account a pronounced preemptive turn in policing, as displayed most visibly at international meetings such as the G20. Techniques such as "kettling," the practice of rounding up protestors en masse even before any enforceable infractions have occurred, blur the lines between criminality and contestation by treating anyone present as a potential threat, applying ad hoc extrajudicial powers of exception against formally legal activity.[7]

The tendency of the operative logic of preemption to produce what it aims to attack was starkly demonstrated by the policing strategies employed at the 2010 G20 meetings in Toronto. A perimeter fence was built around the meeting venue to keep protestors at a distance. Understandably, protestors understood that they could assemble around the perimeter, up to the fence. However, the Toronto city council had passed a special law making it illegal to come within five meters of the fence—and had kept the law secret. Protestors were caught unawares when they were arrested for what, for all they knew, was a legal assembly. The idea, apparently, was that the more "forward" of the protesters represented a less unemerged threat, closer to an actual danger. "It was just done surreptitiously, like a mushroom growing under a rock at night," said a lawyer representing those arrested (Yang 2010). Productive preemption has long been practiced in another form, that of police entrapment. Entrapment flirts with the border between detection and incitement. In U.S. counterterrorism practices, the line to incitement is crossed as a matter of course. Virtually all of the highly publicized cases of domestic terrorism plots claimed to have been foiled thanks to the vigilance of a watchful government turn out to have been originated, actively planned, and materially supported by the FBI, in some cases over strong resistance on the part of the "perpetrators" (Ackerman 2014; Human Rights Watch 2014).

A similar preemptive turn has occurred in surveillance, as can be seen in the Obama administration's internal guidelines outlining the criteria for placing individuals in its terrorism database and no-fly list (National Counterterrorism Center [NCC] 2013; Scahill and Devereaux 2014). The guidelines require a "reasonable suspicion" before someone is listed. Reasonable suspicion, however, is defined circularly. To be placed on the list with reasonable suspicion it must be determined that an individual "is known or *suspected to be* or has been knowingly engaged in conduct constituting, in preparation for, in aid of, or *related to* terrorism and/or terrorist activities" (NCC 2013, 33; emphasis added). In other words, one is reasonably suspected if one has been suspected (see chapter 7 on the tautologies of preemption). "Irrefutable evidence or concrete facts are not necessary" (NCC, 34). All that is necessary is being part of a "possible nexus" (NCC, 23) that is in some even refutable and unconcrete way "related to" terrorism. This expands surveillance to cover threats that have not yet fully emerged. Traditional profiling based on an individual's belonging to a predetermined category is replaced by "encounter movement management and analysis" (NCC, 58–77). Surveillance seeks to perceive the not-yet-fully-emerged on the fly, in ongoing patterns of movement. The profiling consists not in a checklist of characteristics for cross-checking, but in the assembling of "encounter packages" (NCC, 58). The base concept is encounter, making the practice of surveillance more event-based than identity-based. What is profiled is a potential future, through an extrapolation of a movement curve. It is no longer the individual per se who is profiled, based on an interpretation of his or her past as indicated by identifying marks of belonging. Of course traditional profiling, based for example on skin color or religious garb, is still practiced. But it is more often responsible for spectacular misfires that build resentment and resistance among affected communities (witness the events in Ferguson, Missouri, in 2014) than it is an effective tool for crime and terrorism control. Operationally, it is an anachronism that does not serve its stated purpose of keeping the peace (serving instead to reassert a racist status quo). In any case, traditional profiling is a preventive tool that is maladapted to the present-day preemptive environment (on the difference between prevention and preemption, see chapter 1). But then, it is perhaps its very maladaptation as a preventive mechanism that gives it a productive preemptive function: its misfires produce situations perceived by the authorities as situations of potential threat, like the protests sparked in Ferguson by the shooting of an unarmed black man, that then become pretexts for the deployment of preemptive policing. The policing tends to take highly militarized forms that it has acquired by virtue of its strategic home-front role on the full spectrum of post-9/11 power (Balko 2013).

One Bush-era practice that has ostensibly been left behind is torture. Torture, like the "preventive detention" with which it is closely associated in the U.S. carceral archipelago of largely secret prisons ("black sites") whose crown jewel is Guantánamo, participates in the operative logic of preemption by treating a perceived threat as if it were a present danger, setting in motion a judicial time-loop by making the punishment precede criminal charges, let alone trial (chapter 7 analyzes this paradoxical temporality of preemption). The general perception is that Obama ended torture and closed Bush's black sites. Soon after becoming president, in 2009, Obama did issue an executive order closing black sites. What is often overlooked is that the order only applied to CIA-operated black sites. Any sites operated by other U.S. agencies remained in service (Horton 2010). In addition, floating black sites aboard navy ships were created (Lendman 2013). These are primarily short-term holding stations. Detainees can be transferred from the ships to civilian courts or special military commissions, after interrogations unencumbered by the constitutional rights in force on land. But, lifting a page from the capitalist playbook, they can also be shipped off to other countries: outsourced. The practice of torture, the kidnapping of suspects for preventive detention ("rendition"), and the large-scale operation of black sites continue by proxy (Whitlock 2013). U.S. Special Forces still practice extralegal "rendition" (a polite word for kidnapping) but transfer captives to cooperative nations (those hosting U.S. bases in return for military aid, training, and other assistance) for detention, not excluding treatment with what the Bush administration called "enhanced interrogation techniques." Obama's refusal to allow the prosecution of Bush administration officials involved in torture and other infractions of international law leaves the door wide open for future presidents to re-enhance their own techniques with a confident expectation of impunity.[8]

Another obvious difference is Obama's diffidence as regards "nation-building" and his reluctance to employ "boots on the ground." This is not difficult to understand, in view of the harsh retrospective criticism of Bush's endeavors in these areas. (In too many cases these criticisms have a distinct odor of deathbed conversions on the part of former accomplices, which, when it came to the invasions of Afghanistan and Iraq as well as the central piece of legislation that gave a gloss of legitimacy to the "war on terror's" politics of exception—the Patriot Act—included the near-totality of the Democratic Party.) Obama's preference has been for rapid airborne attack over boots on the ground, using the tendentially global space-filling network of U.S. bases for punctual Special Forces missions and frequent unmanned drone attacks. The disintegration of Iraq and worsening situation in Afghanistan following the withdrawal of U.S. ground troops, along with a string of crises in Libya, Syria, Somalia, and the Ukraine, to name just the most talked about in the media, ensure that calls for another wholesale turn toward the hard end of the spectrum will continue. In the eyes of some, particularly of the neoconservative persuasion, the absence of spectacular military engagements under Obama qualifies this "Bush on steroids" as disappointingly "passive" (Krauthammer 2014).

In sum: preemption, and the politics of exception associated with it, is still very much with us. As Andrew Bacevich, a career military man and self-described conservative political theorist who has been a vocal critique of American interventionism abroad, wrote, "even as the enterprise once known as the global war on terror continued [under Obama], it lost all coherence and began to metastasize" (Bacevich 2011, 185). It has mushroomed, following its own self-driving momentum, colonizing new arenas on the domestic front and extending its will to power beyond the borders of its U.S. homeland (Canada, the UK, and Australia offering particularly amenable rocks for it to grow under).

This is a complex process. One analyst (Miller) sees a unified "consensus" while another (Bacevich) sees a total lack of "coherence." As discussed above, an operative logic possesses great powers of self-transformation. It is always mutating, morphing to new circumstances. The Bush-like tendencies extending through the Obama administration have not been without pushback, from Congress, the judiciary, and the public. An operative logic affirms each obstacle it encounters, in the form of a positive shift in its own processual shape. This makes a historical analysis of its course an extremely arduous task. But even when the analysis is carefully conducted, the situation can still appear at once clearly unified and totally incoherent. This is because the "coherence" of an operative logic is on the transhistorical level. Its historical expressions are riven with intervals of "rupture" that Foucault argues are as crucial to an understanding of the process of history as the full-spectrum infra-patterning of their shared field of emergence (what Foucault in his earlier work called the "epistemè," a term that is not adopted here because of its accent on knowledge and its still-structuralist flavor; chapters 3 and 4 discuss the embodied unknowing operationalized by the logic of preemption). The field of emergence, Foucault further argued, is dispersive. An operative logic can appear both unified and incoherent because of the disjunction between the ruptures occurring on the empirical level of actually appearing historical orderings on the one hand, and the dynamic unity-in-dispersion of the infra-empirical tendential commotion that quasi-cause both the orderings and their fits and starts.

The dispersive dynamic unity of the operative logic is difficult to grasp. It is not simply dispersive, but redistributive. Each irruptive emergence of a tendential movement ripples across the full spectrum of power, entailing a correlative adjustment all along the line (in much the way the punctual actuation of a spline in animation software propagates a continuous movement of variation all along the curve). Even more challengingly, its actuations do not fit itself into a preexisting spatial or temporal ordering. As chapters 3, 4, and 7 argue, an operative logic extrudes its own spatiality and temporality. It is productive of the space-times of its own operativity. It is this power of spatiotemporal genesis that epitomizes operative logics' ontopower.

It is not the aim of this book to conduct a historical analysis, nor even to follow all of the accompanying infra-twists and turns of the operative logic of preemption from the Bush administration through the Obama administration. Its aim is more modest (but still exacting): to diagnose the tendencies of the present field of life, in their overall lines, but at precise splines. Occasional indications of the lines from Bush through Obama are included, most often in endnotes. Chapter 2 discusses the historical/transhistorical complexity of the field of preemptive power in terms of an "ecology of powers." Chapters 6 and 7 present some of its media-borne convolutions on the U.S. home front.

Chapter 2 tackles the question of how the operative logic of preemption cohabits the field of power that is coextensive with the field of life, and with what other operative logics. A crucial distinction not foregrounded elsewhere in this afterword is broached: between *process* and system. Each system has its own logic. But systems logics are combinatorics of function and/or meaning. The operative logic of processes is of the singularity of events under varying repetition. They are predicated not on combinatorics but on "mutual inclusion," in immanence and working-out; not on arrangement, but on potential for relation coming to actual expression. Systems are powerful. Processes are ontopowerful. Systems desire the reproduction of their constituted apparatus, if not in all its specifics, at least in its general form. Processes will the carrying of their constitutive tendency to higher and higher degrees of intensity, accepting, in the name of the augmentation of their ontopower, to become, even to become wholly other. Processes mobilize a singular force of becoming, without content. Systems cling to general forms of functioning and meaning, and the reproduction of the contents they construct. Systems strive to hold variation within the general parameters of their constituted forms. A system, of course, is not unconnected to process. In fact, a system is an expression of a process. It is an actual expression of an operative processual logic, as concretized in a historically specific apparatus.

The system-process distinction is crucial because it is in the interplay between systems (as concretized in actual formations) and process (as the immanent motor of history, in-forming and overspilling every such concretization) that the relation between philosophy as the history of the present and the fabled histories of the long duration is negotiated. It is the interplay between system and process that forms the hinge (itself processual!) between empirically existing historical formations and the superempirical more-than-being of transhistorical becoming.

Chapter 2 considers the only other operative logic that rivals the processual reach and virulence of the operative logic of preemption: capitalism. The problematic node for *neoliberal* capitalism specifically has a short-hand formula: "corporations are people too." This operatively logical (if illogical in every other way) conceptual formula has been validated in the United States in two Supreme Court decisions.[9] Its longer, once again threefold, formulation goes as follows: corporations are people too; corporations have rights; their rights are guaranteed by the free market, as are the rights of people.[10] The first part-concept posits "human capital" as the privileged part-subject expressing the neoliberal process's subjectivity without a subject. Part-concepts two (corporate rights) and three (free market) combine with part-concept one to pose the problem of the individual actor. This is the problem of the operative logic of neoliberalism, despite its rhetoric of individualism and free choice: what agency is left for the individual subject of action when its field of life, coterminus with the market, has the right to be corporately self-organizing, free of the encumbrance of meddling by actors possessed of countervailing tendencies. The problem, in a word, is the question of freedom. Its cases of solution are provisional resolutions of the constitutive tension arising from the difference that neoliberalism's formula strives to suppress: that between the freedom of the market, as enjoyed by corporate persons, and the freedom of choice reserved for people persons (on all of these points, and on the inadequacy of the neoliberal notions of freedom, choice, and the economic actor even for describing neoliberalism's own operations, see Massumi 2015a).

The capitalist process operates in the same threat-environment as the process of preemption. It approaches it, however, from a different angle. It is dedicated to the production and accumulation of *quantitative* surplus-value. It also attends to the not-yet-fully emerged, but in order to channel into market mechanisms that leverage emergence for the production of monetized value. Like preemption, neoliberal capitalism operates as an ontopower: it brings to be what its apparatus captures. It is a power of becoming leveraging the field of emergence of life.

In this chapter, the process of preemption is labeled, for reasons of historical convenience, the *neoconservative* process. Both the warlike neoconservative process and the neoliberal capitalist process ply the same field of emergence. But as operative logics, they do so with a tendential autonomy that requires their operative logical differences to be respected. It is too simple to say, for example, that the apparatus of war is in the service of capitalist imperialism. In certain ways, historically, there is no doubt that it is. But to be content with that connection is to remain on the systemic level, and attribute a hegemony to a general form of functioning: that of capital, subsuming war. The concept of hegemony is always too general, and therefore insufficiently processual. Processually, neoliberalism and neoconservatism interlace and enter into a singular symbiosis. But what their respective operative logics will is only themselves, only their own governing tendency. This means that their symbiosis is an adventitious outgrowth of their cohabiting the same field of emergence. In other words, it is a processual marriage of convenience. There is no destiny in the historical expression of processes. It is always possible that capitalism and war, neoliberalism and neoconservatism, uncouple. It is always possible that there is an event-series in potential following which one may wane as the other waxes at its expense (as some elements of the Christian right as well as many libertarian circles in the United States would like to see). But for the present, these two processes are in tight processual embrace, in a mutually reinforcing way.

In order to grasp this co-operation, it is helpful to situate this ontopowerful couplet of neoliberalism and neoconservatism in the wider ecology of modes of power (each of which encapsulates an operative logic but strikes a different balance between systemic reproduction and processual becoming). Chapter 2 goes about this task of understanding complexion of the ecological field of power by adopting and adapting Michel Foucault's typology: sovereign power, disciplinary power, and biopower (pastoral power is neglected for reasons of expository succinctness). The argument is that ontopower is more processually intense and far-reaching than any of these modes. This is true of both species of ontopower, neoliberal and neoconservative—and all the more so of the processual couple of their mutual preemptive embrace. In particular, it is argued that ontopower is conceptually distinct from biopower, and that it processually encompasses it, along with its companion modes of power. For modes of power, to the extent that they are effectively powered by an operative logic, know not how to die. They only know how to tend—that is to say, to return, under variation, in new spacings and timings of their actual expressions, at different degrees of intensity. Ontopower exceeds and encompasses the other modes, even biopower. In Foucauldian terms, ontopower is the coming into its own of the "environmental" mode of power whose emergence Foucault passingly hypothesizes in *The Birth of Biopolitics* (Foucault 2008, 271). This mode of power is closely akin to what Deleuze termed "control" (Massumi 2015a). In the ecology of powers it characterizes overall, environmental control (the power to modulate emergence immanently to the field of life) contracts a special symbiotic relationship with sovereign power, resurgent. This takes the form of sinkholes of exception (Agamben 2005) dropped into the environmental fabric: extralegal escape hatches for the arbitrary exercise of war powers, of the kind described above in the note on ObamaBush.

Chapter 3 is the opening sally in an extended exploration, which continues across chapters 4 and 5, of the history of the present of the theory and practice of war, as in-formed by the thinking of process. Chapter 3 focuses on the time implications of the logic of preemption. In order to flush out the not-yet-fully-emerged into a taking-determinate-form that enables its threat to be preempted, it is necessary not only to perceive potential, but to perceive it before the enemy perceives your perceiving it—or even perceives itself on the verge of an event. A perceptual arms race ensues. The ontopower mobilized by the apparatus of war is under intense pressure, exerted by its own operative logic, to telescope into an interval smaller than the smallest perceivable, and to leverage battle-ready surplus-value of perception from it. This surplus-value immediately folds back into the processual field in the form of rapid attack, operationalizing the fractions-of-a-second scale of the incipiency of perception as its own "readiness potential." This operationalization means that as perception telescopes into the interval of events' not-yet-taking-place, action reciprocally telescopes into perception: action-perception. The activation of action-perception occurs in the vanishingly short interval of a coming experience's incipiency. It strikes too fast for conscious cognition: it strikes the *body*. The body must be reconceptualized as the crucible of potentiating action-perception. It must be understood as constitutively open to the cutting into the interval of leading edges of preemptive power. It must be a mode of perpetual readiness potential for the unperceivable onset of action-perception. Although unperceivable, the incipience of action-perception is promptable, and its unfolding modulatable. This concept of the body, presupposed by today's theory and practice of war, is here termed *bare activity*. The concept of bare activity regularly returns throughout the book, developed in different chapters from different angles. It is the animated (immanently activated), problematically agitated ("inner-vated") body.

All of this raises the issue of nonconscious perception and the way in which it can be prompted and modulated so as to orient, if not completely determine, a dynamic taking-form. Chapter 3 introduces pertinent concepts from the experimental psychology of nonconscious perception, most prominently that of *priming*. The chapter studies the leveraging of nonconscious perception into warlike action-perception, through central texts in war theory belonging to the "Revolution in Military Affairs" current that in-formed U.S. military strategy of the early twenty-first century, as well as through on-the-ground events in the Iraq War. The discussion of military strategy in this chapter revolves around an interpretation of the infamous "shock and awe" doctrine in perceptual-processual terms. Philosophically, a central assertion is that the perceptual time-pressure exerted by the operative logic of preemption makes the theory and practice of war directly epistemological, even downright metaphysical. However, the epistemology is suffused in an ontology, and the ontology, concerning as it does emergence, or the coming-to-be in a determinate form, is an *ontogenetics* (a metaphysics of becoming). The approach to epistemology, given this telescoping into ontogenetic action-perception, has to remain steadfastly non-cognitive. The leveraging of nonconscious perception to produce a surplus-value of attack must be distinguished from the older model of "subliminal influence." Subliminal influence is still a cognitive concept. It rests on the idea that a meaningful content is subconsciously communicated. In priming, the meaning and content come after, in effect. And the model is not one of communication to pass a message, but of activation for producing something that has never come to pass before—a novel modulation.

Chapter 4 is by far the longest in the book. Its project is to evaluate the tendency animating present-day warfare. As explained earlier in this chapter, the evaluation of a tendency bears on its limits. The immanent limit of operative logic of preemption was at stake in chapters 1–3 and continues centrally to be developed throughout the book. But what of its ulterior limit? Military theory of the late 1990s and 2000s designates the virtual attractor of preemptive war. This ideal limit, which co-operates in animating and orienting preemptive action-perception, is explicitly posited in the discourse of "network-centric war." *Self-synchronization* is its name. Self-synchronization is when information is so rapidly and effectively distributed throughout "battlespace," or the unbounded processual field of asymmetric war, that even the lowest level "battlespace entities" are empowered to decide autonomously, in the interval. This distribution of decision at the most immediate level of action-perception makes the apparatus of war maximally self-organizing. The impossible ideal of self-synchronization is reached when the machinery of war becomes so instantaneously self-organizing that the military hierarchy becomes the functional equivalent of a purely horizontal organization. In other words, information is so quickly transduced throughout the military apparatus into action-perception that the differential between the hierarchy and ground-level battlespace entities (which are sometimes soldiers, but increasingly often nonhuman) diffuses into the network.

Suggestively, the military theory texts never speak of this in terms of a transparency of information, or a striving for complete information. Quite the contrary, the entire enterprise is predicated on the conviction that in a complex threat-environment information is by nature incomplete. The "fog of war" cannot be overcome. It is an epistemo-ontological given. The challenge, then, is to operationalize lack of information. This is done by ensuring that what little information there is is instantaneously transformed into action-perception. Information becomes "pointy." It becomes a weapon, directly and unmediatedly, despite its incompleteness. It becomes the cutting edge of preemptive power, striking at the bare-active heart of the becoming of war. The unrectifiable incompleteness of information is compensated for by its pointedness: the speed of the transduction of information into action-perception, which enables the rapid generation of series of interventions whose power curve is self-correcting, as a function of the war machine's network-centric self-organizing capabilities.

After establishing the non-cognitive nature of the project, chapter 4 moves step by step through how a military abstractly builds itself a self-synchronizing body of bare activity. This is done through a close reading of central military texts. As an assist, the concept of nonconscious priming is further developed at length, centering on the role of *cueing*. Extensive excursions into the philosophy of perception and the philosophy of time are made to cue in to self-synchronization in its movement to the limit.

Chapter 5. The becoming effectively metaphysical of war, and the correlative becoming warlike of power across the full spectrum in response to the ubiquity of the threat-environment, make a philosophical take on history absolutely necessary for the understanding of what is afoot in the realm of power. Chapter 5 undertakes a brief meditation returning to the main topics of the first part of this chapter: the difference between historiography and the philosophy of history. This tension, as explained earlier, bears on the processual reality of tendency, as an abstract force of history. Chapter 5 discusses the problem of the mixity of actually existing empirical formations, and the resulting need to conceptually evaluate the polyphony of tendential forces at whose crossroads each formation is located. This involves assessing which tendency is most intensely in-forming a given formation's functioning. This distillation of singular transhistorical tendencies from their historical in-mixing with other tendencies, and with other orders (of function, of meaning), requires an evaluation of the ideal end points co-animating and orienting them. The chapter drafts William James's concept of the processual *terminus*, a key element of his radical empiricism, into service toward this end.

Chapter 6 moves to the "home front" of the "war on terror." It discusses the terror color-alert system set in place by the Bush administration as an exercise in media-based priming of the population for asymmetric war across the spectrum. The color-alert system made the not-yet of threat present, in the form of *fear*. The thesis of the chapter can be summed up in the formula: threat is the prospect of fear; fear is the project of threat. In other words, operating in an all-encompassing threat-environment does not mean reducing insecurity. That is as impossible as filling the lack of information. It means producing it. The production of insecurity registers in fear. The production of fear is not a political negative. It is a prime opportunity to modulate the unfolding of bare activity into action-perception.

Here, bare activity is infused with the affective tonality of fear in a way that orients people's responses to the bare-active fact that they have no choice but to participate in the acting-out of insecurity. Priming by fear-producing threat-cues does not ensure a unanimity in response. People's reactions vary enormously, depending on any number of individual and situational factors. The success is at best statistical (and according to the statistics, it worked—in the first years of the alert system's operation, Bush's approval rating rose an average of 2.75 percent after each increase in the threat-level; Willer 2004). Priming cannot, of itself, linearly determine a result. It is a quasi-causal mode of intervention. It cannot create uniformity of response. But what it can do is transport people together into a new field—an affective landscape to whose dominant tonality, namely fear, everyone without exception is in some way attuned. What it can do is catalyze an *affective attunement*. The attunement is differential, given the variability of response, but it is universal in its bracing the population for what may (or may not) come. It is immaterial whether what may come does come. A threat that does not take place—that does not eventuate as an actual danger—still carries this quasi-causal power of inducing a *collective individuation*. For that is exactly what the differential bracing of all into the singular universality of an emergent affective attunement is: the complexly correlated individuation of an entire population. In the heat of a collective individuation, the individual lives itself as a part-subject. The collective here—"collective" in its truly processual meaning—is not an aggregate of individuals. It is a singularly multiple subjectivity without a subject, expressing itself through part-subjects in a synchrony of correlated becomings-different, from each other and from what each had been.

Chapter 6 dedicates a substantial amount of time to charting how the quasi-causal power of fear as the project of threat takes on more and more autonomy as a self-deciding subjectivity-without-a-subject of becoming. Fear-production is one of the main avenues by which the operative logic of preemption becomes more intensely self-conducting, driving itself to higher and higher degrees of ontopower. The highest power of self-causation is reached when an operative logic gets to the point that it can forgo to the greatest extent possible the assistance of reproductive apparatuses and assumes the power to enact itself, purely formulaically (that is to say purely abstractly, hinging only on a "thought-sign"). This point is reached when fear catches its own tail to become a self-performing "fear of fear itself."

Chapter 7 further explores the operative-logical process of enactive self-causation. Its analyses delve into the way in which the prospect of threat produces self-validating *affective facts*. The processual logic of preemption implies a singular kind of logic, in the normal sense of the word: a conditional logic. This makes perfect sense: quasi-causality is nothing other than a form of conditioning (see also chapter 3 on conditioning versus classical causality). The quasi-causal efficiency of priming, and other leading edges of ontopower, are not linearly causal, and are not completely determining of its effects. Neither is there the proportionality between cause and effect that is demanded of classical linear causes. In a linear causality, there should be no excess of effect over the input of causal force: no leveraging of effects. But that is exactly what ontopower is all about. Ontopower does not cause in any traditional sense. It conditions. It reconditions the field of emergence, in order to modulate and orient what becomingly unfolds from it. The conditional logic that the operative onto-logic of preemption brings to the fore can be summed up in the formula: "could have, would have, just as good as was." In other words, even if a threat did not eventuate into an actual danger, it always could have, so preemptive action will always have been right. This is a tautological logic, but one that does not self-destruct. Instead, in produces: affective facts.

The production of affective facts rests on the ambiguous empirical status of threat: threats may be "real" (i.e., correspond to an actual danger), or they may be *felt* into existence. If I am afraid, I felt a threat. It is immaterial whether it was present or not. Threat, in any case, comes from the future. It doesn't present itself. Danger presents itself. Threat looms. And its looming casts a shadow in the present in the form of fear. So if I have felt fear, it is because the futurity of threat made itself felt. Once a futurity, always a futurity: the threat always *could have* eventuated. That's the affective fact of the matter. It makes whatever actions that were taken to ward off the threat legitimate and justified. That the danger did not present itself is proof that the threat is *still* there. Bush: I was right to invade Iraq, because Saddam Hussein could have had weapons of mass destruction, and if he had, he would have used them. The "would have" used them is, of course, the Achilles' heel of this conditional logic. It asserts an empirical fact about the state of mind of an actual individual—when in affective fact, it is all about the radically empirical reality of the abstract, quasi-causal force of futurity.

This conditional logic is an odd bird. It creates a feedback loop between futurity and pastness: could have, would have . . . was a fact. This time-loop is a characteristic of the operative logic of preemption, and wherever it is found, preemptive ontopower is also found. This is even the case of popular culture, especially where it co-operates with notions of community and national origins. The film director Steven Spielberg performed a classic production of a nationalistic affective fact. Speaking of the American kitsch-community painter Norman Rockwell, he cooed: "I look back at these paintings as America the way it could have been, the way someday it may again be" (Gopnik 2010). What a loop! He looks back to the paintings as they exist in the present and sees the future America was because it could have been. Unspoken affectively factual conclusion: everything America has ever done is a priori right. Greatest country on earth. Et cetera. This time-recursive production of rightness is endemic to the fables of history aimed at producing the "right" national origins. National origins (all origins) are by nature ontopowerfully loopy. Popular culture is full of the loopiness, which is shored up, for those with long-duration attention spans, by many strains of traditional historiography. It is the loopiness of the play of origins, seen here in pop-culture form, that makes conceptual formulae like "of-by-for the people" operative logics by giving them the force of productive paradox. The loopiness is not necessarily reflected in the semantics of the formulation, as it is in Spielberg's phrase. It can also be effected as an implicit presupposition activated by the performative conditions of the formula's utterance that in-forms the conceptual formula's in-forming of its carry-on expressions (as was the case with Lincoln's Gettysburg Address formula).[11]

As discussed in chapter 2, the logic of preemption is also processually active in the modus operandi of neoliberal capitalism. It edges into popular culture through marketing. Steve Goodman (2010) develops a convincing preemptive analysis of the logo and branding. "A product does not necessarily preexist the contact between brand and consumer. Rather, the contact in terms of the viro-sonic production of allure [i.e, priming by such mechanisms as advertising jingles] serves to produce memories of

contact with products that do not yet exist. When capital becomes speculative in this way, it forces critical analysis onto the same speculative terrain" (145). "Brands close in on you from the future" (146).

The operative logic of preemption and its signature production of affective facts is endemic to the present-day field of the emergence of life,
in multiple and proliferating forms. When the world becomes speculative
in this way, the history of the present is forced onto the same speculative
terrain.

## Counter-Power

How will one hide from that which never sets?
—Heraclitus (1981, CXXII, 83)

The necessary becoming-speculative of the analysis of power creates enormous challenges for any potential political response to neoliberalism,
neoconservativism, and the many other avatars of ontopower afield in the
world. It can be maintained that the operative logic analyzed in this book
is not limited to these formations. It can be argued that it is the core logic
of power as such, and that what this book is diagnosing is simply the coming into its own of power's productively preemptive, world-emergent conditioning nature, ever rising. This is certainly consonant with Nietzsche's
understanding of power: "at any precise moment of a force, the absolute
conditionality of a new distribution of all its forces is given: it never stands
still" (Nietzsche 1968, 547). This leaves the traditionally logical thought of
history and rational calculation as to how to respond to its seemingly in-
exorable course off balance, if not off their hinges. "No reason, internal to
history, can be assigned why that flux of forms, rather than another flux,
should have been illustrated" (Whitehead 1968, 90). How do you hide from
that which not only never sets but never rests—the perpetual conditional
futurity in the present? How do you act politically under such conditioning, in the absence of any reasonable assurance that the quantum of causal
force you apply will bring expected results in any linear fashion?

The problem is there is no place to hide. Ontopowers of perception
never rest in their recurring to the bare-active interval of each moment's
arising. The challenge is enormous because this field of emergence, which

has become a full-spectrum battlespace for preemptive power—which never sets because a spectrum has no horizon, only passages to the limit—is precisely the terrain to which radical forms of political resistance have turned to hatch their own emergent counter-powers. Much of the vocabulary this book has found it necessary to use toward understanding the processes of power it is dealing with are familiar to the post-1968 radical left, up to and including the antiglobalization movements of the turn of the millennium and such movements as Occupy and the Indignados, among others, of the early 2010s: the demanding of the "impossible"; elegies to immediacies of potential and the invention of possibility; the strange time of the future-past corresponding to this self-fast-forwarding retroactive invention of possibility; the praise of continual variation and change; the project of self-organizing collective individuation; the refusal of representative forms of democracy and political mediation in general, in favor of enactive or performative modes of intervention with a creative edge; the shift away from ideological analysis and programmatic politics demanding unity of action on the level of practice, and on the level of ideas mediating that action through demands for a uniformity of adhesion, toward modes of direct action fostering a concertation of differences on all levels. Instead of sheltering emergent counter-powers from the dominant power structure (which is not in fact a structure, or a system, but a process), all of this places their movements in the oddest of convergences with the powers that be (or more accurately, the powers that become, and make-become). Some commentators have taken this as a sign of the archaism and obsolescence of these paradigms. This is not the conclusion to which this book is meant to point. Because there is no place to hide, there is no going back. There is only the option of going forward, with the flow—inflecting the current on the fly toward a different terminus.

The "absolute conditionality" of power and the fact that there is no reason internal to history is something to rejoice about. That there is no reason internal to history for the flux of forms means that there is also "no reason why there could be no alternative flux" (Whitehead 1968, 90). "Could be." Could be, would be . . . no noncontingent reason why it wasn't. What the antiwar, anticapitalist left needs is not to discard the modes of action-perception that have characterized its enactive history of the present for a few short decades. It needs to hone them. It needs to continue to engage the battle on the only terrain there is: becoming. It needs to become more and more ontopowerful, under the quasi-causal influence of effective tendencies governed by virtual attractors of its own inventing. It needs to inflect its ontopowerfulness toward forms of surplus-value of *life living*[12] that refuse capitalism's quantifying capture of their excess of animation, as well as refusing forms of still qualitative surplus-value that brand one with the role of human capital, or fuel the apparatus of war, or reproduce popular notions of fabled community and nation that make dangerous kitsch of collective individuation. Engaging on this terrain necessarily involves engaging in a politics of affect—even to the point of practicing a counter-politics of the production of affective facts, of another color.

"No fact of history, personal or social, is understood until we know what it has escaped and the narrowness of the escape" (Whitehead 1968, 89–90). For every "could have, would have . . . was" of the dominant processing of ontopower, there is a "could have, would have . . . no reason why it wasn't" of an alternative unfolding into and across history: a narrowly missed escape. What shakes out to have been the dominant tendency has narrowly escaped veering into a countertendency at every turn. Correspondingly, the part-subjects of the potential countertendency have narrowly missed their exit from the dominant tendency's barreling on. The left needs to hit its escape stride—but inventively. Escape is not a negation: it is an alternative affirmation of the world's potential, spilling out from its bare-active overfullness with forms of life not yet fully emerged. Escape is untimely. That is to say:

> acting counter to our time and thereby acting on our time and, let us hope, for the benefit of a time to come (Nietzsche 1983, 60).[13]

# NOTES

## 1. The Primacy of Preemption

Chapter 1 originally appeared as "Potential Politics and the Primacy of Perception," *Theory and Event* 10, no. 2 (2007). Republished with permission.

1. Enshrined in the Bush administration's National Security Strategy of the United States issued September 17, 2002 (United States Government, 2002).

2. The change in tactics, announced in Bush's January 2007 State of the Union address, came in the form of the "surge" in U.S. troop numbers in Iraq beginning the next month.

3. It has been politically necessary for Obama to distance himself from the Bush administration at certain conjunctures. Obama's distancing from Bush administration vocabulary has not been consistent. The Obama administration's vocabulary fluctuates according to the political expediency of the moment, but is always poised to re-Bushify, as this 2014 news report of comments by Obama's attorney general exemplifies: "Attorney General Eric H. Holder Jr. on Tuesday implored more European countries to adopt American-style counterterrorism laws and tactics, including undercover stings to prevent potential terrorists from traveling to Syria. . . . Mr. Holder applauded Norway and France for recently adopting laws criminalizing the intent to commit terrorism. . . . 'In the face of a threat so grave, we cannot afford to be passive,' Mr. Holder said in prepared remarks. 'Rather, we need the benefit of investigative and prosecutorial tools that allow us to be pre-emptive in our approach to confronting this problem" (Apuzzo 2014).

4. "Given the goals of rogue states and terrorists, the United States can no longer solely rely on a reactive posture as we have in the past. The inability to deter a potential attacker, the immediacy of today's threats, and the magnitude of potential harm that could be caused by our adversaries' choice of weapons, do not permit that option. We cannot let our enemies strike first" (Bush 2002).

5. This is reflected in General Stanley McChrystal's reflections on his role as head of the U.S. Joint Special Operations Command under Bush and commander of NATO operations in Afghanistan under Obama: "When the counterterrorist effort against al Qaeda started, it was narrowly focused and centralized; you only did occasional operations with a high degree of intelligence and a tremendous amount of secrecy. That worked well for the pre-9/11 environment, but in the post-9/11 environment— particularly the post–March 2003 environment in Iraq—the breadth of al Qaeda and

associated movements exploded. *This gave us an enemy network* that you couldn't just react to but actually had to dismantle. It also gave us a very complex battlefield—not just terrorism but also social problems, an insurgency, and sectarian violence. So the first thing we did when I took over in late 2003 was realize that we needed to understand the problem much better. To do that, *we had to become a network ourselves*—to be connected across all parts of the battlefield, so that every time something occurred and we gathered intelligence or experience from it, information flowed very, very quickly" (McChrystal 2013). On "network-centric war" and the role of information, see chapter 4.

6. Donald Rumsfeld (2002b): "Our challenge in this new century is a difficult one: to defend our nation against the unknown, the uncertain, the unseen, and the unexpected. . . . We must put aside comfortable ways of thinking and planning . . . so we can deter and defeat adversaries that have not yet emerged to challenge us" (23) even though "they will likely challenge us asymmetrically" (23). Although he still uses the term "deterrence," it is clear by his comments on the Cold War that its old meaning has been entirely evacuated in favor of the new doctrine of preemption. Rumsfeld recommends lightening the military apparatus to enable "lightning strikes" and "shifting on the fly." This requires a reorientation on "capabilities-based" planning: "one that focuses less on who might threaten us, or where, and more on how we might be threatened" (24; for more on capabilities-based planning, see chapter 4). Since the enemy is by nature unspecified, the *manner* of the attack is all that can be planned for. What is important is the capability to respond with lightning speed and absolute tactical "shift ability" even before we know what hit us. This is a kind of *military mannerism* that closes the distance between being and knowing. Response capability is potentialized so that it is on a trip wire and acts immediately without waiting for analysis or understanding. It is based on actuatable *know-how* rather than a reflective and empirical *knowing-that*. This kind of knowledge is fundamentally *affective* rather than cognitive per se: "capability-based" means based on the ability to be affected in such a way as to transduce the affection directly into action. Perceptually, in this affective mode *detection* is primary in relation to *perception*. Detection is the bare registering of a presence (actually, not necessarily yet a presence, only a *movement*). Perception involves a recognition of the who or what of it: an identity subsuming and explaining the movement. Detection is non-identitarian, and even *preindividual*, since the base determination is of the manner of the threat and not of the threat in all its specificity. In the preemptive regime, perception always begins in detection and is operationally subordinated to it.

7. "The military seeks to reorganize in a way that is influenced by the organization of a guerrilla network. This act of mimicry is based on the assumption, articulated by military theorists John Arquilla and David Ronfeldt, that 'it takes a network to combat a network'" (Weizman 2006, 64).

8. In the words of Donald Rumsfeld: "Defending against terrorism and other emerging threats requires that we take the war to the enemy. The best—and, in some cases, the only—defense is a good offense" (Rumsfeld 2002b, 31).

9. Bush to Rumsfeld, September 26, 2001: "Look, our strategy is to create chaos, create a vacuum, to get the bad guys moving. We get 'em moving, we can see them, we can hit them" (Woodward 2002, 153).

10. For more on the would have/could have and the political conditional, see chapter 7.

11. See note 9 above.

12. For more on the politics of fear, see chapter 6.

13. Bush: "I'm not a textbook player. I'm a gut player" (Woodward 2002, 137). Bush often made reference to operating on "gut instinct" and was widely quoted to that effect in the press during his presidency.

14. "The aide said that guys like me were 'in what we call the reality-based community,' which he defined as people who 'believe that solutions emerge from your judicious study of discernible reality.' I nodded and murmured something about enlightenment principles and empiricism. He cut me off. 'That's not the way the world really works anymore,' he continued. 'We're an empire now, and when we act, we create our own reality. And while you're studying that reality—judiciously, as you will—we'll act again, creating other new realities, which you can study too, and that's how things will sort out. We're history's actors . . . and you, all of you, will be left to just study what we do' " (Suskind 2004).

15. For more on affective politics and virtual causality, see chapters 6 and 7.

16. The conditions of operative closure in which deterrence functions qualify it as an *autopoietic* system by Humberto Maturana and Francisco Varela's definition. Preemption's conditions of openness mean that it does not fit the definition. Both deterrence and preemption are ontogenetic, in the sense of being self-producing, or actively producing the elements that compose them. Deterrence keeps what it produces in the closed loop (a circular arms race). Preemption, however, actively incites an *otherness* to itself to emerge. It self-produces by producing its own alterity: its logic needs the otherness of the terrorist in order to legitimate itself affectively and in order to self-actuate. Otherness is immanent to its logic, whereas deterrence is self-referential and needs only its own criterion of mutuality to legitimate and actuate. Since preemption is an open ontogenetic system productive of otherness, it is what Félix Guattari would call a *heterogenetic* system rather than an autopoietic system strictly speaking (Guattari 1995, 33–42).

17. The Bush administration asserted a radical interpretation of the Unitary Executive Theory that gave the president virtually unlimited discretionary power in his role as commander in chief, up to and including torture (Calabresi and Yoo 2008, 410–411). In accordance with this interpretation, it passed two major legislative measures enshrining powers of exception. First, the Military Commissions Act of 2006 codified the status "unlawful enemy combatant" and the president's discretion to apply it. The same legislation created a system of military courts for enemy combatants in which the constitutional right to due process was suspended (including habeas corpus and provisions against hearsay evidence and evidence obtained through torture). Second, amendments to the Insurrection Act of 1807

contained in the National Defense Authorization Act of 2006 overturned one of
the basic principles of the U.S. system of government: that the military could not
be called into action domestically against the civilian population. The radicality
of the Military Commissions Act was tempered by a 2008 Supreme Court decision
reinstating habeas corpus for enemy combatants as well as the right to a civilian
trial, but it has made little practical difference for the "enemy combatants" held at
secret black sites (see afterword) and more visibly at Guantánamo Bay, in the latter
case because of political opposition to transferring detainees from Guantánamo
to the mainland (which also made closing the facility a political impossibility
for Obama). The amendments to the Insurrection Act were repealed in toto in
2008. Despite these moderating measures, the general tendency toward the
encroachment of executive power into the domains of the judiciary and the military
has not been reversed. Pressures from the right to veer once again toward Bush-era
practices are frequently felt (for example, ongoing criticism of terrorism suspects
being tried in normal criminal courts, and calls to further militarize the policing
of the U.S.-Mexico border; Roberts 2014a). The possibility of exceptional measures
sinking escape hatches into the legal and juridical fabric of the U.S. government
is still very much in place, both formally and informally (again, see the afterword
for further discussion of this point). For example, congressional action can be
sidestepped by formal "signing statements." This is a practice used by Bush and
adopted (albeit used less frequently) by Obama (Tumulty 2014) in which the
president appends a statement to a legislative bill he is signing that asserts his
executive privilege to ignore certain of its provisions in the interests of national
security, as circumstances demand. In a more wildcat manner, the principle of
the unitary executive can be invoked at will as assertion of the president's role as
commander in chief of the armed forces. Once again, this was a prominent Bush
practice, but always with mitigating provisions (for example, a time-limit for the
intervention in the absence of post facto congressional approval). Obama took this
practice to the limit with his 2011 decision to bomb Libya, becoming the first U.S.
president to simply flat out ignore the War Powers Act (the fundamental legislation
regulating the balance of power between the executive branch and the legislature
which requires congressional approval for the use of military force; Greenfield 2011).

## 2. National Enterprise Emergency

Chapter 2 originally appeared in *Theory, Culture & Society*, no. 6 (2009): 153–185.
DOI: 10.1177/0263276409347696. Republished with permission.

1. Unless otherwise noted, all quotes in this section are from this presidential
address. For a description of the staging of the event, see Englehart (2005).

2. The Greek government's allegations of arson were criticized by conservation
groups and the opposition Socialist Party for want of empirical evidence.

3. For an analysis of the process by which a felt conditional possibility becomes a
tautological truism, see chapter 7.

4. This was later overturned by an act of Congress. See chapter 1, note 17. However, this retreat was compensated for by the continuing militarization of the police itself.

5. On processual isomorphism as an operative identity independent of structure, form, and content (and therefore not a homology), see Gilles Deleuze and Félix Guattari, "Apparatus of Capture," (1987, 424–473). In this chapter Deleuze and Guattari also provide a prescient theorization of full-spectrum war-in-peace, and of the convergence of the capitalist process and the war-powers process (discussed below).

6. Within hours of the news of swine flu, the Internet was buzzing with tens of thousands of posts speculating that it was a bioterrorist attack. The virus as terrorist agent made a comeback in 2014 with Ebola. The CNN expert analyst Dr. Alexander Garza called Ebola "the ISIS of biological agents." "If you think about Ebola as an agent that spreads throughout and kills innocent people, it's directly like ISIS, right? It infects people and it kills people, and so the response, if we're calling this a national security issue, needs to be equivalent to if this was a form of terrorism, meaning we have to attack the problem overseas, like we do with terrorism and like the president is doing, sending the military. But we also have to protect the homeland" (CNN 2014).

7. This point was forcefully advanced by Bruno Latour (1993): the emergent "actors" in today's world are nature-culture "hybrids." For present purposes, the notion of the hybrid carries the inconvenience of still presupposing as its starting point oppositional definitions of nature and culture, even if only to neutralize the opposition. The strategy that will be followed here (one which Latour would not endorse) is to redefine nature in a way that already includes the potential for "culture," making culture an emergent expression of nature.

8. This is in no way an argument against taking measures against global warming, or a belittling of the fundamental role of human activity in its triggering. Quite the opposite, it is an argument for taking radical measures toward a post-carbon economy constitutionally disinclined toward these kinds of global-environmental synergies. The only post-carbon economy that would meet that description would also be a postcapitalist economy, given that capitalism's process of self-valorization is predicated not only on perpetual growth but on perpetually accelerating growth, posited to be unlimited in principle. This makes capitalism constitutionally unsustainable.

9. In the vocabulary of the introduction, the singular-generic is the felt force of the singular-multiple as it irrupts from the untimely interval into the history that will register its determination to be determined in the emergence of a particular form.

10. On the logic of mutual inclusion, see Massumi (2014a, 6, 33–35, 45–47).

11. In What Animals Teach Us about Politics a distinction in made between the accident understood as a lack of determination, or pure contingency, and spontaneity. Spontaneity concerns mutual disjunctive inclusion in potential, moved

by a determination-to-be-determined (Massumi 2014a, 48–49). Here, the distinction is not insisted upon because the felt force of the accident in the contemporary threat environment oscillates between these figures of the accident, even though ontogenetically the determination-to-be-determined is primary. The accident as pure contingency is a perspective effect of a particular system faced with intrusions from the outside for which it lacks a workable understanding, and so must launch into action to produce one. See chapter 5, in particular note 13, for a further discussion of the accident and its relation to chaos.

12. Whitehead, for his part, does not bar God. He, does, however, define god as the "primordial accident" (1978, 7). Spinoza's *deus sive natura* holds God and Nature in inclusive disjunction. As discussed below, Deleuze and Guattari develop a similar notion of a "nature-culture continuum," but as a resolutely atheological proposition.

13. For an analysis that updates the Marxist theory of value to take into account the ways in which capitalism produces historically-specific natured natures immanent to its operation, how that production drives capitalism's process of accumulation, and how taking it into account requires an abandonment of the oppositions that have traditionally underpinned Marxist theory (human/nature, base/superstructure, and so on), see Jason W. Moore (2014a, 2014b). Moore's term for what is being called here natured nature is "abstract social nature."

14. For more on preemptive power and the force of time, see chapter 3. With respect to extensive distinctions and spatialization, the infamous theses of the "clash of civilizations" and the accompanying rhetoric of "culture wars" make an extensive distinction of cultural difference, enabling cultures to be grasped as territorialized entities, in spite of the premise of transnational globalism impelling this very theorization. This spatialization of culture presupposes a prior externalization of nature, figuring as a reserve of prospectable raw materials rather than of formative forces, and prioritizing the model of the passive deposit. This simply located, spatialized nature is passive before the industry of the human, whose own space is dynamically fragmented into opposing cultures. All formative force and conflict, all dynamism, falls to the side of the human. The spatialization of culture and correlative passification of nature is the signature trait of humanism in its many incarnations. Posthumanisms and antihumanisms strive to avoid this extensive dichotomization. However, those who assign the ascension to language as a limit between the human and the animal (such as those of Heidegger, Lacan, and Agamben, among others) are led to miss or misconstrue constitutive power, or what Deleuze calls the "real conditions of emergence" of individuations human, animal, and otherwise: the real, and really felt, impelling potential of incipient formative forces creatively agitating an intensive field disjunctively including nature and culture (in other words, folding their potential differentiations together in the same event, in a kind of occurrent continuum of any and all extensive distinctions they potentially unfold into on constituted levels of systemic organization; for an extended account of the nature-culture continuum from this perspective, see Massumi 2014a). Deleuze's "virtual" (on the edge of actualization),

Whitehead's "real potential," and Gilbert Simondon's "associated milieu" are ways of conceptualizing the real conditions of emergence of constitutive power (ontopower).

15. This distinction corresponds to Guattari's distinction in *Chaosmosis* between autopoietic systems as conceived by Varela and Maturana and heteropoietic process or "machinic heterogenesis" (1995, 33–57). See chapter 1, note 16.

16. On process as nature and nature as process, see Deleuze and Guattari: nature lived "not as nature but as a process of production" (1983, 2–5 and passim). The account of system in this chapter is loosely based on the work of Niklas Luhmann, with major deviations pertaining to the principle of "operational closure."

17. It should be borne in mind that the sense in which the term "bare activity" is used here is in close dialogue with the work of Whitehead, it does not correspond to his own usage of the term. In fact, he uses it in an opposite sense, to designate the Newtonian notion that activity consists of extensive displacement occurring mechanically in a pregiven spatial frame at a durationless present point. See Whitehead 1968 (145–146). Here, the term "bare" is repurposed to construct a concept that functions as a counterweight to Agamben's "bare life." This usage accords with that of James: "Now it is obvious that we are tempted to affirm activity wherever we find anything *going on*. Taken in the broadest sense, any apprehension of something *doing*, is an experience of activity. Were our world describable only by the words 'nothing happening,' 'nothing changing,' 'nothing doing,' we should unquestionably call it an 'inactive' world. Bare activity then, as we may call it, means the bare fact of event or change. 'Change taking place' is a unique content of experience, one of those 'conjunctive' objects which radical empiricism seeks so earnestly to rehabilitate and preserve. The sense of activity is thus in the broadest and vaguest way synonymous with the sense of 'life'. . . . We are only as we are active" (James 1996a, 161).

18. My use of "undifferentiation" follows the French translation. It is "indistinction" in the English translation.

19. For more on these points in relation to Agamben, including comments on Agamben's book on the animal (2003), see Massumi (2014a, 67–68, 111n60, 115n5).

20. For an extended concept of animality as part of an incorporeal materialism, see Massumi (2014a).

21. This extended, in the years following Katrina, to privatizing the entire New Orleans public school system (Layton 2014).

22. For a detailed account of Bremer's decrees, see Juhasz (2006, 185–260). For a history of the IMF's model of neoliberalism and its imposition on developing nations, see Klein (2008). The neoliberal model extends to the prosecution of war itself, with outsourcing of military operations a ubiquitous feature of the U.S. practice of present-day warfare.

23. Foucault's theory of disciplinary power is developed throughout *Discipline and Punish: Birth of the Prison* (1977a). Foucault returns to the topic in relation to sovereignty and biopower in *"Society Must Be Defended"* (2003).

24. On governmentality as "transactional," see Foucault (2008, 12–13, 297).

25. Foucault defines raison d'état as a twofold limitation on the arbitrariness of sovereign power. On the one hand: the transcendent limitation of higher law: "the government of the state must obviously respect a number of principles and rules which are above or dominate the state and are external to it. The government of the state must respect divine, moral, and natural laws as laws which are not homogeneous with or intrinsic to the state" (Foucault 2008, 4). On the other hand: the becoming immanent of sovereign power to its own field of application in the form of security and regulative mechanisms, pertaining to the control and rationalization of circulation (policing) and of contractual relation (the legal-juridical apparatus), which create the conditions for the emergence of liberal governmentality as a mode of power in its own right (2008, 5–10). Liberal governmentality is animated by a tendency for immanent regulation to assert independence from the state (deregulation). This tendency toward state deregulation in the name of the self-regulation of the economic system, which has become synonymous with the environment of life, is taken to an extreme under neoliberalism. The process of deregulation, however, is never (and can never be) complete, due to the presence of countervailing tendencies in the ecological field of power. To what extent deregulation can be considered a counter-form of "rationality" to the reason of state, or whether a concept of "affectivity" is needed to grasp its dynamic, is a question that is taken up in Massumi (2015a).

26. For an excellent theorization of the interconnections between emergence, preemptive power, and neoliberal capitalism, see Melinda Cooper (2008).

27. The work of William E. Connolly (2008, 2013) is particularly attuned to the paradoxical symbiosis between renascent stability-seeking particularisms and self-organizing neoliberal expansionism.

## 3. Perception Attack

An abridged earlier version of chapter 3 appeared as "Perception Attack: Brief on War Time," in Theory and Event 13, no. 3 (2010).

1. Early in Obama's administration, the "war on terror" was replaced by the anodyne "overseas contingency operations," but the more fear-inducing phraseology of "terror" quickly returned (Alberts 2010; Obama 2010).

2. For the original research introducing the term attentional blink, see Raymond et al. (1992). For a summary of the research, see Shapiro et al. (2009).

3. For an overview of DARPA's "AugCog" program coauthored by a longtime director of the project (Dylan Schmorrow), see St. John et al. (2004). For a popular account of attentional blink in the context of DARPA, see Motluk (2007).

4. On the immeasurability of surplus-value, see Negri (1996, 151–154).

5. Cebrowski and Garstka's "Network-Centric Warfare—Its Origin and Future," from which this phrase is quoted, is a foundational text in the development of full-spectrum military doctrine, articulated as a shift from hardware-based "platform-

centric warfare" to capabilities-based "network-centric warfare." The dynamics of network-centric warfare is analyzed at length in chapter 4.

6. Cebrowski and Garstka also make the link: "The organizing principle of network-centric warfare has its antecedent in the dynamics of growth and competition that have emerged in the modern economy. The new dynamics of competition are based on increasing returns on investment, competition within and between ecosystems, and competition *based on time*" (1998, emphasis added). In many passages, the authors draw an equation between "competitor" and "enemy."

7. See chapter 2, "Discursus on Bare Life." On bare activity, see also Massumi (2011, 1–3, 10–11).

8. Cebrowski and Garstka speak of an integrated "warfighting ecosytem" (1998). Ulmann and Wade speak of the need to "control the environment" rather than win punctual engagements (1996, xxvii).

9. On posture in this sense, see Erin Manning (2009). See also Deleuze and Guattari (1986, 3–8).

10. It is a constant of full-spectrum-force military doctrine to motivate the need for new strategies by evoking the "dynamic and unstable" nature of the new economy as a complex system. War and the economy, it is then argued, are isomorphic. Both require what amounts to an ecological approach in order to find ways of managing the uncertainty inherent to complex systems. The three key texts most heavily drawn on here, including those by Ulman and Wade (1996), Cebrowski and Garstka (1998), Arquilla and Ronfeldt (2001), and (in chapter 4) Alberts and Hayes (2003), contextualize themselves in this manner (the quoted phrase is from Cebrowski and Garstka), as does the Revolution in Military Affairs current embraced by Donald Rumsfeld as U.S. secretary of defense during George W. Bush's first term (Rumsfeld 2002b). For a technical study of complexity theory and recent military strategy, see Moffat (2003).

11. It is here that the homology between war and economics signaled in the brief discussion of surplus-value above becomes dramatic. See Klein (2008).

12. In a more restricted technical sense, signature management refers to making weapons and equipment undetectable.

13. This has been the Israeli strategy in Gaza since its dismantling of Jewish settlements and withdrawal of ground forces in 2005. All ingress and egress, of goods and people, are controlled from the periphery and from the airspace above. Information is collected and controlled through the use of such means as satellite surveillance, informants, and Israeli control over the population registry and cell phone frequencies. This maintains in permanent readiness the conditions for a sudden shift to shock tactics and hard power, in the form of targeted assassinations, shelling, and ground incursions of various magnitudes. The occupation of Gaza never ended. It just changed modes.

14. Eyal Weizman (2007) has analyzed the Israeli military's conscious practices of battlespace creation using timing and movement techniques in the West Bank: "It was not the given order of space that governed patterns of movement, but movement

itself that produced space around it. . . . The tactics . . . involved a conception of the city as not just the site, but as the very *medium* of warfare—a flexible, almost liquid matter that is forever contingent and in flux (186). . . . War-fighting is no longer about the destruction of space, but rather is about its 'reorganization' " (218). Weizman describes in detail how the Israeli Defense Force strategy of military intervention functions to destructure and restructure the territory by means of a syncopated becoming-imperceptible that operationalizes time as the main battlespace factor, blurring the traditional distinctions between offense/defense and civilian/military.

15. In the context of this theorization, philosophically it would be more accurate to say "incorporeal" than "immaterial," with the incorporeal understood *as* a dimension of the body: the dimension of its potential. In potential, the body's felt force of existence exceeds its actuality, overspills its physical position in space, and outpaces the metric time of its physical movement. On this concept of the body (or more precisely, "bodying") in the framework of an incorporeal materialism, see Massumi (2002, 5–6; 2014a, 28–30, 53)

16. As an early theorist of full-spectrum war asks, what if one viewed war less as the application of physical force than "as the quest for metaphysical control" achieved through "non-fighting"? His answer: one would practice "neo-cortical warfare," which "attempts to penetrate the adversaries' recurring and simultaneous cycles of observation, orientation, decision and action" in order to "exercise reflexive influence, almost parasympathetic influence, over products of the adversary's neo-cortex." In a word, one would perfect the art of what is being called here the perception attack: hitting the enemy at the level at which he "processes and organizes visual and kinesthetic perceptions" (Szafranski 1994, 43, 47, 48). For a discussion of neo-cortical warfare in the context of the Revolution in Military Affairs, see Baxstrom et al. (2005).

17. For a journalistic account of the establishment by the Pentagon of "Human Terrain Teams" in response to the impasse in Iraq, see Shachtman (2007). Pendulum shifts to the "human terrain"/soft power end of the full spectrum are reflected in a vocabulary shift from "counterterrorism" operations to "counterinsurgency." A much ballyhooed shift of this kind was made in the U.S. *Army Field Manual No.* 3–24 issued in December 2006 in the face of the glaring failures of the counterterrorism operations following the invasion of Iraq (Sewell et al. 2007). President Obama's *National Security Strategy* (United States Government 2010) and *National Security Review* (Jaffe 2012) attempt a synthesis of counterinsurgency and counterterrorism, the latter recentered on rapid response with a minimum of "boots on the ground" rather than outright occupation.

18. On the superempirical, see Massumi (2002, 16, 58, 76–77, 152, 160). The concept of the superempirical is closely allied to Whitehead's concept of nonsensuous perception mentioned earlier (1967a, 180–183; Massumi 2014b).

19. Chapter 5 analyses this infra-relation in terms of Simondon's concept of collective individuation.

20. As Obama indirectly underlined in his speech marking the beginning of the end of the U.S. pullout from Afghanistan and the beginning of a new phase of more diffuse war when he mentioned the need in the future to strike the right balance between hard and soft power in order to avoid "stirring up resentments" (Obama 2014a).

## 4. Power to the Edge

1. "Control" should be read here in the sense Deleuze gives it in his "Postscript on Control Societies," as the immanent modulation of a field of emergence (Deleuze 1995, 177–182). See also Massumi 2015a.

2. Here, the theory of the performative is extended beyond the purview of Austin's original formulation to unconventional situations. It is used to refer to speech acts or gestures that catalyze, with no prior guarantee of success, an excess of eventful effect over what the conditions, conventionally considered, would be expected to yield. In this understanding, the performative coincides with Deleuze and Guattari's concept of "incorporeal transformation" (Deleuze and Guattari 1987, 80–85).

3. Sorry, Erin.

4. Recognition primed, naturalistic decision making: this is a reference to Gary Klein (1999), a consultant for that military and a representative of the cognitive-rationalist alternative to the kinds of approaches presented here.

5. James on the specious present: "The practically cognized present is no knife-edge, but a saddle-back, with a certain breadth of its own on which we sit perched, and from which we look in two directions into time. The unit of composition of our perception of time is a *duration*, with a bow and a stern, as it were—a rearward- and a forward-looking end. It is only as parts of this *duration-block* that the relation of *succession* of one end to the other is perceived. We do not first feel one end and then feel the other after it, and from the perception of the succession infer an interval of time between, but *we seem to feel the interval of time as a whole, with its two ends embedded in it* [emphasis added]. The experience is from the outset a synthetic datum, not a simple one; and to sensible perception its elements are inseparable, although attention *looking back* [emphasis added] may easily decompose the experience, and distinguish its beginning from its end" (James, 1950, 2:609–610).

This description applies to the consciously sensed present. What is being argued here is that there is a "knife-edge" to it: the unperceived, or unconsciously perceived cue. The cue is like an imperceptible cursor skip from one consciously lived "saddle-back" to another whose durations overlap.

6. The concept of commanding form is adapted from Susanne Langer's concept for the "matrix" of the musical theme (Langer 1953, 122–123, 131, 138), inflected by James's description of the "terminus" and Whitehead's account of the relation between past, present, and future in *Adventures of Ideas* (Whitehead 1967a, 191–200). As used here, the concept of commanding form is closely allied to Raymond Ruyer's concept of "priming theme" (*thème-amortisseur*; Ruyer 2012, 160).

7. On the associated milieu as the "dynamic ground in which schema [of action] confront each other and combine, and in which they participate," see Simondon (1989, 58; this passage is translated in the excerpt published in Brouwer and Mulder 2007, 208). The back-set primes composing the associated milieu are Whitehead's "welter of alternatives" (Whitehead 1978, 187) forming the "background" of every experience (Whitehead 1967a, 226, 260, 270).

8. Embodied cognition and enactive perception theories usually go no further than the level of implicit knowledge and as such content themselves with the preconscious, failing to develop tools to deal with the nonconscious incipience where action, perception, and dawning qualities of experience come together at a level at which modes of activity we separate out as bodily or mental are in complex co-animation, in an effective zone of indiscernibility. This strategic choice to ground experience in implicit knowledge functions to retain a thoroughly cognitivist paradigm. For one thing, implicit knowledge supposes an implicit subject of the knowing. For another, the purported form implicit knowledge takes ("schema") can be adequately described in the standard terms used to describe the function-oriented general ideas usually assumed to constitute conscious know-how (affordances provided by a particular type of context, suggesting sequences of actions usefully adapted to that context and executable in logical, stepwise fashion). Implicit knowledge is formally identical to conscious knowledge—just without the conscious attending, as Alva Noë makes explicit: "The presence of detail [in occluded parts of the visual field] consists not in its representation now in consciousness, but in our implicit knowledge now that we can represent it in consciousness if we want" (Noë 2004, 99). From the point of view of the present account, this amounts to a cognitivist/functionalist imperialism limiting the potential force of "embodied" and "enactivist" approaches. A further indication of this is the accompanying reduction of action to sensorimotor sequencing. Maxine Sheets-Johnstone critiques the concept of "embodiment" in embodied cognitions studies on similar grounds (2009a, 221; 2009b, 377, 394–395). She strenuously argues for the primacy, for an understanding of action, of the concept of animation over that of the sensorimotor. For an account of movement beyond the sensorimotor, see Manning and Massumi (2014, 37–48).

9. On the "retrograde movement of the truth," see Bergson 2007, 10–13: "The premonitory signs are therefore, in our eyes, signs only because we now know the course, because the course has been completed. Neither the course, nor its direction, nor in consequence, its end were given when these facts came into being; hence they were not yet signs" (13). In these passages, Bergson is critiquing the cognitive illusion that the possibility of an event preexists its unfolding, so that it is in a sense preformed rather than enactively emergent. In the present account, the prime or cue is a noncognized sign (an asignifying sign, or enactive signal) that catalyzes a field of potential for variable emergence. It can only be cognized through the retrograde movement of the truth that Bergson discusses. In cognition, the cue is retroactively translated into a signifying sign of a premonitory nature.

10. This is what Whitehead terms a negative prehension: "A negative prehension is the definite exclusion of [an] item from positive contribution to the subject's own real internal constitution. This doctrine involves the position that a negative prehension expresses a bond" (Whitehead 1978, 41).

11. On capabilities-based operations, see also Rumsfeld (2002b).

12. The process of "decision" described here can in fact be correlated to Bergson's theory of intuition, which occurs in a zone of indiscernibility between concept and perception, where these coincide with incipient action: "It is in concepts that the system develops; it is into images that it contracts when it is driven back to the intuition from which it descends" (Bergson 2007, 98).

13. The concept of mission capability packages was first introduced by David S. Alberts in "Mission Capability Packages" (Alberts 1995).

14. This is stretching the sense of affordance as given to the term by its inventor, James J. Gibson, for whom "the affordance of something does *not change* as the need of the observer changes. . . . Being invariant, it is always there to be perceived" (Gibson 1986, 138–139). Here, nothing (neither the affordance, nor the observer, nor the observer's need) is taken to be invariant. No factor is simply "always there." Everything is in continual variation, in the time-loop of the future-past as it cycles through bare activity.

15. On page 80, Guattari links the concept of complexion to that of "fusion" mentioned earlier.

16. This relates to Peirce's concepts of abduction and perceptual judgment mentioned in chapter 3 (Peirce 1997, 199–201; Peirce 1998, 155, 191–195, 204–211, 226–242; Massumi 2015a, 44–47).

17. Direct perception is a controversial concept embraced by Gibson's ecological theory of perception, embodied cognition, and enactive perception theory, but rejected by mainstream psychology and cognitive theory. Both of the latter posit a state of "raw" perception, consisting of the disorganized registering of sense-impressions. The sense-impressions are construed as "information," which is then "processed" and ordered upstream of its reception by the mediating operations of the brain. Mediation-based, information-processing models of perception typically uncritically embrace the metaphor of the brain as a computer (forgetting that in an earlier technological period, the brain was a telephone exchange, and before that a clockwork mechanism). Mediation-based theories of perception are hard-pressed not to fall into two mutually exclusive propositions, often at the same time: the implicit presupposition of a subject of the mediation, hovering somewhere behind the brain, to which the sense-impressions are presented (the "homunculus" problem); and the reduction of perceptual awareness, and consciousness in general, to an epiphenomenon entirely reducible to the physical operations of the brain's computerlike processing and having no reality of its own. Whitehead's metaphysics necessitates a doctrine of direct perception (Whitehead 1978, 116; Whitehead 1985, 30, 39–42). The theory of direct perception requires a toolbox of concepts, like those mobilized here, that are not information- and mediation-based: the bare-active

interval of perception, action-perception, thought in the act, fusion, commanding form, abduction/perceptual judgment, and so forth.

18. It has been experimentally verified that what are normally multistep mathematical operations can be performed instantaneously in the interval of perception (Sklar et al. 2012).

19. Erin Manning analyzes this proprioceptive in-bracing for self-differentiating unfolding "preacceleration" (Manning 2009, 5–7, 15–19). Proprioception is by nature nonconscious. The proprioceptors in the muscles and joints do not directly produce conscious feeling. Proprioception is felt only in its other-sense effects (as inhabiting the sense-modes of sight, touch, hearing, and smell, and in fusion with them, as explained below in the discussion of synchresis). For more on proprioception, see Massumi (2002, 58–61, 168–169, 174–186; 2011, 124–125).

20. This is analyzed in *Semblance and Event* (Massumi 2011) in terms of the "semblance."

21. Time as measure is a second-order development of prime time, produced by submitting different moments of prime time, each of which is absolutely, qualitatively singular in its own right, to a common standard of comparison (a periodic movement). Time as measure is invented by the technical apparatus of comparison. The measurement is a transduction of qualitative experience into quantity. On this process, see Bergson (2001, 104–106). For more on shock, affect, and the production of the space-time of life, see chapter 6.

22. Experiential event: or "actual entity," in Whitehead's terminology. Whitehead also emphasizes that the production of the extensive continuum in the standing-out of each event occurs in no-time: "There is a becoming of something with temporal [and spatial] extension; but the act itself is not extensive, in the sense that it is divisible into earlier and later acts of becoming which correspond to the extensive divisibility of what has become. . . . The creature is extensive, but . . . its act of becoming is not extensive" (Whitehead 1978, 69).

23. On nonsensuous perception see Whitehead (1967a, 180–183) and Massumi (2011, 17–18, 23–24, 109–110).

24. This full-spectrum analysis of the virtual ground of actual experience forbids theories that identify its generative field with one sense or another, such as theories that critique vision in the name of an originary tactility, under the auspices of the "haptic" (Marks 2002; Noë 2004, 73). There is always an interstitial proprioception that immanently effects the relay. It is imprecise to call the immanent relay between experiences in different sense modalities a modality in its own right. Because it is by nature nonconscious, it is itself *amodal*: not actually in any one modality of experience. The amodal is more akin to thought than to any particular modality of sensing. Whitehead and Benjamin analyze forms of the amodal under the concepts of nonsensuous perception and nonsensuous similarity respectively (see Massumi 2011, 17–18, 74, 105–110, 123–124, 138–142). The "haptic" in Deleuze (2003) is more profitably understood less as a relaying of tactility into vision than as a "synchresis": a modality of its own singular kind, just as Chion argues that

audiovision is irreducible to either vision or audition, but an emergent third: "It is as if the duality of the tactile and the optical were surpassed visually" (Chion 1994, 129), under pressure of a differential "between two planes," from whose "interval" an "emergence" self-effects (Chion 1994, 111; in this case, the differential is between different dimensions of vision itself, different aspects of color). In light of these considerations, the term "synesthetic" as used in the preceding paragraph in this text, becomes problematic. It is serviceable, but for conceptual precision it is best replaced by "amodal."

25. On the topology of experience as the production of a "biogram," see Massumi (2002, 177–207).

26. The classic text on swarming and military theory is Arquilla and Ronfeldt (2000).

27. The "superject" is a concept from Whitehead (1978, 45). "Attention to life" is a concept of Bergson's referring to the infra-individual, proprioceptive in-bracing for action-perception, which he calls a forward-looking "pantomime" that is continuous background operation in the intervals of conscious attending: "I do not mean voluntary attention, which is momentary and individual" (Bergson 1975, 94–95). But what does voluntary attention mean at this point? It can only mean a momentarily dominant tendency operating as a selective posturing for a next action-perception.

28. The usage of "datum" here coincides with that of Whitehead, which concerns a resultant fusional unity as opposed to separable bits, and is intimately bound up with creative emergence: "Whatever is a datum for a feeling has a unity *as felt*. Thus the many components of a complex datum have a unity: this unity is a 'contrast' of entities. In a sense this means that there are an endless number of categories of existence, since the synthesis of entities into a contrast in general produces a new existential type" (Whitehead 1978, 24).

29. On analogy, see Simondon (2005, 559–566) and Combes (2013, 9–12, 14–16). For Simondon, thought itself is analogical. Modes of thought that embrace operative analogy, thinking concertedly not only about it but through it, he calls "allagmatics." Instead of representing or describing, an allagmatic thought enacts in itself operations congruent to those of the concerned system. In this way, thought itself enters eventfully into double becoming with that system. It stages an encounter. Rather than purporting to stand outside or above, in analogic encounter thought co-individuates in aparallel evolution with its "object." In so doing, it remains in "strict coincidence with the real" (Simondon 2005, 109–110) grasped from the angle of its ontogenetic potential (to correlate and differ). Allagmatic thinking is thought itself practiced as an ontopower, as capable of creative emergence. It is "neither deductive nor inductive, but transductive" (Simondon 2005, 32). Transductive thought "grasps being not outside space and time, but prior to the division into a spatial systemization and temporal schematism" (Simondon 2005, 565). It grasps germinal being. The present project attempts to put in practice a transductive approach in its encounter with contemporary war. Also on

transduction, see Deleuze and Guattari (1987, 81, 313). On processual isomorphy in relation to social formations, see Deleuze and Guattari (1987, 4, 458, 477). Deleuze and Guattari understand isomorphy not as a correspondence between forms, but as an operative interchangeability and mutual transformability between formations linked effectively, processually, not through resemblance, and which may display the most disparate of formal differences. On aparallel evolution, see Deleuze and Guattari (1987, 10, 60).

## 5. Embroilments and History

1. The post-Rumsfeld David Petraeus doctrine of improved intelligence, emphasis on the human terrain, more attention to the mechanics of "nation-building," and reengaging diplomacy and a certain degree of multilateralism was enshrined in a new edition of the U.S. Army/Marine Corps *Counterinsurgency Field Manual* (2007). Interestingly, one of the main authors of the manual was an anthropologist, Susan Sewell. At the same time, the neoconservative hardline remained ensconced in the Bush administration around its fiercest proponent, Vice President Dick Cheney. The Obama administration's *National Security Strategy* of 2010 attempted to strike a balance between counterinsurgency and counterterrorism, deemphasizing nation-building while retaining key Revolution in Military Affairs terminology such as synchronization: "We must balance and integrate all elements of American power and update our national security capacity for the 21st century. We must maintain our military's conventional superiority, while enhancing its capacity to defeat asymmetric threats. Our diplomacy and development capabilities must be modernized, and our civilian expeditionary capacity strengthened, to support the full breadth of our priorities. Our intelligence and homeland security efforts must be integrated with our national security policies, and those of our allies and partners. And our ability to synchronize our actions while communicating effectively with foreign publics must be enhanced to sustain global support" (United States Government 2010, 5).

2. The adviser in question was David Kilcullen; see Ignatius (2008). The desired "low footprint" in Iraq presumably included the fifty permanent bases throughout the country demanded by the United States as a condition of its departure—part of a revised full-spectrum strategy at the heart of which would lie the force-to-own time in the form of the ever-present threat of rapid-dominance attack. The negotiation of the U.S. postwar presence fell to Obama, who, controversially, was unable or insufficiently motivated to bring Iraqi prime minister Nouri al-Maliki around. As a result, an initial micro-footprint of three hundred U.S. Special Operations forces, quickly growing to sixteen hundred, was restationed in Iraq in 2014 in the face of the Islamic State of Syria (ISIS; also known as ISIL) offensive from across the Syrian border. It is lost on few commentators that it was the U.S. invasion, in part justified as part of a campaign to contain militant Islamist groups, that created the conditions for this conflict—more evidence, if any is needed, that

preemptive war is productive, that it produces what it fights against. The strategies of preemptive war, as described throughout this book, were quickly revived by the Obama administration for the occasion. On the same day—the thirteenth anniversary of 9/11—that Homeland Security Secretary Jeh Johnson admitted that the administration had "no credible information that [ISIS] is planning to attack the homeland" (Roberts 2014b), President Obama gave a major speech announcing airstrikes against ISIS that was replete with Bush-like war-on-terror terminology revolving around not-fully-emerged threat: "Although we have not yet detected specific plotting against our homeland, ISIL leaders have threatened America and our allies. . . . We continue to face a terrorist threat. . . . If you threaten America you will find no safe haven. . . . We will degrade, and ultimately destroy, ISIL through a comprehensive and sustained counter-terrorism strategy" (Obama 2014b). The production of ISIS by the preemptive war meant to ward off just such threats was vividly communicated in a *Guardian* newspaper interview with a senior ISIS commander. The commander is quoted as saying that confinement in a U.S. military prison had been a golden "opportunity" to plan the movement that would later become ISIS. "We could never have all got together like this in Baghdad, or anywhere else. It would have been impossibly dangerous. Here, we were not only safe, but we were only a few hundred metres away from the entire al-Qaida leadership. . . . We had so much time to sit and plan. It was the perfect environment. We all agreed to get together when we got out. . . . For us it was an academy" (Chulov 2014).

3. This is, of course, an evocation of the virtual. Critiques of Deleuze's thought, such as Peter Hallward's (2006), which see it as "lacking a politics" or, like Badiou (1999) as well as Hallward, which see it as an "otherworldly" Platonic idealism in spite of itself, misunderstand this integral implication of the potential or the virtual in the event of the actual. Deleuze's most condensed statement of their processual identity of the virtual and the actual as dimensions of the same event is "The Actual and the Virtual" (Deleuze and Parnet 2007, 148–152). Potential and virtual are not synonymous terms, but the distinctions that may be drawn between them are not immediately pertinent for the specific purposes of this study. In Whiteheadian terms, "potential" here is assimilated to "real potential" and the virtual to "pure potential." On real potential: "Indetermination, rendered determinate in the real concrescence, is the meaning of 'potentiality.' It is a conditioned indetermination, and is therefore called a 'real potentiality'" (Whitehead 1978, 23). On pure potential: "An eternal object [corresponding to Deleuze's "singularity" in *The Logic of Sense* (1990)] in abstraction from any one particular actual entity is a potentiality for ingression into actual entities. . . . The definite ingression into a particular actual entity is not to be conceived as the sheer evocation of that eternal object from 'not-being' into 'being'; it is the evocation of determination out of indetermination. Potentiality becomes reality; and yet retains its message of alternatives which the actual entity has avoided. In the constitution of an actual entity:—whatever component is red, might have been green; and whatever component is loved, might

have been coldly esteemed. The term 'universal' is unfortunate in its application to eternal objects. . . . If the term 'eternal objects' is disliked, the term 'potentials' would be suitable. The eternal objects are the pure potentials of the universe" (Whitehead 1978, 149).

4. On the necessary relation of philosophy to non-philosophy, see Deleuze and Guattari (1994, 41, 218).

5. Matters of fact are "opposed to intelligible relations (of objects or ideas)." They concern not clearly and distinctly discernible individual entities or states of affairs, but relations of mutual inclusion in a "zone of indiscernibility" that is one with the hit of sensation, as "a force of coupling" (here, sensation is styled as bare activity, and the force of coupling is tendency, triggered by shock) (Deleuze 2003, 4, 66). On tendency, interpreted as part of a logic of mutual inclusion, see Massumi (2014a, 46–47).

6. On extra-being, see Deleuze (1990, 7, 123, 221). On the "penumbra" of potential surrounding every event, see Whitehead (1978, 185–186).

7. On this kind of abstract cause as "quasi-cause," and the quasi-cause as relational cause, see ch. 5, afterword, and Massumi (2002, 225–228).

8. In Guattari's vocabulary, the terminus is the kernel around which a "refrain" forms: "The refrain holds together partial components without abolishing their heterogeneity. Among these components are lines of virtuality that are born of the event itself and reveal themselves, at the very moment of their self-creation, in the mode of always having been, with time itself conceived as a nucleus of temporalization and mutation" (Guattari 2002, 244).

9. See, for example, James (1996a, 46–47, 56, 61, 68, 78, 104). For more on the terminus in James, see Massumi (2011, 29–38).

10. On the rise and fall of the "groundless" ground of experience (le sans-fond), see Deleuze (1994, 275).

11. The "left-under" of the terminus, inhabiting the generative fissure of time, cursored from emergence to emergence by the cueing-in of action-perception, is akin to what Deleuze calls the "dark precursor," the "differenciator" that triggers a "forced movement" (Deleuze 1994, 119–121).

12. In Simondon, "solidarity" refers to a mutual conditioning of operations, successive and simultaneous, that tends to the point of "saturation" (maximum actualization of potential). In the case of a technical object, at the saturation point, its operativity takes on an autonomy that makes it self-driving. This process is that of "concretization." Concretization is "naturalization." The more concretized a system becomes (the more "synergistic" its operations), the more "naturalized" it becomes. At the limit of naturalization, a system has achieved "oversaturation" (pregnancy with maximum potential). In the theory of war as discussed in chapter 4, this coincides with the limit of self-synchronization (the successive and the simultaneous coming together). See Simondon (1989, 43–46, 156–158, 285; 2005, 517). Many parallels can be drawn between Simondon's concept of concretization and Whitehead's "concrescence" (Whitehead 1978).

13. See chapter 2 for further discussion of contingency and accident, in particular note 11. Pure chaos cannot sustain itself. A purely chance event is either captured by the field of coindividuation and modulates its iterative reordering (in which case it becomes other than pure chaos), or it disappears without a trace the moment of its arising, like the virtual particles of physics in the pure potential of the void, which instantaneously pop into and out of existence. Chaos is virtual. Actuality is quasi-chaotic. James on quasi-chaos as characteristic of the iterative coevolutionary system of experience populated by cresting events tendentially related by wavelike transitions: "Experience as a whole is a process in time, whereby innumerable particular terms lapse and are superseded by others that follow upon them by transitions which, whether disjunctive or conjunctive in content, are themselves experiences, and must in general be accounted at least as real as the terms which they relate. . . . The whole system of experiences as they are immediately given presents itself as a quasi-chaos through which one can pass out of an initial term in many directions and yet end in the same terminus, moving from next to next by a great many possible paths. . . . We live, as it were, upon the front edge of an advancing wave-crest, and our sense of a determinate direction in falling forward is all we cover of the future of our path. It is as if a differential quotient should be conscious and treat itself as an adequate substitute for a traced-out curve. Our experience, *inter alia*, is of variations of rate and of direction, and lives in these transitions more in the journey's end. The experiences of tendency are sufficient to act upon" (James 1996a, 63, 69).

On chaos as virtual, and on its different forms of capture by philosophy, art, and science, see Deleuze and Guattari (1994, pages 118, 201–203). It must be emphasized along with Deleuze and Guattari, that although chaos cannot exist, nothing would become without it. As captured, it is the creative factor in the universe's unfolding. In itself, it cannot be conceptualized as "an" accident but only as *the* accident: the "primordial accident" of the world's creative advance. This primordial accident is, for Whitehead, "God" (a metaphysical, atheological god) (Whitehead 1978, 7).

14. The "lure for feeling" is the Whiteheadian term corresponding to the terminus: "the final cause guiding the concrescence of feelings" (Whitehead 1978, 185). The abstract end point enveloped in the terminus in Whiteheadian terms is an "eternal object" (in the present context, a "complex eternal object" most especially; Whitehead 1978, 24, 186). Tendency correlates in Whiteheadian terms to "appetition," and fulfillment to "satisfaction." On decision and "cut," see Whitehead (1978, 43).

15. On failure as a necessary part of the advance of creative process, see Deleuze and Guattari (1983, 42, 152).

16. On the processual embrace of the finite expression and infinite potentiality, see Guattari (1995, 54, 100, 110–116).

17. William E. Connolly has extensively developed the idea of contestability as the enabler of a pluralistic politics practicing an ethos of engagement. See Connolly (1995), among other works.

18. This extraction of a "pure" form (using the word "pure" in a technical sense synonymous with "virtual") is a fundamental strategy of Deleuze and Guattari's philosophic approach. It can be seen clearly in action in relation to political processes in the "Nomadology" and "Apparatus of Capture" chapters of *A Thousand Plateaus*, and in relation to thought processes in *What Is Philosophy?* The most common misreading of these aspects of their thought is produced by mistaking this processual typology by extremum with a typology of actual formations as approached "in the middle," that is to say, as embroiled in the coevolutionary field of historical cross-tendencies (in "mixity"). There is, for example, no actual separation between art, philosophy, and science in *What Is Philosophy?* They separate out tendentially, at their virtual limits, in order to enter effectively into mixity. The limits are active and constitutive, if ideal, exerting a force of attraction on all that runs through the middle (which is everything, actually). In their actual interplay, they determine degrees of mixity. Evaluation of actual formations bears on this degree of tendential mixity in their processes (as discussed in the afterword). The concept of ideal recursive causality associated with terminus in its co-operation with tendency is explicitly developed in "Apparatus of Capture" (using the term limit for terminus).

## 6. Fear

The translation of the Tarde epigraph has been modified. The second epigraph is one of the many "Bushisms" that circulated in the press and on the Internet during the Bush years. This one appears to be apocryphal. It seems actually to belong to Dan Quayle, vice president under George H. W. Bush. As regularly attributed to George W. Bush, however, it squarely belongs to his corpus.

1. The color alert system remained in operation throughout the Bush administration and for the first two and a half years of President Obama's first term. It was discontinued in April 2011 by then Homeland Security Secretary Janet Napolitano. A two-part verbal alert system replaced it: "imminent" for a specific attack expected in a short time; "elevated" for a more general threat. The new National Terrorism Advisory System is only intermittently activated, with alerts expiring after two weeks unless specifically renewed. Under the new system, the ubiquitous color alert charts formerly seen in public spaces such as airports and in the corner of cable television news screens have been replaced by Twitter and Facebook feeds. During the life of the color alert system, the low-threat colors of blue and green were never used. The system was almost permanently on orange, with occasional toggles to yellow or red. In her announcement of the demise of the color alert system, Secretary Napolitano cited as the reason for the change that the old system instilled fear without providing helpful information (Korling 2011). The life of the Bush-era system may not have been prolonged by the admission by Napolitano's predecessor at Homeland Security, Tom Ridge, in his post-service

memoirs that declarations of higher alert level under the color-alert system were used for political purposes, in particular to increase Bush's chances of reelection in 2004 (Weiner 2009). An empirical study published in 2004 confirmed that increased terror alert levels translated into higher levels of support for Bush and, interestingly, found that the support transferred over from Bush's handling of national security to his handling of the economy: "Results showed a consistent, positive relationship between terror warnings and presidential approval. I also found that government-issued terror warnings increased support for President Bush's handling of the economy" (Willer 2004).

2. Television's arc as the event-medium reached its high point in 1990 with the Gulf War and its bringing to prominence of cable news network CNN to the detriment of traditional broadcast news. Twenty years later, it had visibly waned. The completion of television's integration into an internet-dominated media ecology was evident by 2011, as attested to by the prominence of social media in the collective experience of that year's events of the Arab Spring and Occupy Wall Street. On the central role of television in the Gulf War, see Kellner (1992) and Baudrillard (1995).

3. "Our natural way of thinking about these coarser emotions is that the mental perception of some fact excites the mental affection called the emotion, and that this latter state of mind gives rise to the bodily expression. My theory, on the contrary, is that *the bodily changes follow directly the perception of the exciting fact, and that our feeling of the same changes as they occur IS the emotion.* Common-sense says, we lose our fortune, are sorry and weep; we meet a bear, are frightened and run; we are insulted by a rival, are angry and strike. The hypothesis here to be defended says that this order of sequence is incorrect, that one mental state is not immediately induced by the other, that the bodily manifestations must first be interposed between, and that the more rational statement is that we feel sorry because we cry, angry because we strike, afraid because we tremble, and not that we cry, strike, or tremble, because we are sorry, angry, or fearful. . . . It makes us realize more deeply than ever how much our mental life is knit up with our corporeal frame, in the strictest sense of the term" (James 1950, 2:449–450, 467).

4. On affect as "the primary ground for the continuity of nature," see Whitehead (1967a, 183–184) and Massumi (2002, 208–218).

5. This formula was suggested by Alfred North Whitehead's theorization of "the sensa as qualifications of affective tone." The experience, he writes, "starts as that smelly feeling, and is developed by mentality into the feeling of that smell." This applies as well to the "affective tones" we call "moods," which must be considered "direct perceptions . . . on equal terms with the other sensa" (Whitehead 1967a, 246). In other words, philosophically, the theory of affect and emotion and the theory of perception strictly coincide. The concept of affective tone will be discussed further on.

6. Kathleen Stewart (2010) develops a theory of affective atmosphere that converges in certain respects with the present account.

7. For an earlier theorization of fear as ground of existence and way of life, see Massumi (1993).

8. On dephasing, see Simondon (2005, 14, 25–26, 320–323).

## 7. The Future Birth of the Affective Fact

1. By "actual fact," I mean the situation as defined (by rule, convention, or consensus) by a normative system for the establishment of publicly recognized fact under whose jurisdiction the question normally falls, when that system's operation is not preempted (for example, a judicial system, an administrative review process, a peer-review process, etc.).

2. As discussed in chapter 1, the classical doctrine of war allows preemptive action in cases where there is a "clear and present danger" of attack. Preemption is only allowed defensively, in the face of actual danger. The contemporary neoconservative doctrine of preemption justifies offensive action against threats that are not fully emergent or, more radically, that have not even begun to emerge.

3. The Abu Ghraib images first came to light in April 2004. For a compendium of Bush administration documents justifying the use of torture, see Greenberg and Dratel (2005).

4. See, for example, Knowlton (2007).

5. See chapter 1 and chapter 5, note 2.

6. See, for example, La Presse (2005a). See in particular the photo and caption.

7. The affective tainting of objects or bodies implicated in a threat-event can go so far as to functionally substitute the affective fact of the matter for what is accepted as actual fact (as defined above in note 1). The actual fact is neither directly contested nor forgotten, yet is disabled. It slips behind the affective fact, which comes to the fore to take over as the operative reality. To cite an example of this affective-factual eclipse, in August 2007 President Bush retracted earlier statements expressing an intent to close the extraterritorial prison camp at Guantánamo Bay. Guantánamo Bay had become a political liability after the torture scandal at Abu Ghraib, revelations of shady "black site" prisons into which "enemy combatants" disappeared without a trace, and criticism of CIA kidnapping of suspects on foreign soil for delivery to third nations known systematically to use torture (known euphemistically as "rendition"). What placed Guantánamo Bay in the same category as these other extraterritorial practices is that they all aim to preempt regulated governmental treatment of suspects according to standard juridical procedures. The strategy is to surge in, in order to rush the production of the results of normal juridical procedures before they have had a chance to operate. Imprisonment and punishment come suddenly, before any actual crime is proven. The grabbed bodies are treated, a priori, as guilty. This is done purely on the basis of signs of threat that happened to actualize in their vicinity. Some of the inhabitants of Guantánamo who were subsequently released after years of imprisonment were swooped up in Afghanistan during the U.S. invasion and turned out simply to have been in the wrong

place at the wrong time. The treatment of the detainees as a priori guilty attaches this quality to them for life, regardless of their actual actions and the actual danger they posed. They are stained, *as if* they had been guilty all along. The felt quality of guilt has its own affective ambience, which can transmute into a number of specific emotions: hatred, resentment, disgust, distrust. The detainee becomes an affective pariah. According to the Bush administration, certain prisoners scheduled for release will not be taken in by any country, even their own country of origin. These are detainees whom the U.S. military has not been able to bring to trial, meaning that their cases are not strong enough to transfer into the domestic criminal system—or even bring before the newly established Military Commissions where the bar of the burden of proof is set extravagantly low and the accused's possibilities of defense are sorely limited. Bush explained, without displaying a hint of irony or in any way acknowledging the paradox, that it is because of cases such as these that Guantánamo Bay must be kept open. The prison doors must remain closed in order to detain those who are technically innocent. "This is not as easy a subject as some may think on the surface," the explanation went. "A lot of people don't want killers in their midst, and a lot of these people are killers." "These people" should be released because they are innocent, but can't be released because they are "killers" (Bush 2007). Bush's reasoning is not as illogical as it might be supposed as judged by the standards of normative logic. The apparent inconsistency corresponds to a change in factual level occurring between the recognition of innocence and the assertion of guilt. A shift has occurred mid-logic from actual to affective fact. The affective fact is that these innocents are as good as killers. Nothing will change the fact that those preemptively treated as guilty are now, as a result of affective tainting, permanently guilty *in effect*. They are *effectively* guilty (presumably, they would have if they could have). Indefinite internment is now the hard, life-wasting affective fact of their situation. Affective facts stand only on their own preemptive occurrence. Yet they may come effectively to stand in for actual facts.

8. After this incident, there was no questioning in the press about who had been preemptively attacked based on the now incredible information, or what their present circumstances might be. Had they been killed? Had they been "renditioned" to a third country? Disappeared into a "black site" prison? Sent to Guantánamo for indefinite detention? Would their cases ever be heard? The question, it seemed, occurred to no one. The event was not taking place at that actual-factual level, but rather on the affective level where threat plays itself out through fear. See note 7 above.

9. The invocation of 9/11 makes good populist political sense given that, according to a Zogby International Poll, a full six years after the event 81 percent of Americans listed it as the most important event of their lives. The percentage rises to 90 percent on the East Coast (*Montreal Gazette* 2007).

10. *La Presse* (2005b; report on comments by then Homeland Security "Czar" Tom Ridge). The French headline of this article ("Plus de panique!") captures the ambivalence of preemption: taken in isolation it can be read either as "more panic"

or "no more panic" (the latter interpretation being the one suggested in the body of the article).

11. This is Peirce's "material quality," as discussed in chapter 6.

12. Deleuze and Guattari analyze the relations between modes of power in terms of "a threshold or degree" beyond which what is already active as a tendency "takes on consistency" (1987, 12). See the discussion of tendency and mixity in chapter 5.

13. What is being called operative logics here correspond to what Deleuze and Guattari (1987) call "machinic processes" or "abstract machines." "We define social formations by *machinic processes* and not by modes of production (these on the contrary depend on the processes). . . . Precisely because these processes are variables of coexistence that are the object of a social topology, the various corresponding formations are coexistent" (435). "There is not only an external coexistence of formations but also an intrinsic coexistence of machinic processes. Each process can also function at a 'power' other than its own; it can be taken up by a power corresponding to another process" (437). "Everything coexists, in perpetual interaction" (430). Machinic processes operate according to "reverse causalities that are *without finality* but testify nonetheless to an action of the future on the present" which implies "an inversion of time. . . . These reverse causalities shatter evolution. . . . It is necessary to demonstrate that what does not yet exist is already in action, in a different form than that of its existence" (431). The machinic processes of most concern to Deleuze and Guattari in this chapter form "apparatuses of capture." "As a general rule, there is a primitive accumulation whenever an apparatus of capture is mounted, with that very particular kind of violence that creates or contributes to the creation of that which it is directed against, and thus presupposes itself" (447). Violence creative of that which it is directed against employs "anticipation-prevention mechanisms" (439)—in other words, it acts productively by acting preemptively. "Anticipation-prevention mechanisms have a high *power of transference*" or of contagion between processes and their corresponding formations (437). In deleuzo-guattarian terms, the preemptive power analyzed here is an emergent species of highly virulent apparatus of capture effecting a "primitive accumulation" of threat-value, and spreading its operative logic through affective contagion (Deleuze and Guattari 1987, 430, 431, 435, 437, 447). One of the modes in which there is effective interaction between operative logics "in a different form than that of their existence" is Whitehead's negative prehension, previously mentioned in chapter 4: "A negative prehension is the definite exclusion of [an] item from positive contribution to the subject's [the process's] real internal constitution. . . . The negative prehension expresses a bond. . . . Each negative prehension has its own subjective form, however trivial and faint. . . . It adds to the emotional complex [the affective atmosphere], if not to the objective data. . . . [Negative prehensions] are required to express *how* any one item is felt. . . . The negative prehension of an entity [a process] is a positive fact with its emotional subjective form [it is an affective fact]; there is a mutual sensitivity of the subjective

forms of prehensions [there is an ecology of reciprocal presupposition effectively extending to what is negatively prehended]" (Whitehead 1978, 41–42).

In Deleuze and Guattari's vocabulary, the "bond" constituted by a negative prehension is an example of the "non-localizable liaisons" characteristic of capture (1987, 446). Threat, at the limit where it is "trivially and faintly" felt only as an atmospheric quality independent of any actual instance of itself, constitutes such a nonlocalized bond, even when it is not specifically expressed in a sign of alarm. It still contributes in a real but abstract way to the "how" of the mutual sensitivity of subjective forms, even when it is not positively felt. It still adds to the shared "emotional complex" that is the affective environment conditioning *how* forms feelingly pursue their individuation. This is particularly the case once the "primitive accumulation" of threat-value has reached a certain level and extension throughout the environment due to the "high transference power" of its processual mechanisms. Threat operating in this way, at the limit where it is not actually signed but still negatively prehended, felt vaguely and purely qualitatively, constitutes what in earlier work I described as "low-level" background fear capable of insinuating itself into the constitution of subjectivities. It is affective fact at its most abstract. See Massumi (1993).

14. In the adaptation of Peircean terms as they are mobilized here, the bare-active body as "material quality" (as discussed in chapter 6) is the same dynamic form considered from the angle of its potential feeling (actually felt or unfelt) as a content of experience. In other words, the dynamical object is the singular form in which the *threat* takes effect as it hits the body (the feeling of the catapulting into an imperative transition), and the material quality is the *fear* in which threat's taking effect is immediately expressed, but in a way that can be generally reflected upon and compared post facto (again, as analyzed in chapter 6). The latter would correspond to Peirce's "immediate object" ("the emotional object and the immediate object coincide"; Peirce 1998, 410). In Daniel Stern's vocabulary, the feeling of the dynamical object is a "vitality affect." The fear is a germinal "categorical" affect (Stern 1985, 53–61; see also Massumi 2011, 43–44, 111, 152–153; Massumi 2014a, 25–30, 56–58, 78–80). At impact, these are co-occurrent aspects of the same event.

## Afterword: After the Long Past

Translation of the opening epigraph has been modified.

1. All quotations from Whitehead in this paragraph and the next are from *Adventures of Ideas* (1967a), 191–192.

2. Whitehead does, of course, retain an important role for history, in spite of (or more to the point, because of) its fabulatory nature. For Whitehead, every event begins with an initial phase of "reenaction" in which patterns of activity inherited from the immediate past are "reenergized" for the forming present (Whitehead 1967a, 192). Because the reenactions are of inherited patterns, they renew for the

present modes of relation that have been formative of presents past. This enables a speculative reconstruction of the line of inheritance that brought the patterns of activity forward. This reconstruction is fabulatory for two reasons. First, the reenaction is felt before and more fully than it is cognized (it is "prehended" rather than "apprehended"). The feeling hits in an interval of incipient formation that cannot be fully brought into reflective consciousness, whose very nature is to selectively edit the commotion of experience's arising (Whitehead 1967a, 217, 244). This means that the past is always inflected by the conditions of the present, so that any reconstruction is watermarked by the regions of nonconsciousness, indeterminacy, and vagueness that are a necessary part of the present's constitution. The second reason the reconstruction is fabulatory is that the reenaction of the past coincides with the immanence of the future in the present. "This immediate future is immanent with some degree of structural definition" (Whitehead 1967a, 217, 244) in the form of embryonic orientations and tendencies continuing the patterns of activity inherited from the past and modulated or improvised upon as the present moment unfolds. The patterns of the past presenting itself are alloyed with structures of futurity. This gives any back-casting of the past a tinge of speculative fiction in reverse. The important point is that "the history of the present" as it can be understood from such thinkers as Foucault, Nietzsche, and Whitehead does give an effective grasp on the past, for the feeling of the past's reenaction at the heart of every moment's rising is real and unrefusable (Whitehead 1967a, 210). It is lived, and it is bodily. It is its own occurrent truth. In relation to current debates, the notion of the history of the present converts the question of the past into an ontological question—or better, an ontogenetic one (bearing on the genesis of moments, the structures they settle into, and the becomings that surpass them). The consideration of epistemology, by this approach, is not separable from an inquiry into ontogenesis. This is in stark contrast to the purely epistemological way such questions have been formulated in recent speculative realist debates, particularly around Quentin Meillassoux's concept of the "arche-fossil": the question of events occurring on a scale beyond human experience, like the death of stars in distant galaxies whose light we still see eons later (Meillassoux 2008, 1–28). Meillassoux speaks as if the problem were the impossibility of a direct cognitive relation between a present subject and the distant event. From the point of view of the history of the present, this is a false problem. It brackets the fact that light of the past event hits in the present with patterns of activity (inflected by the intervening events through which the light has passed en route) that enable an inferential reconstruction thanks to "our experience of the stability of the orders involved"— assisted by "an imaginative leap" (Whitehead 1967a, 248). The problem is not—and never is, even for present perception—that of the relation of the subject of cognition to an external event. Rather, the problem is that of the internal relations immanent to the present's constitution (in the "interval" of formation) that give rise to an occasion of thought. It is more fundamentally a question of the untimely relations of the dimensions of time to each other, from which the subject of thought will emerge, than it is a question of the relation of a preconstituted subject to a given object. Ontogenesis presupposes no preformed subject or field of consciousness in "correlation" with objects, but rather sees subjects and objects as co-emergent from events. Whitehead discusses the light of dead stars and other "arche-fossil" topics related to the knowledge of the past in 1964 (151–153), 1967a (247–248), and 1967b (89–90). On "historic routes" of transmission from the past always passing through the immanence of an occasion's arising, see 1967a (195–197).

3. The theory of the apparatus of capture is extensively developed in Deleuze and Guattari (1987, 424–473).

4. On "singularities" as composing a pure, disjunct multiplicity, yet always already extending themselves toward each other, see Deleuze (1990, 68, 109). On "remarkable points" (translated as "distinctive points"), see Deleuze (1994, 46–48, 253–254).

5. For a discussion of Deleuze and Guattari's concept of the "abstract machine" in relation to that of "operative logic," see chapter 7, note 13.

6. For more on full-spectrum force, see chapter 3.

7. For analyses of the turn to preemptive policing, including discussions of exception, the placing of policing on a continuum with military action, and the extrusion of spatialities specific to preemption, see Lafleur (2014), Gillham (2011), and Starr, Fernandez, and Scholl (2011).

8. "We tortured some folks," Obama admitted in 2014, using the word "torture" for the first time during his tenure in office to describe the CIA's enhanced interrogation techniques. He criticized the CIA's "mistake"—but went on to say that he "understood" why it happened and that the folks who did it to some other folks were "patriots." He gave a one-word summary of the reason why the mistake was understandable (and, the message was clear, pardonable): "fear." He went on to express unflinching support for his current CIA director, John Brennan, under fire for having unconstitutionally spied on the U.S. Senate committee investigating Bush-era CIA torture practices (Lewis 2014). Following the release of the Senate committee's report in December 2014, calls have increased for prosecution, most vocally in the form of a joint initiative between the ACLU and Human Rights Watch. At the center of these groups' concern is the worry that the lack of a full criminal investigation by a special prosecutor "would contribute to the notion that torture remains a permissible policy option for future administrations" (Pilkington 2014).

9. The two Supreme Court decisions extending constitutionally guaranteed rights of persons to corporate entities are Citizens United vs. Federal Election Commission (2010) and Burwell vs. Hobby Lobby (2014).

10. The repetition in this chapter of three-part conceptual formulae is just a convenience. Given the reciprocal mutual inclusion of part-concepts in each other, as discussed above, any enumeration of them is heuristic. The multiplicity of the conceptual formula is not numerical. Three parts are convenient because it makes it easier to conceive of a circuit—and one that does not close itself down into a dualistic opposition or suggest a dialectic. The three of the conceptual formula does

not suggest the synthesis of a dialectical contradiction. It's a conviviality of three that cheerfully invites a fourth (and the fourth a fifth, and so forth). A conceptual formula can be accordioned out into any number of part-concepts, or conversely telescoped into a seemingly unitary expression (such as "corporations are people too"). The enumeration depends on the conceptual-historical problem at hand, and what tasks that problem assigns the hunter of the snark of tendencies, and what tendencies the hunter him- or herself brings to the task. The philosophy of the event, or of process or becoming, is always a constructive undertaking.

11. On implicit presupposition as a nonlinguistic formative force immanent to language acts, see Deleuze and Guattari (1987, 78–85).

12. "Life living" is a concept developed throughout Erin Manning's *Always More Than One* (2013), in dialogue with Deleuze's concept of "a" life (2007).

13. A fuller discussion of counter-power is outside the scope of this book. It is the topic, particularly as regards the question of affect, of *The Power at the End of the Economy* (Massumi 2015a) and *Politics of Affect* (Massumi 2015b).

# REFERENCES

Ackerman, Spencer. 2014. "Government Agents 'Directly Involved" in Most High-Profile Terror Plots." *Guardian*, July 21. http://www.theguardian.com/world/2014/jul/21/government-agents-directly-involved-us-terror-plots-report. Accessed July 22, 2014.

Agamben, Giorgio. 1998. *Homo Sacer: Sovereign Power and Bare Life*. Trans. Daniel Helen-Roazen. Stanford, CA: Stanford University Press.

Agamben, Giorgio. 2003. *The Open: Man and Animal*. Trans. Kevin Attell. Stanford, CA: Stanford University Press.

Agamben, Giorgio. 2005. *State of Exception*. Trans. Kevin Attell. Chicago: University of Chicago Press.

Alberts, David S. 1995. "Mission Capability Packages." Department of Defense Command and Control Research Program. http://www.dodccrp.org/events/13th_iccrts_2008/CD/library/html/pdf/Alberts_Mission.pdf. Accessed June 29, 2014.

Alberts, David S., John J. Garstka, and Frederick P. Stein. 2000. *Network Centric Warfare: Developing and Leveraging Information Superiority*. Washington, DC: Department of Defense C4ISR Cooperative Research Program, 2nd revised edition. http://www.dodccrp.org/htm14/research_ncw.html. Accessed May 26, 2010.

Alberts, David S., and Richard E. Hayes. 2003. *Power to the Edge: Command and Control in the Information Age*. Washington, DC: Department of Defense Command and Control Research Program, 3rd printing 2005. http://www.dodccrp.org/files/Alberts_Power.pdf. Accessed May 26, 2010.

Alberts, Sheldon. 2010. " 'Terror' Has Returned to the White House: The Obama Administration Wanted to Move Away from the 'Politics of Fear,' but Politics and Fear Got in the Way." *Ottawa Citizen*, January 9. http://www.ottawacitizen.com/news/Terror+returned+White+House/2424122/story.html?utm_source=feedburner&utm_medium=feed&utm_campaign=Feed%3A+canwest%2FF239+(Ottawa+Citizen+-+News). Accessed January 11, 2010.

Apuzzo, Matt. 2014. "Holder Urges Europeans to Step Up Antiterrorism Tactics." *New York Times*, July 8. http://www.nytimes.com/2014/07/09/world/europe/holder-urges-better-antiterror-tactics-for-europe.html?_r=0. Accessed July 8, 2014.

Arquilla, John, and David Ronfeldt. 2000. *Swarming and the Future of Conflict*. Santa Monica, CA: RAND.

Arquilla, John, and David Ronfeldt. 2001. *Networks and Netwars: The Future of Terror, Crime, and Militancy.* Santa Monica, CA: RAND.

Associated Press. 2004. "Cheney Arrives in N.Y. via Ellis Island." August 29. http://www.msnbc.msn.com/id/5859896/. Accessed May 26, 2010.

Austin, J. L. 1975. *How to Do Things with Words*, 2nd edition. Cambridge, MA: Harvard University Press.

Bacevich, Andrew J. 2011 (reprint). *Washington Rules: America's Path to Permanent War.* New York: Metropolitan Books.

Badiou, Alain. 1999. *Deleuze: The Clamor of Being.* Trans. Louise Burchell. Minneapolis: University of Minnesota Press.

Bajaj, Vkas. 2005. "Bloomberg Cites 'Specific Threat' to NY Subways." *New York Times*, October 6, A5.

Balko, Radley. 2013. *The Rise of the Warrior Cop: The Militarization of America's Police Forces.* New York: PublicAffairs.

Barnett, Roger W. 2003. *Asymmetrical Warfare: Today's Challlenge to U.S. Military Power.* Washington, DC: Brassey's.

Barr, Andy. 2008. "Cheney: Obama Not Likely to Cede Authority." Politico.com, December 15. http://www.politico.com/news/stories/1208/16594.html. Accessed July 26, 2014.

Baudrillard, Jean. 1995. *The Gulf War Did Not Take Place.* Trans. Paul Patton. Bloomington: Indiana University Press.

Baxstrom, Richard, Naveeda Khan, Deborah Poole, and Bhrigupati Singh. 2005. "Networks Actual and Potential: Think Tanks, War Games and the Creation of Contemporary American Politics." *Theory and Event* 8 (4). http://muse.jhu.edu/journals/theory_and_event/summary/v008/8.4singh.html. Accessed July 27, 2014.

Becker, Jo, and Scott Shane. 2012. "Secret 'Kill List' Proves a Test of Obama's Principles and Will." *New York Times*, May 29. http://www.nytimes.com/2012/05/29/world/obamas-leadership-in-war-on-al-qaeda.html?pagewanted=all. Accessed July 26, 2014.

Benjamin, Walter. 2003. "On the Concept of History." In *Selected Writings. Volume 4 1938–1940.* Trans. Edmund Jephcott et al. Ed. Howard Eiland and Michael W. Jennings. Cambridge, MA: Harvard University Press, 389–400.

Bergson, Henri. 1975. *Mind-Energy: Lectures and Essays.* Trans. H. Wildon Carr. Westport, CT: Greenwood.

Bergson, Henri. 2001. *Time and Free Will: An Essay on the Immediate Data of Consciousness.* Mineola, NY: Dover.

Bergson, Henri. 2007. *The Creative Mind: An Introduction to Metaphysics.* Mineola, NY: Dover.

Berkowitz, Bruce. 2003. *The New Face of War: How War Will Be Fought in the 21st Century.* New York: Free Press.

Boyce, Peter. 2008. "Army to Accelerate Future Combat Systems (FCS) Deliveries to Infantry Brigade Combat Teams" (U.S. Army news release), June 26. http://www

.army.mil/article/10392/Army_to_Accelerate_Future_Combat_Systems__FCS
__Deliveries_to_Infantry_Brigade_Combat_Teams. Accessed July 27, 2014.

Bremer, Paul L, III. 2001. "New Risks in International Business." *Viewpoint: The Marsh
and McLennan Companies Journal* 2. http://www.bettermanagement.com/library
/library.aspx?i=4521&pagenumber=1. Accessed April 21, 2009.

Brouwer, Joke, and Arjen Mulder. 2007. *Interact or Die!* Rotterdam: V_2/Nai Publishers.

Bush, George W. 2000. *Dallas Morning News*, May 10, 2000. Cited in Miller (2002, 251).

Bush, George W. 2002. "President Bush Delivers Graduation Speech at West Point."
The White House, June 1. http://georgewbush-whitehouse.archives.gov/news
/releases/2002/06/print/20020601-3.html. Accessed April 21, 2014.

Bush, George W. 2005a. President's Radio Address. The White House, June 18.
http://georgewbush-whitehouse.archives.gov/news/releases/2005/06/20050618
.html. Accessed April 21, 2014.

Bush, George W. 2005b. "President Bush Delivers Remarks on Hurricane Katrina
Recovery." *Washington Post*, September 15. http://www.washingtonpost.com
/wp-dyn/contentarticle/2005/09/15/AR2005091502252_pf.html. Accessed
September 16, 2005.

Bush, George W. 2006. Transcript: Bush's News Conference. CNN.com, October 11.
http://www.cnn.com/2006/POLITICS/10/11/bush.transcript. Accessed April 21,
2014.

Bush, George W. 2007. "The President's News Conference," August 9. The American
Presidency Project. http://www.presidency.ucsb.edu/ws/index.php?pid=75649.
Accessed July 3, 2014.

Calabresi, Steven G., and Christopher S. Yoo. 2008. *The Unitary Executive: Presidential
Power from Washington to Bush*. New Haven, CT: Yale University Press.

Cebrowski, Vice Admiral Arthur, and John Garstka. 1998. "Network-Centric
Warfare—Its Origin and Future." *Proceedings of the United States Naval Institute* 124
(1) (January): 28–35. http://www.oft.osd.mil/initiatives/ncw/presentations/ncw
.cfm. Accessed 26 May 2010.

Chion, Michel. 1994. *Audio-Vision: Sound on Screen*. Trans. Claudia Gorbman New
York: Columbia University Press.

Chulov, Martin. 2014. "ISIS: The Inside Story." *Guardian*, December 11. http://
www.theguardian.com/world/2014/dec/11/-sp-isis-the-inside-story. Accessed
December 12, 2014.

Clausewitz, Carl von. 1946. *On War*. Trans. Col. J. J. Graham. London: N. Trübner.
Online. Gutenberg Galaxy e-text. Originally published 1874. http://www
.gutenberg.org/etext/1946. Accessed May 26, 2010.

CNN. 2014. *Legal View with Ashleigh Banfield*. October 6. http://transcripts.cnn.com
/TRANSCRIPTS/1410/06/lvab.01.html. Accessed October 13, 2014.

Combes, Muriel. 2013. *Simondon and the Philosophy of the Transindividual*. Trans.
Thomas Lamarre. Cambridge, MA: MIT Press.

Connolly, William E. 1995. *The Ethos of Pluralization*. Minneapolis: University of
Minnesota Press.

Connolly, William E. 2008. *Capitalism and Christianity, American Style*. Durham, NC: Duke University Press.

Connolly, William E. 2013. *The Fragility of Things: Self-Organizing Processes, Neoliberal Fantasies, and Democratic Activism*. Durham, NC: Duke University Press.

Cooper, Melinda. 2008. *Life as Surplus: Biotechnology and Capitalism in the Neoliberal Era*. Seattle: University of Washington Press.

DARPA. 2014. "President's Funding Request for DARPA Aims to Fund Promising Ideas, Help Regain Prior Levels" (press release), March 4, 2014. http://www .darpa.mil/NewsEvents/Releases/2014/03/05.aspx. Accessed June 14, 2014.

Deleuze, Gilles. 1988. *Foucault*. Trans. Séan Hand. Minneapolis: University of Minnesota Press.

Deleuze, Gilles. 1990. *The Logic of Sense*. Trans. Mark Lester and Charles Stivale. Ed. Constantin V. Boundas. New York: Columbia University Press.

Deleuze, Gilles. 1993. *The Fold: Leibniz and the Baroque*. Trans. Tom Conley. Minneapolis: University of Minnesota Press.

Deleuze, Gilles. 1994. *Difference and Repetition*. Trans. Paul Patton. New York: Columbia University Press.

Deleuze, Gilles. 1995. *Negotiations*. Trans. Martin Jouglin. New York: Columbia University Press.

Deleuze, Gilles. 2003. *Francis Bacon: The Logic of Sensation*. Trans. Daniel W. Smith. London: Continuum.

Deleuze, Gilles. 2007. "Immanence: a Life." In *Two Regimes of Madness: Texts and Interviews 1975–1995*. Trans. Ames Hodges and Mike Taormina. New York: Semiotext(e).

Deleuze, Gilles, and Félix Guattari. 1983. *Anti-Oedipus*. Trans. Robert Hurley, Mark Seem, and Helen R. Lane. Minneapolis: University of Minnesota Press.

Deleuze, Gilles, and Félix Guattari. 1986. *Kafka: Toward a Minor Literature*. Trans. Dana Polan. Minneapolis: University of Minnesota Press.

Deleuze, Gilles, and Félix Guattari. 1987. *A Thousand Plateaus*. Trans. Brian Massumi. Minneapolis: University of Minnesota Press.

Deleuze, Gilles, and Félix Guattari. 1994. *What Is Philosophy?* Trans. Graham Burchell and Hugh Tomlinson. London: Verso.

Deleuze, Gilles, and Claire Parnet. 2007. *Dialogues II*. Trans. Hugh Tomlinson. New York: Columbia University Press.

Dorrien, Gary. 2004. *Imperial Designs: Neoconservatism and the New Pax Americana*. New York: Routledge.

Dougherty, Kevin. 2007. "Province to Rid Schools of Junk Food. Youth Obesity a Pandemic: Couillard." *Montreal Gazette*, September 14: A8.

Englehart, Tom. 2005. "The Can-Do Bush Administration Does . . . and the Presidency Shines (for Twenty-Six Minutes). http://www.tomdispatch.com/post /22726/. Accessed November 30, 2014.

Fanon, Frantz. 1965. *A Dying Colonialism*. Trans. Haakon Chevalier. Ed. Adolfo Gilly. New York: Grove Press.

Foucault, Michel. 1977a. *Discipline and Punish: Birth of the Prison.* Trans. Alan Sheridan. New York: Pantheon.

Foucault, Michel. 1977b. "Nietzsche, Genealogy, History." In Donald F. Bouchard, ed., *Language, Memory, Counter-practice.* Ithaca, NY: Cornell University Press. 139–164.

Foucault, Michel. 1978. *The History of Sexuality.* Vol. 1, An Introduction. Trans. Robert Hurley. New York: Vintage.

Foucault, Michel. 1979. *Discipline and Punish: The Birth of the Prison.* Trans. Alan Sheridan. New York: Vintage.

Foucault, Michel. 1982. "The Discourse on Language." Trans. Rupert Sawyer. In *The Archaeology of Knowledge.* Trans. Alan Sheridan. New York: Pantheon. 215–237.

Foucault, Michel. 2003. *"Society Must Be Defended": Lectures at the Collège de France, 1975–1976.* Trans. David Macey. New York: Picador.

Foucault, Michel. 2007. *Security, Territory, Population. Lectures at the Collège de France, 1977–1978.* Ed. Michel Snellart. Trans. Graham Burchell. New York: Palgrave Macmillan.

Foucault, Michel. 2008. *The Birth of Biopolitics: Lectures at the Collège de France 1978–1979.* Trans. Graham Burchell. New York: Palgrave Macmillan.

Gibson, James J. 1986. *The Ecological Approach to Visual Perception.* Hillsdale, NJ: Lawrence Erlbaum.

Gillham, Patrick F. 2011. "Securitizing America: Strategic Incapacitation and the Policing of Protest since the 11 September 2001 Terrorist Attacks." *Sociology Compass* 5 (7): 636–652.

Giuliani, Rudolph. 2007. "Towards a Realistic Peace: Defending Civilization and Defeating Terrorists By Making the International System Work." *Foreign Affairs* 86 (5): 8.

Goodman, Steve. 2010. *Sonic Warfare: Sound, Affect, and the Ecology of Fear.* Cambridge, MA: MIT Press.

Gopnik, Blake. 2010. "Norman Rockwell Exhibit Opens at the Smithsonian American Museum." *Washington Post,* July 3: E1. http://www.washingtonpost.com /wp-dyn/content/article/2010/07/01/AR2010070107266.html. Accessed July 7, 2014.

Greenberg, Karen L., and Joshua L. Dratel, eds. 2005. *The Torture Papers: The Road to Abu Ghraib.* Cambridge: Cambridge University Press.

Greenfield, Kent. 2011. "Obama, Libya, and Executive Power." *Huffington Post,* May 20. http://www.huffingtonpost.com/kent-greenfield/obama-libya-and -executive_b_864529.html. Accessed July 27, 2014.

Greenwald, Glenn. 2012. "Attorney General Holder Defends Execution without Charges." *Salon,* March 6. http://www.salon.com/2012/03/06/attorney_general _holder_defends_execution_without_charges/. Accessed July 26, 2014.

Grey, Stephen, and Dan Edge. 2011. "Kill/Capture: Transcript." *Frontline,* May 10. http://www.pbs.org/wgbh/pages/frontline/afghanistan-pakistan/kill-capture /transcript/. Accessed July 26, 2014.

Grimmett, Robert F. 2004. "Instances of Use of United States Armed Forces Abroad, 1798–2004." Congressional Research Service Report RL30172. http://www.au.af .mil/au/awc/awcgate/crs/r130172.htm. Accessed July 29, 2014.

Guattari, Félix. 1995. *Chaosmosis*. Trans. Paul Bains and Julian Pefanis. Bloomington: Indiana University Press.

Guattari, Félix. 2002. "From Transference to the Aesthetic Paradigm." In Brian Massumi, ed., *A Shock to Thought: Expression After Deleuze and Guattari*. London: Routledge. 240–245.

Hallward, Peter. 2006. *Out of This World: Deleuze and the Philosophy of Creation*. London: Verso.

Henderson, D. A. 2009. "Disease and Terror: The Swine-Flu Outbreak Caught Health Officials Completely by Surprise—Just as a Bioterror Attack Would." *Newsweek*, April 30. http://www.newsweek.com/id/195422. Accessed May 6, 2009.

Heraclitus. 1981. *The Art and Thought of Heraclitus: An Edition of the Fragments with Translation and Commentary*. Ed. Charles H. Kahn. Cambridge: Cambridge University Press.

Herman, Arthur. 2006. "Getting Serious About Iran: A Military Option." *Commentary*, November. http://www.commentarymagazine.com/article/getting-serious-about -iran-a-military-option. Accessed April 21, 2014.

Horton, Scott. 2010. "Obama's Black Sites." *Harper's*, May 29. http://harpers.org/blog /2010/05/obamas-black-sites/. Accessed July 28, 2014.

Human Rights Watch. 2014. "U.S.: Terrorism Prosecutions Often an Illusion. Investigations, Trials of American Muslims Rife with Abuse," July 21. http://www .hrw.org/node/127456. Accessed July 27, 2014.

Ignatius, David. 2008. "The Right Iraq Footprint." *Washington Post*, June 19: A19. http://www.washingtonpost.com/wp-dyn/content/article/2008/06/18 /AR2008061802635.html. Accessed July 1, 2014.

Jaffe, Greg. 2012. "Obama Announces New, Leaner Military Approach." *Washington Post*, January 5. http://www.washingtonpost.com/world/national-security/obama -announces-new-military-approach/2012/01/05/gIQAFWcmcP_story.html. Accessed January 10, 2012.

James, William. 1950. *Principles of Psychology*. 2 volumes. New York: Dover.

James, William. 1983. "What Is an Emotion?" In *The Works of William James*, vol. 13, *Essays in Psychology*. Cambridge, MA: Harvard University Press.

James, William. 1996a. *Essays in Radical Empiricism*. Lincoln: University of Nebraska Press.

James, William. 1996b. *A Pluralistic Universe*. Lincoln: University of Nebraska Press.

Johnson, Chalmers. 2004. *Sorrows of Empire: Militarism, Secrecy, and the End of the Republic*. New York: Henry Holt.

Juhasz, Antonia. 2006. *The Bush Agenda: Invading the World One Economy at a Time*. New York: Regan Books/HarperCollins.

Kellner, Douglas. 1992. *The Persian Gulf TV War*. Boulder, CO: Westview.

Kierkegaard, Søren. 1983. *Fear and Trembling, and Repetition.* Trans. Howard V. Hong and Edna H. Hong. Princeton, NJ: Princeton University Press.

Klein, Gary. 1999. *Sources of Power: How People Make Decisions.* Cambridge, MA: MIT Press.

Klein, Naomi. 2008. *The Shock Doctrine: The Rise of Disaster Capitalism.* New York: Picador.

Knowlton, Brian. 2007. "Bush Insists Al Qaeda in Iraq Threatens U.S." *New York Times,* July 24. http://www.nytimes.com/2007/07/24/washington/24cnd-prexy.html?_r =2&hp=&adxnnl=1&adxnnlx=1185307982-HUTcmjEuKEuIonU+qEttPQ&oref =slogin&module=Search&mabReward=relbias%3Ar&. Accessed July 27, 2014.

Korling, Paul. 2011. "Say Goodbye to Orange Terrorist Alerts. *Globe and Mail,* April 20. http://www.theglobeandmail.com/news/world/americas/say-goodbye-to-orange -terrorist-alerts/article1993741. Accessed April 20, 2011.

Krauthammer, Charles. 2014. "The Vacant Presidency." *Washington Post,* July 25. http://www.washingtonpost.com/opinions/charles-krauthammer-the-vacant -presidency/2014/07/24/0b110fdc-1363-11e4-9285-4243a40ddc97_story.html. Accessed July 25, 2014.

Lafleur, Sylvain. 2014. "Analyse foucaldienne d'un dispositif policier à l'ère des manifestations altermondialistes et assembléistes." PhD dissertation, University of Montreal.

Langer, Susanne. 1953. *Feeling and Form.* New York: Charles Scribner's Sons.

*La Presse* (Montreal). 2005a. "ADM (Aéroports de Montréal) soutient que la sécurité des passagers a été améliorée." May 10: A7.

*La Presse* (Montreal). 2005b. "Plus de panique!" May 17: A2.

Lardner, George Jr. 2002. "Nixon Archives Portray Another 'War' on Terror. Response to '72 Massacre and '73 Mideast War Has Many Echoes in Bush Administration's Challenges." *Washington Post,* May 7: A04.

Latour, Bruno. 1993. *We Have Never Been Modern.* Trans. Catherine Porter. Cambridge, MA: Harvard University Press.

Layton, Lyndsey. 2014. "In New Orleans, Major School District Closes Traditional Public Schools for Good." *New York Times,* May 28. http://www.washingtonpost .com/local/education/in-new-orleans-traditional-public-schools-close-for -good/2014/05/28/ae4f5724-e5de-11e3-8f90-73e071f3d637_story.html?wpisrc =nl%5Fhdtop. Accessed May 29, 2014.

Lendman, Stephen. 2013. "U.S. Globalized Torture Black Sites." Global Research. http://www.globalresearch.ca/us-globalized-torture-black-sites/5353706. Accessed July 28, 2014.

Lewis, Paul. 2014. "Obama Admits CIA 'Tortured Folks' but Stands by Brennan over Spying." *Guardian,* August 1. http://www.theguardian.com/world/2014/aug/01 /obama-cia-torture-some-folks-brennan-spying. Accessed August 2, 2014.

Libet, Benjamin. 2005. *Mind Time: The Temporal Factor in Consciousness.* Cambridge, MA: Harvard University Press.

Lippmann, Walter. 1920. *Liberty and the News.* New York: Harcourt, Brace and Howe.

Loughlin, Sean. 2003. "Bush Warns Militants Who Attack US Troops in Iraq." CNN .com, July 3. http://www.cnn.com/2003/ALLPOLITICS/07/02/sprj.nitop.bush/. Accessed April 21, 2014.

Manning, Erin. 2009. *Relationscapes: Art, Technology, Philosophy*. Cambridge, MA: MIT Press, 43–48.

Manning, Erin. 2013. *Always More Than One: Individuation's Dance*. Durham, NC: Duke University Press.

Manning, Erin, and Brian Massumi. 2014. *Thought in the Act: Passages in the Ecology of Experience*. Minneapolis: University of Minnesota Press.

Marks, Laura U. 2002. *Touch: Sensuous Media and Multisensory Media*. Minneapolis: University of Minnesota Press.

Massumi, Brian. 1993. "Everywhere You Want to Be: Introduction to Fear." In Brian Massumi, ed., *The Politics of Everyday Fear*. Minneapolis: University of Minnesota Press. 3–38.

Massumi, Brian. 2002. *Parables for the Virtual: Movement, Affect, Sensation*. Durham, NC: Duke University Press.

Massumi, Brian. 2011. *Semblance and Event: Activist Philosophy and the Occurrent Arts*. Cambridge, MA: MIT Press.

Massumi, Brian. 2014a. *What Animals Teach Us about Politics*. Durham, NC: Duke University Press.

Massumi, Brian. 2014b. "Envisioning the Virtual." In Mark Grimshaw, ed., *The Oxford Handbook of Virtuality*. Oxford: Oxford University Press. 55–70.

Massumi, Brian. 2015a. *The Power at the End of the Economy*. Durham, NC: Duke University Press.

Massumi, Brian. 2015b. *Politics of Affect*. London: Polity Press.

McChrystal, Stanley A., General. 2011. "It Takes a Network: The New Front Line of Modern Warfare." *Foreign Policy* 90 (2) (March/April): 66–70. http://www .foreignpolicy.com/articles/2011/02/22/it_takes_a_network. Accessed July 18, 2011.

McChrystal, Stanley A., General. 2013. "Generation Kill: A Conversation with Stanley McChrystal." *Foreign Policy* 92 (2) (March/April). http://www.foreignaffairs .com/discussions/interviews/generation-kill. Accessed July 28, 2014.

Meillassoux, Qentin. 2008. *After Finitude: An Essay on the Necessity of Contingency*. Trans. Ray Brassier. London: Continuum.

Miller, Aaron David. 2012. "Barack O'Romney." *Foreign Policy*, May 23. http://www .foreignpolicy.com/articles/2012/05/23/barack_oromney?page=0,0&wp_login _redirect=0. Accessed July 26, 2014.

Miller, Mark Crispin. 2002. *The Bush Dyslexicon*. New York: Norton.

Moffat, James. 2003. *Complexity Theory and Network Centric Warfare*. Washington, DC: US Department of Defense, Command and Control Research Program Publications. http://www.dodccrp.org/files/Moffat_Complexity.pdf. Accessed November 30, 2014.

*Montreal Gazette.* 2007. "Attacks Were the Most Important Historical Events in Our Lives: Poll." September 11: A17.

Moore, Jason W. 2014a. "The Capitalocene. Part 1: On the Nature and Origins of Our Ecological Crisis." Personal website Jason W. Moore. http://www.jasonwmoore .com/uploads/The_Capitalocene__Part_I__June_2014.pdf. Accessed December 10, 2014.

Moore, Jason W. 2014b. "The Capitalocene. Part 2: Abstract Social Nature and the Limits to Capital." Personal website Jason W. Moore. http://www.jasonwmoore .com/uploads/The_Capitalocene___Part_II__June_2014.pdf. Accessed December 10, 2014.

Motluk, Allison. 2007. "How Many Things Can You Do at Once?" *New Scientist* 2598 (April): 28–31.

Nagourney, Adam. 2000. "Bush and Gore Mix Jokes and Barbs at Smith Dinner." *New York Times*, October 20. http://www.nytimes.com/2000/10/20/nyregion/bush-and -gore-mix-jokes-and-barbs-at-smith-dinner.html. Accessed July 2, 2014.

National Counterterrorism Center. 2013. *Watchlisting Guidance.* March. Electronic Frontier Foundation: https://www.eff.org/files/2014/07/24/2013-watchlist -guidance_1.pdf. Accessed October 13, 2014.

Negri, Antonio. 1996. "Twenty Theses on Marx." In Saree Makdisi, Cesare Casarino, and Rebecca E. Karl, eds., *Marxism beyond Marxism.* London: Routledge. 149–180.

*New York Times.* 2008. "Transcript: Obama's National Security Team Announcement," December 1. http://www.nytimes.com/ 2008/12/01/ us/politics/ 01text-obama .html?ref=politics. Accessed December 2, 2008.

Nietzsche, Friedrich. 1968. *The Will to Power.* Ed. Walter Kaufmann. Trans. Walter Kaufman and R. J. Hollingdale. New York: Vintage.

Nietzsche, Friedrich. 1983. *Untimely Meditations.* Trans R. J. Hollingdale. Cambridge: Cambridge University Press.

Noë, Alva. 2004. *Action in Perception.* Cambridge, MA: MIT Press.

Obama, Barack. 2010. "Remarks by the President on Strengthening Intelligence and Aviation Security." The White House, January 7. http://www.whitehouse.gov /the-press-office/remarks-president-strengthening-intelligence-and-aviation -security. Accessed July 27, 2014.

Obama, Barack. 2014a. "Transcript of President Obama's Commencement Speech at West Point." *New York Times*, May 28. http://www.nytimes.com/2014/05/29/us /politics/transcript-of-president-obamas-commencement-address-at-west- point.html. Accessed May 29, 2014.

Obama, Barack. 2014b. "Barack Obama's TV Address on ISIS: Full Text." *Guardian*, September 11. http://www.theguardian.com/world/2014/sep/11/barack-obama-tv -speech-on-isis-full-text. Accessed October 13, 2014.

Paphitis, Nicholas. 2007. "Greek Government Points to Arson for Fires." *Guardian*, August 28. http://www.guardian.co.uk/worldlatest/story/0,,-6880199,00.html. Accessed September 1, 2007.

Peirce, C. S. 1992. *The Essential Peirce: Selected Philosophical Writings*. Vol. 1. Bloomington: Indiana University Press.

Peirce, C. S. 1997. *Pragmatism as a Principle and Method of Right Thinking: The 1903 Lectures on Pragmatism*. Albany: State University of New York Press.

Peirce, C. S. 1998. *The Essential Peirce: Selected Philosophical Writings*. Vol. 2. Bloomington: University of Indiana Press.

Perera, Suvendrini, and Joseph Pugliese. 2011. "Introduction: Combat Breathing: State Violence and the Body in Question." *Somatechnics* 1 (1): 1–14. doi: 10.3366/soma.2011.0002

Pilkington, Ed. 2014. "Human Rights Groups Call for Special Prosecutor to Investigate CIA Torture." *Guardian*. December 22. http://www.theguardian.com/law/2014/dec/22/aclu-human-rights-watch-ask-eric-holder-prosecute-cia-torture. Accessed December 24, 2014.

Raymond, J. E., K. L. Shapiro, and K. M. Arnell. 1992. "Temporary Suppression of Visual Processing in an Rsvp Task: An Attentional Blink?" *Journal of Experimental Psychology: Human Perception and Performance* 18: 849–860. doi: 10.1037/0096-1523.18.3.849.

Roberts, Dan. 2014a. "Texas Governor Pushes for Troops on US Border amid 'Refugee Crisis.' " *Guardian*, July 3. http://www.theguardian.com/world/2014/jul/03/texas-governor-troops-border-refugee-crisis-child-migrants. Accessed July 3, 2014.

Roberts, Dan. 2014b. "Barack Obama Authorises Air Strikes against ISIS Militants in Syria." *Guardian*, September 11. http://www.theguardian.com/world/2014/sep/10/obama-speech-authorise-air-strikes-against-isis-syria. Accessed October 13, 2014.

Rumsfeld, Donald. 2001. US Department of Defense News Briefing with Secretary of Defense Donald Rumsfeld and Chairman of the Joint Chiefs of Staff General Richard B. Myers, October 12. http://www.defenselink.mil/transcripts/transcript.aspx?transcriptid=2068. Accessed July 27, 2014.

Rumsfeld, Donald. 2002a. Department of Defense News Briefing, February 12. http://www.defense.gov/Transcripts/Transcript.aspx?TranscriptID=2068. Accessed May 30, 2014.

Rumsfeld, Donald. 2002b. "Transforming the Military." *Foreign Affairs* 81 (3) (May–June): 20–32.

Ruyer, Raymond. 2012. *Néo-finalisme*. 2nd edition. Paris: PUF.

Scahill, Jeremy. 2013. *Dirty Wars: The World Is a Battlefield*. New York: Nation Books.

Scahill, Jeremy, and Ryan Devereaux. 2014 "The Secret Government Rulebook for Labeling You a Terrorist." *Intercept*, July 23. https://firstlook.org/theintercept/article/2014/07/23/blacklisted/. Accessed October 13, 2014.

Schmitt, Eric, and Richard W. Stevenson. 2004. "Admitting Intelligence Flaws, Bush Stands by Need for War." *New York Times*, July 10: A9.

Sewell, Sarah, John A. Nagi, David H. Petraeus, and James F. Amos. 2007. *The US Army/Marine Corps Counterinsurgency Field Manual*. Chicago: University of Chicago Press.

Shachtman, Noah. 2007. "How Technology Almost Lost the War: In Iraq, the Critical
Networks Are Social—Not Electronic." *Wired Magazine* 15 (12). http://archive
.wired.com/politics/security/magazine/15-12/ff_futurewar?currentPage=all.
Accessed July 27, 2014.

Shapiro, Kimron L., J. Raymond, and K. Arnell. 2009. "Attentional Blink."
*Scholarpedia* 4 (6): 3320.

Sheets-Johnstone, Maxine. 2009a. *The Corporeal Turn: An Interdisciplinary Reader*. Exeter,
UK: Imprint Academic.

Sheets-Johnstone, Maxine. 2009b. "Animation: the Fundamental, Essential, and
Properly Descriptive Concept." *Continental Philosophy Review* 42 (2009): 375–400.

Simondon, Gilbert. 1989. *Du mode d'existence des objets techniques*. Paris:
Aubier-Montagne.

Simondon, Gilbert. 2005. *L'individuation à la lumière des notions de forme et d'information*.
Grenoble, France: Millon.

Sklar, Aseal Y., Nir Levy, Ariel Goldstein, Roi Mandel, Anat Maril, and Ran R.
Hassin. 2012. "Reading and Doing Arithmetic Nonconsciously." PNAS *Early
Edition*, October 5. http://www.pnas.org/cgi/doi/10.1073/pnas.1211645109.
Accessed July 27, 2014.

Soucy, Louise Maude Rioux 2005. "Le virus de la prochaine pandémie de grippe
n'existe pas encore." *Le Devoir*, October 19: A1. http://www.ledevoir.com/2005/10
/19/92964.html. Accessed October 19, 2005.

Starr, Amory, Luis Fernandez, and Christian Scholl. 2011. *Shutting Down the Streets:
Political Violence and Social Control in the Global Era*. New York: New York University
Press.

Stengers, Isabelle. 1997. "Turtles All the Way Down." In *Power and Invention*. Trans.
Paul Bains. Minneapolis: University of Minnesota Press. 61–75.

Stern, Daniel N. 1985. *The Interpersonal World of the Infant*. New York: Basic Books.

Stewart, Kathleen. 2010. "Atmospheric Attunements." *Rubric* 1: 2–14.

St. John, Mark, David A. Kobus, Jeffrey G. Morrison, and Dylan Schmorrow.
2004. "Overview of the DARPA Augmented Cognition Technical Integration
Experiment." *International Journal of Human–Computer Interaction* 17 (2): 131–149.

Suskind, Ron. 2004. "Without a Doubt." *New York Times Magazine*, October 17. http://
query.nytimes.com/gst/fullpage.html?res=9C05EFD8113BF934A25753C1A9629C8
B63. Accessed April 21, 2014.

Szafranski, Col. Richard. 1994. "Neocortical Warfare?" *Military Review* (November):
41–55.

Tarde, Gabriel. 1903. *The Laws of Imitation*. Trans. Elsie Clews Parsons. New York:
Henry Holt.

Trudel, Dominique. 2013. "Guerre, communication, public: Walter Lippmann et
l'émergence d'un problème." PhD dissertation, University of Montreal.

Tumulty, Karen. 2014. "Obama Circumvents Law with 'Signing Statements,' a Tool
He Promised to Use Lightly." *Washington Post*, June 2. http://www.washingtonpost
.com/politics/obama-circumvents-laws-with-signing-statements-a-tool-he

-promised-to-use-lightly/2014/06/02/9d76d46a-ea73–11e3–9f5c-9075d5508f0a
_story.html. Accessed July 27, 2014.

Turse, Nick. 2011. "The Pentagon's Planet of Bases." *TomDispatch*, January 9. http://
www.tomDispatch.com/blog/175338/. Accessed July 26, 2014.

Turse, Nick. 2012. "The Pentagon's Bases of Confusion." *Tomdispatch*, September 4.
http://www.tomdispatch.com/post/175588/tomgram%3A_nick_turse%2C_the
_pentagon%27s_bases_of_confusion/. Accessed July 26, 2014.

Ullman, Harlan K. 2002. "Muscular Containment. Assertive Policy Could Be
Applied to Iraq, North Korea" (op-ed). *Washington Times*, October 30. http://www
.highbeam.com/doc/1G1–93607082.html. Accessed July 27, 2014.

Ullman, Harlan K. 2006. "Hard Lessons in 2006. Will White House, Congress Act
Differently?" (op-ed). *Washington Times*, January 4. http://www.highbeam.com
/doc/1G1–140492296.html. Accessed July 27, 2014.

Ullman, Harlan K., and James P. Wade. 1996. *Shock and Awe: Achieving Rapid
Dominance*. Washington, DC: National Defense University Press. http://www
.dodccrp.org/files/Ullman_Shock.pdf. Accessed May 26, 2010.

United States Government. 2002. "The National Security Strategy of the USA,"
September 20. http://georgewbush-whitehouse.archives.gov/nsc/nss/2002/index
.html. Accessed April 21, 2014.

United States Government. 2010. *National Security Strategy*. http://www.whitehouse
.gov/sites/default/files/rss_viewer/national_security_strategy.pdf. Accessed
May 30, 2014.

Virilio, Paul. 1975. *L'insécurité du territoire*. Paris: Stock.

Von Drehl, David. 2003. "For 'Shock and Awe' Author, Concern." *Washington
Post*, March 22. http://www.highbeam.com/doc/1P2–252425.html. Accessed
December 10, 2014.

Walker, Peter M. B. 1991. *Chambers Science and Technology Dictionary*. Edinburgh:
Chambers.

Warrick, Joby. 2011. "Cheney: After Yemen Strike, Obama Owes an Apology to
Bush." *Washington Post*, October 2. http://www.washingtonpost.com/world
/national-security/cheney-after-yemen-strike-obama-owes-apology-to-bush/2011
/10/02/gIQADug9FL_story.html. Accessed July 26, 2014.

Weinberger, Sharon. 2008. "Army Looks to Save Its 'Future,'" June 26. http://blog
.wired.com/defense/2008/06/army-looks-to-s.html. Accessed June 28, 2008.

Weiner, Rachel. 2009. "Tom Ridge: I Was Pressured to Raise Terror Alert to Help
Bush Win." *Huffington Post*, September 20. http://www.huffingtonpost.com/2009
/08/20/tom-ridge-i-was-pressured_n_264127.html. Accessed July 2, 2014.

Weissenstein, Michael. 2005. "Officials: NYC Terror Plot Uncorroborated." *Star Leger*
(Newark, NJ), October 9: 6.

Weizman, Eyal. 2006. "Lethal Theory." *Log* 7 (winter/spring): 53–130.

Weizman, Eyal. 2007. "Urban Architecture: Walking through Walls." In *Hollow Land:
Israel's Architecture of Occupation*. London: Verso. 185–220.

Whitehead, Alfred North. 1964. *Concept of Nature*. Cambridge: Cambridge University Press.

Whitehead, Alfred North. 1967a. *Adventures of Ideas*. New York: Free Press.

Whitehead, Alfred North. 1967b. *Science and the Modern World*. New York: Free Press.

Whitehead, Alfred North. 1968. *Modes of Thought*. New York: Free Press.

Whitehead, Alfred North. 1978. *Process and Reality*. New York: Free Press.

Whitehead, Alfred North. 1985. *Symbolism: Its Meaning and Effect*. New York: Fordham University Press.

Whitlock, Criag. 2013. "Renditions Continue under Obama, Despite Due-Process Concerns." *Washington Post*, January 1. http://www.washingtonpost.com/world /national-security/renditions-continue-under-obama-despite-due-process -concerns/2013/01/01/4e593aa0–5102–11e2–984e-f1de82a7c98a_story.html?wpisrc =nl_cuzheads. Accessed July 27, 2014.

Willer, Robb. 2004. "The Effects of Government-Issued Terror Warnings on Presidential Approval Ratings." *Current Research in Social Psychology* 10 (1): 1–12.

Woodward, Bob. 2002. *Bush at War*. New York: Simon and Schuster.

Yang, Jennifer. 2010. "G20 Law Gives Police Sweeping Powers to Arrest People." *Toronto Star*, June 25. http://www.thestar.com/news/gta/g20/2010/06/25/g20_law _gives_police_sweeping_powers_to_arrest_people.html. Accessed July 27, 2014.

# INDEX

logic, 46–47; affect and, 88. *See also*
    operative logic
Luhmann, Niklas, 251n16

Manning, Erin, 258n19
Manturana, Humberto, 247n16, 251n15
Massumi, Brian: *Power at the End of the
    Economy*, 272n13; *Semblance and Event*,
    258n20; *What Animals Teach Us about
    Politics*, 249n11
materiality, 49; experience and, 203; life
    and, 186; operation and, 36; threat
    and, 3–4, 30; violence and, 83, 87.
    *See also* immateriality
Meillassoux, Quentin, 270n2
memory, 110; bare activity and, 107;
    consciousness and, 116; perception
    and, 63–64, 67, 95, 178; priming and,
    108–109. *See also* recollection
metaphysics: violence and, 83, 87–88
metastability: deterrence and, 8;
    neoliberalism and, 52–53; politics
    and, 175
micro-perception, 145, 149, 151
micropolitics: emergence and, 46 (*also
    see* politicsmilitary, 11, 17); civilian
    and, 28–29, 34; mutually assured
    destruction and, 8; neoconservatism
    and, 43, 50; potential and, 12; pre-
    emption and, 4–5; threat and 27
military, 8, 11–12, 50, 69, 103, 120, 138,
    212, 165–166, 230, 246n6, 246n7,
    249n6; action and, 86, 195, 271n7;
    attentional blink and, 67; body and,
    121, 123; civilian and, 17, 28, 34, 81,
    89, 91, 105–106, 248n17, 254n14;
    cognition and, 151; force and, 76, 145;
    full-spectrum and, 252n5, 253n10;
    information and, 99; life and, 79, 83;
    neoconservatism and, 43; neoliberal-
    ism and, 251n22; network and, 93–94,
    96–98; nonbattle and, 72; operation
    and, 67–68; perception and, 73, 123;

power and, 77–78, 84; preemption
    and, 5, 56; repetition and, 64; security
    and, 29; skill and, 122; uncertainty
    and, 27; war and, 57, 237
military commissions, 229, 247–248n17,
    267n7
Military Commissions Act, 247–248n17
Miller, Aaron David, 226
modulation, 74, 80, 119, 144, 160, 186,
    200, 211–212; action and, 76, 118,
    132, 134; affect and, 171–173, 185; bat-
    tlespace and, 146, 151; change and,
    163; control and, 150; emergence
    and, 123, 255n1; event and 48, 66,
    102, 162; experience and, 75; feeling
    and, 172; human and, 83; interval
    and, 84; life and, 50, 235; operation
    and, 75; perception and, 70–71, 108,
    116; posture and, 76, 79; potential
    and, 85–86, 97, 117; system and, 57;
    violence and 88
momentum, 103, 139–141; action and,
    110, 112; neoconservatism and,
    57–58; neoliberalism and, 52–53, 57;
    tendency and, 163; terminus and,
    158–159; war on terror and, 230
Moore, Jason W, 250n13
movement, vii, 7–8, 12, 25, 147, 201,
    214; affect and, 81; antiaccident
    and, 40; attentional blink and, 97;
    bare activity and, 44; body and, 131,
    254n15; habit and, 64; incipience
    and, 180; interval and, 110; military
    and, 80, 93; neoconservatism and,
    50; network and, 143; ontogenesis
    and, 39; perception and, 71; power
    and, 34, 55, 84; preemption and,
    14–15; priming and, 109–110; self-
    synchronization and, 141; technique
    and, 253n14; terminus and, 160–161.
    *See also* tendency
multiplier effect, 31; economy and,
    50–52; nature and, 35. *See also* effect